ENABLING LEARNING

Language Teaching for
Australian Universities

ENABLING LEARNING

Language Teaching for
Australian Universities

Edited by John Kinder, Nicola Fraschini
and Marinella Caruso

ANU PRESS

LCNAU STUDIES IN
LANGUAGES AND CULTURES

ANU PRESS

Published by ANU Press
The Australian National University
Canberra ACT 2600, Australia
Email: anupress@anu.edu.au

Available to download for free at press.anu.edu.au

ISBN (print): 9781760466671
ISBN (online): 9781760466688

WorldCat (print): 1452280387
WorldCat (online): 1452280552

DOI: 10.22459/EL.2024

This title is published under a Creative Commons Attribution-NonCommercial-NoDerivatives 4.0 International (CC BY-NC-ND 4.0) licence.

The full licence terms are available at
creativecommons.org/licenses/by-nc-nd/4.0/legalcode

Cover design and layout by ANU Press

This book is published under the aegis of the LCNAU Studies in Languages and Cultures editorial board of ANU Press.

This edition © 2024 ANU Press

Contents

Editors and contributors	vii
Abbreviations	xiii
Foreword: Keeping the faith in languages and cultures Jean Fornasiero	xv
Introduction: Resilience, renewal and revival: Language teaching in the 2020s John Kinder, Nicola Fraschini and Marinella Caruso	1

Part 1: Policies and access

1.	The L2 learning experience as the Cinderella of the L2 motivational self system Giuseppe D'Orazzi	13
2.	Transitioning to university: Online video resources for language students Joshua Brown, Manuel Delicado Cantero and Solène Inceoglu	43
3.	Korean language education in Western Australia: Development and challenges Nicola Fraschini, Joanna Elfving-Hwang and Yu Tao	63
4.	The role of universities in training Indigenous language workers: Developing an Australian Indigenous Languages Institute Cathy Bow	93

Part 2: Language pedagogy

5.	Flipping the classroom in beginner Italian: Implications for teaching and learning Marinella Caruso and Federica Verdina	125
6.	Administrative and pedagogical considerations for collaborative online Korean courses: A case study Nicola Fraschini and Adrienne Gonzales	157

7. Connections between learners' communities of practice and their use of social language learning strategies: A case study 177
Mary Grace Quigley

Part 3: Intercultural language teaching

8. Humanising translator and interpreter ethics for critical language users: A case of what the impartial model can learn from the 'empathetic' model 205
Maho Fukuno

9. Teacher–student and student–student interaction in live online classes 233
Xiaoping Gao and Leimin Shi

10. Equipping Australian Defence Force (ADF) members with the ability to influence the outcome of interactions conducted in an intercultural environment 263
Anna Ivanova

Index 277

Editors and contributors

Cathy Bow. We are humbled and proud to be able to include in this volume the contribution from Cathy Bow. She died, tragically and unexpectedly, in October 2021. We already had her chapter, its two readers had given enthusiastic reviews and, in collaboration with the LCNAU Committee, we decided to publish the chapter posthumously as our tribute to a respected and mourned colleague. Cathy moved to Darwin in 2012, working at the Northern Institute of Charles Darwin University (CDU). There she gained a Graduate Certificate in Yolngu Studies and, in 2020, a PhD on 'Entanglements of Digital Technologies and Indigenous Language Work in the Northern Territory'. To future researchers and language users, she bequeathed major digital resources for Indigenous languages in the Territory. The Living Archive of Aboriginal Languages houses over 4,000 digitised books in languages of the Northern Territory. Within the Northern Institute at CDU, she used the Digital Language Learning Shell to help Bininj people teach their language at The Australian National University (ANU) and CDU. She then helped language centres to set up similar courses in Kriol and Gumbaynggirr. Cathy became a member of the committee of LCNAU in 2020 and was quietly dynamic in contributing to new initiatives. She is remembered for the humble and respectful way she carried out all her work, for her generosity and energy.

Joshua Brown is a senior lecturer in Italian studies at the University of Western Australia. His research interests are historical sociolinguistics, language contact, and digital humanities. He is co-editor of a volume entitled *Languages and Cross-Cultural Exchanges in Renaissance Italy* for Brepols. Recent co-authored publications include 'Women's Literacy in a Late Medieval Religious Community: Organisation and Memorialization at Santa Marta in Milan, 1405–1454' (*Journal of Religious History*, 2021), 'Towards the Elaboration of a Diastratic Model in Historical Analyses of

Koineization' (*Sociolinguistic Studies*, 2020) and 'Language History from Below. Standardization and Koineization in Renaissance Italy' (*Journal of Historical Sociolinguistics*, 2020).

Marinella Caruso is a senior lecturer in the Italian studies program at the University of Western Australia. She has published on language contact, Italian in a migratory context (*Italian Language Attrition in Australia*, FrancoAngeli, 2010), second language education and policy and on the scholarship of teaching and learning. Recent studies include 'Continuity in Foreign Language Education in Australia' (*Australian Review of Applied Linguistics*, 2017) and 'Online Tools for Feedback Engagement in Second Language Learning' (*International Journal of Computer-Assisted Language Learning and Teaching*, 2019). Her current projects are related to Italian language learner motivation using Q methodology (Caruso and Fraschini, 'A Q Methodology Study into Vision of Italian L2 University Students. An Australian Perspective', *The Modern Language Journal*, 2021).

Manuel Delicado Cantero is a senior lecturer in Spanish at ANU. His main research area is the (historical) syntax of Spanish and other Romance languages; his most recent publication in this field is *Noun-Based Constructions in the History of Portuguese and Spanish*, co-authored with Patrícia Amaral (Oxford University Press). He has worked on collaborative projects on L2 Spanish pronunciation teaching and has published in journals such as *The Journal of Spanish Language Teaching* and *The Language Learning Journal*, and in books such as *Key Issues in the Teaching of Spanish Pronunciation: From Description to Pedagogy*, edited by Rajiv Rao (Routledge).

Giuseppe D'Orazzi is a lecturer at the University of Melbourne. Before arriving in Australia, he undertook his undergraduate and graduate studies in Italy, Germany and China, while he received his teaching training in the United Kingdom, United States and Tunisia. His research interests include second language learning and teaching, intercultural communication, sociolinguistics, and European and Italian studies. His current projects focus on motivation and demotivation in learning second languages at Australian universities and COVID-related health communication across Aboriginal and Torres Strait Islander communities in Australia.

Joanna Elfving-Hwang is an associate professor of Korean studies and director of the Korea Research Centre of Western Australia at Curtin University. Her research focuses on beauty cultures and the sociology of the body in South Korea, gender and masculinities in Korean popular culture, as well as Korean studies pedagogies and education policies in Australia.

Jean Fornasiero is a professor emerita of French studies at the University of Adelaide, a fellow of the Australian Academy of the Humanities and an officer in the Ordre des Palmes académiques. She served as president of LCNAU from 2016 to 2021 and was founding secretary, then president of the Australian Society for French Studies from 1993 to 2002. She continues to promote the cause of language education through research and other projects. During her career, she taught languages and culture courses at all levels, taking a particular interest in translation studies. She is widely published in nineteenth-century French studies and is currently engaged in bringing intercultural French-Australian histories to the wider public through writing and exhibitions.

Nicola Fraschini is a senior lecturer in Korean studies at the University of Melbourne. Dr Fraschini has served two terms as president of the Australian Association of Teachers of Korean and introduced the first Korean language teacher training program in Victoria. His research interests are foreign language learner and teacher emotions, motivation and Q methodology. His research has been published in journals such as the *Modern Language Journal*, *System* and the *Annual Review of Applied Linguistics*. He is also the co-author of *Mission Accomplished: Korean* (co-authored with Hyun Mi Kim), a two-volume textbook series for beginner university learners of Korean.

Maho Fukuno is a lecturer in Japanese studies at RMIT University, holding a PhD in linguistics and translation studies from ANU. Her research interests span the interdisciplinary fields of translation studies, intercultural communication, language education and moral philosophy. Her research aims to reimagine translators' ethics with a humanising approach, reflecting diverse versions of moral negotiation in translation practice. This vision extends to her research project, focusing on enabling fair, empathetic and morally sensitive language practices, education and services as critical infrastructure in a multicultural society.

Xiaoping Gao is an associate professor of Chinese and a former discipline leader for Languages and Linguistics in the School of Humanities and Social Inquiry at the University of Wollongong. She has published widely on language pedagogy, second language acquisition, technology-enhanced teaching and learning, teacher education and intercultural communication. She is co-editor of *Frontiers of L2 Chinese Education: A Global Perspective* (Routledge, 2022) and a recipient of several prestigious national teaching awards and grants. She serves on the Editorial Board of *International Journal of Chinese Language Teaching* and the Committee of the *Languages and Cultures Network for Australian Universities*.

Adrienne Gonzales is the associate dean in the School of Liberal Arts at the Central New Mexico Community College. Previously, she was dean of language learning and director of the Language Learning Center at Tulane University in New Orleans, Louisiana. Her work as a language program administrator focuses on program design and curriculum development that increase access to language and intercultural education, particularly in support of less commonly taught languages and heritage language learners.

Solène Inceoglu is a senior lecturer at ANU where she teaches French courses and supervises postgraduate students in applied linguistics. Her main research interests include the effects of instruction on pronunciation development, individual differences in L2 speech perception/production, and technology in L2 pronunciation teaching/learning. Her research has been published in journals such as the *Modern Language Journal*, the *Journal of Second Language Pronunciation*, *Language and Speech*, *Language Awareness*, the *Journal of Asia TEFL*, *Applied Psycholinguistics* and *Studies in Second Language Learning and Teaching*.

Anna Ivanova is the head of development at the Australian Defence Force (ADF) School of Languages. Anna leads the design and development of over 50 ADF language courses in 16 different languages, as well as all assessment, blended learning and faculty development programs. Anna has received senior military commendations for her work and leadership in the development of tailored and enhanced military-specific language courses. Anna represents the ADF at the North Atlantic Treaty Organization Bureau for International Language Coordination conferences.

John Kinder is an emeritus professor of Italian at the University of Western Australia. From early research on the Italian language and dialects in migrant communities in Australia and New Zealand, he published on a wide range of topics in language teaching and learning, the external history of Italian and, most recently, the presence of Italians and Italian in colonial Australia. In retirement, he plans to learn at least two new languages.

Mary Grace Quigley holds a PhD in German studies from the University of Adelaide and an MA in teaching German as a foreign language from the Technical University of Berlin. She identifies as both a teacher and a language learner herself. Her research spans across the fields of German studies and applied linguistics, with a focus on language learning and identity, and the potentials for learners' use of language learning strategies. Mary's investigations take a strong practical focus, looking for possibilities to incorporate research outcomes into teaching practices, promoting learner autonomy and improving learning outcomes.

Leimin Shi is a lecturer at the University of Wollongong. She has around 20 years of language teaching experience across universities in China and Australia. Her area of expertise is related to teacher knowledge and beliefs, and their relationship with the teaching of English and Chinese as a second language. Her most recent publications can be found in *RELC Journal*, *Professional Development in Education*, *Australian Review of Applied Linguistics* and *System*.

Yu Tao is an associate professor in the discipline of Asian studies at the University of Western Australia, where he coordinates Chinese studies courses and teaches Chinese language, politics, and society. A keen higher education practitioner passionate about evidence-based pedagogy innovations, he has published peer-reviewed articles on the teaching of critical thinking, emotions in online language learning and instrumentalism in contemporary higher education.

Federica Verdina is head of languages at Canning Vale College, Western Australia, where she teaches Italian. She holds a PhD from the University of Western Australia focusing on Italian as a language of communication in colonial Australia. Federica's research interests include the history of the Italian language and teaching and learning in language education. As a secondary teacher, she has been involved in developing resources for WA language teachers and supporting other educators in the implementation of the new WA language curriculum.

Abbreviations

ACARA	Australian Curriculum, Assessment and Reporting Authority
ADF	Australian Defence Force
AILI	Australian Indigenous Languages Institute
ALS	Australian Linguistics Society
ANU	The Australian National University
ATAR	Australian Tertiary Admission Rank
AUSIT	Australian Institute of Interpreters and Translators
BILL	Bachelor of Indigenous Languages and Linguistics
CALL	computer-assisted language learning
CDU	Charles Darwin University
CF	corrective feedback
CFL	Chinese as a foreign language
CILLDI	Canadian Indigenous Languages and Literacy Development Institute
COAG	Council of Australian Government
CoEDL	Centre of Excellence for the Dynamics of Language
CWLC	Center for World Languages and Cultures
DFSL	Defence Force School of Languages
EFL	English as a foreign language
EU	European Union
FLCA	foreign language classroom anxiety
FLE	foreign language enjoyment
FLN	Flipped Learning Network

GPA	grade point average
ILA	Indigenous Languages and Arts
ILC	Indigenous Languages Conference
IM	interactional moves
JRGP	Job-Ready Graduates Package
LCNAU	Languages and Cultures Network for Australian Universities
LMS	learning management system
LO	learning outcomes
LOTE	Language Other Than English
LRE	language-related episodes
NAATI	National Accreditation Authority for Translators and Interpreters
NALSAS	National Asian Languages and Studies in Australian Schools
NALSSP	National Asian Languages and Studies in Schools Program
NCP	New Colombo Plan
PASS	Peer Assisted Study Scheme
ROK	Republic of Korea
SCMC	synchronous computer-mediated communication
SCT	sociocultural theory
SD	standard deviation
SE	Strategic Engagement
TA	teaching assistant
TELL	technology-enhanced language learning
UWA	University of Western Australia
VET	vocational education and training
ZPD	zone of proximal development

Foreword: Keeping the faith in languages and cultures

Jean Fornasiero

Making the case for language learning in the Australian education system has become an integral part of the language teacher's role, and one which its practitioners exercise with enthusiasm and talent. And, at present, it needs to be so. Although many disciplines within the humanities and social sciences are currently threatened by educational trends favouring the scientific and vocational sectors, languages have long been on the front line when it comes to closures and budgetary rigours. The core identity of language study as a discipline can even be called into question in ways in which the *raison d'être* of, say, a history or English teacher has not. The status of those disciplines deemed to be at the core of the learning experience has not been eroded so completely over the last century as it has for language study. Today's core disciplines may bear little resemblance to what they once were, in terms of content or methodology, but their status continues to ensure their perennity. In contrast, we would argue that teachers of languages and cultures routinely face existential challenges of a different order from those confronting many of their colleagues in other disciplines. In the 2020s, this has been the lot of increasing numbers of language teachers in the tertiary sector, as funding issues have become more pressing, bringing with them everything from staffing cuts to the complete closure of entire language schools. It was not always so.

The classical languages provided the original model for language study in Australian universities and with them came the status of core discipline. When Greek and Latin lost ground to modern languages, this development paved the way for the discipline's eventual change of status. The curricula that were developed along classical lines for the study of French or German did occupy a space within the core curriculum for a certain time and, while their compulsory status for university entrance or within degree structures was still in place, languages enjoyed strong enrolments. Since the late twentieth century, the field has shifted immensely: modern languages have become effectively multiple, and the field pluridisciplinary, as the discipline in Australia has moved towards its current designation as 'languages and cultures'.

However, as trends in tertiary language education opened up a wider range of languages available for study, the discipline of language study did not on the whole open out to new and larger contingents of students. Only in the larger universities, and particularly in those where language study was made available to students not simply enrolled in arts faculties but throughout the entire university, did enrolment numbers begin to match those not seen since the days of compulsory language study. Elsewhere, language study often came to suffer from competition within its own audience. While the field was undeniably richer from a greater spread of European and Asian languages, and with the appearance of Indigenous language courses in a small number of institutions, student choices had not necessarily expanded. On the one hand, the specific languages proposed to Australian learners were regularly affected by the political climate or the economic interests of the nation. On the other, and more unsettling still, is the situation that prevails in the early twenty-first century: any language taught within a specific educational institution can be discontinued at the whim of its administration, and will not necessarily be replaced by any other. No longer considered a core element of the tertiary curriculum, despite the proven cognitive, social and professional benefits they bestow upon their students, languages have been increasingly driven to the curricular margins.

And yet, languages survive and, in some institutions, they prosper. But in all cases, their teachers share essential characteristics. As long-term inhabitants of an uncertain space, language teachers have become accustomed not only to waging their battle for the resources required to develop linguistic proficiency, intercultural competence and an abiding love of learning in their students, but also to exploiting their own reserves of creativity to produce new modes of classroom practice. Such energetic and resourceful practitioners can be found at all levels of the Australian education system: to identify them would be a vast project. Hence this volume seeks, as a more modest objective, to explore a selection of the ideas and the techniques developed by tertiary language teachers in their constant search for best practice. The editors have chosen well; the chapters included in their varied but well-constructed set of essays offer, in a number of different language settings, a telling sample of the efforts deployed by their fellow academics to identify the means of motivating their students both within and beyond the classroom. Taken individually, and as a whole, these essays all contribute to presenting a compelling reason why universities should continue to value their language teachers as they strive to make themselves ever more globally relevant and globally competent. Without the intercultural competence and linguistic proficiency that only languages and cultures can offer their graduates and future employees, universities are failing to equip themselves adequately for their difficult and highly competitive mission, let alone provide society with functional global citizens.

It is fitting that a volume of this nature should be the first to appear in the collection produced by the Languages and Cultures Network for Australian Universities (LCNAU). Under the title of *LCNAU Studies in Languages and Culture*, the series was conceived as a means for disseminating more widely the research undertaken by the members of the network, but also for acquainting a larger public with the breadth and depth of that research. Often misunderstood, undervalued and even misappropriated through the clumsy mechanisms that evaluate research performance, research conducted by language scholars covers a multitude of fields. It can include pedagogical matters related to language education, cultural, linguistic and societal questions concerning one or more languages or regional areas, fine-grained textual analysis, translation and interpretation, and language policy: the list of potential areas of study is far from exhausted. Languages and cultures is a field where interdisciplinarity is practised as a matter of course. Generally speaking, research in languages and cultures is the work of scholars whose linguistic proficiency and immersion in another culture allows them ready access to resources in a language or languages other than their own, and the capacity to analyse and interpret these resources as well as to exchange findings directly with scholars working in those same languages and to understand the context in which they work. To operate in this way is to be truly part of the global community of scholars. Nor should it be forgotten that languages and cultures provide the educational underpinning for our own multicultural and multilingual society, as together we seek to strengthen the human ties that bind us, rather than succumb to the bitter divisions that threaten our world.

Suspicion of languages and cultures is part of the resurgent isolationship mentality that is a global phenomenon. Encouraging the continued respect for languages and cultures within our society should not be the preserve of language teachers alone, despite their talent for and strong commitment to the task. Nor is it an issue to be carried exclusively by universities, as they confront ever-increasing financial stringencies. However, educational leadership would certainly help to make a new and compelling case for languages. Convincing universities to keep their faith in the discipline might even prepare the terrain for a national language policy, one that not only promotes the teaching and learning of languages and cultures, but recognises them as a force for the greater social and intellectual good.

Introduction: Resilience, renewal and revival: Language teaching in the 2020s

John Kinder, Nicola Fraschini
and Marinella Caruso

Australia has never needed a revival of language teaching and learning more than now. As the world shrinks, horizons expand and our fragile globe becomes more and more a village, Australians are not getting better at learning the languages of neighbours near and far. Attitudes to language diversity and language learning have not improved either, and multilingualism is still not regarded as a normal human characteristic.

This trend characterises both secondary and tertiary education. At the secondary level, the percentage of students taking a foreign language subject in Year 12 in Australian schools has been below 11 per cent since 2011. In 2020 and 2021 it dropped below 10 per cent (Australian Curriculum, Assessment and Reporting Authority [ACARA], n.d.), an extremely low figure by international standards. However, the field is not in a free-fall situation, as the 'health' of languages varies greatly across states and from language to language. For example, Prince (2022) shows that in Western Australia, Indonesian saw a sharp decline between 2000 and 2009 but was stable from 2009 to 2021, although with considerably low numbers. In the same state, in 2023 the Department of Education introduced three new languages in the school curriculum—Korean, Hindi and Tamil. In Victoria, Chinese has been doing exceptionally well (Lo Bianco, 2021), and in New South Wales, Korean has been in constant overall growth since 2016, notwithstanding the decline of heritage learners (Choi, 2022).

At the tertiary level, the language education sector has been shaken by numerous events, at both the local and national levels. Structural changes to degree courses introduced by some universities over the past decade, such as, for example, at the University of Western Australia in 2012, contributed to a growth in language enrolments in those universities (Brown & Caruso, 2016). More recently, in 2021 and 2021, structural changes in the same and other institutions adversely targeted courses in foreign languages and cultures. These changes often meant the closure of entire programs (Lees et al., 2020), the reduction of staff numbers, and limits to the possibility to conduct language and culture-related research despite proven benefits (Fraschini & Tao, 2023). At the national level, the recent Higher Education Support Amendment (Job-Ready Graduates and Supporting Regional and Remote Students) Bill (2020), while on the surface supporting domestic students eager to approach languages, actually makes 'language programs less attractive for universities to run because of the caps placed on Commonwealth-funded places, which means that universities risk running language programs at a loss once the Commonwealth funding gap has been reached' (Fraschini et al., this volume).

These brief remarks may confirm a widespread belief that the situation is critical. However, in the Eleventh Triebel Lecture delivered at the sixth LCNAU (Languages and Cultures Network for Australian Universities) Biennial Colloquium in 2021, at the invitation of the Australian Academy of the Humanities, John Hajek (2021)[1] asked how accurate this widespread sense of crisis that many teachers and researchers are feeling for language education is. Perhaps disseminated by the press, where the word 'crisis' has been identified as a prevalent theme (Mason & Hajek, 2020), and perhaps also reproduced within the disciplinary discourse of the tertiary language education sector (Brown et al., 2019), the feeling of a language *crisis* may not find full justification in the facts. In Hajek's lecture, where he gives a detailed analysis of the language offerings at Australian universities, he shows that in the period 2011–2021, the number of languages offered at Australian universities increased from 45 to 46. For the same period, the number of states offering seven widely taught languages (Chinese, Japanese, French, Italian, German, Indonesian and Spanish) did not change, and while it is true that some languages were no longer taught at some universities, others were now taught more widely (French and Spanish). None of these seven languages has been completely lost, with Indonesian returning to

---

1 For details of the Triebel Lectures, go to humanities.org.au/our-community/triebel-lectures/.

the University of Newcastle in 2023 and Korean studies becoming a major at the University of Melbourne in 2024. Also counteracting the 'crisis' argument is an overall increase in Indigenous language programs across the country. In other terms, Hajek (quoting West-Sooby, 2020) suggested that the metaphor of 'waxing and waning' is possibly better suited to describing the university language education sector, which is characterised more by ups and downs than by a chronic state of decline, and by an overall 'dynamic stability', even as it faces many challenges.

This does not mean that we should be complacent about the current situation, and the policy level is undoubtedly one at which work can be done. Over the past 25 years, policy makers have indeed paid attention to languages, but this attention has been neither consistent over time nor always effective. The National Asian Languages and Studies in Australian Schools (NALSAS) strategy and the National Asian Languages and Studies in Schools Program (NALSSP) represented two efforts carried out at the national level in the area of Asian languages to foster language learning in the secondary sector. These two initiatives, implemented respectively in 1998–2002 and 2009–2012, demonstrated the commitment of significant funding towards languages but also showed the Australian challenges in sustaining an effective long-term national program. The more recent New Colombo Plan (NCP), with a per-student cost three times higher than NALSSP, has been successful in increasing the number of university students studying in Asia and the Indo-Pacific (Prince, 2022). Nevertheless, the NCP, although a very welcome program for the tertiary sector, does not address the issue at the grassroots level, that is, secondary language learning.

Nevertheless, Mason and Hajek (2020) correctly remind us that the policy level is only one among others, and that we must also look at the level of social and public discourse. They point out that what is currently missing in Australian public discourse is the consciousness of language as a social resource and a citizen's right. Others have also provided suggestions on how the situation can be improved. Ingleson (2015) called for a radical change in how Australia addresses the learning and teaching of languages, pointing out that an Australian Institute for Languages could help support a nationally coordinated approach. Lo Bianco (2021) suggested four educational initiatives to address the issue at the most basic level: 1) make languages compulsory, 2) integrate language and content in schools, 3) invest in teacher development and 4) increase the multiculturalisation of the curriculum. Lo Bianco's suggestions were aimed at tackling the issue at the grassroots level, following the principle that early second language learning could positively impact language education at universities and, ultimately, lead to the growth of Australia's intercultural strength as a nation. More recently, in the editorial to the *Melbourne Asia Review* issue dedicated to Asian languages in Australian universities, Ohashi (2023) has argued that what students are looking for, and hence what university courses should offer, is a more intimate and deeper connection with people from other cultures.

Notwithstanding challenges, opportunities and more or less real threats, the field of language teaching is resilient and resourceful. At both secondary and tertiary levels, language teachers are highly qualified, internationally connected and successful at developing motivated and competent language learners. The list of recipients of the national Patji-Dawes Language Teaching Award (CoEDL, 2022) showcases the remarkable efforts being made nationwide by educators in Indigenous and other languages. Such prize-winning teachers are providing passionate and high-quality language education in primary, secondary and university classrooms across the country.

Nowhere is the strength of the language teaching community more on show than in the LCNAU.[2] Established by a team of university language specialists led by professors Colin Nettelbeck, John Hajek and Joseph Lo Bianco of the University of Melbourne, the network became active after a national colloquium staged in February 2009 under the highly symbolic title 'Beyond the Crisis'. As the peak academic body for the field, LCNAU not only promotes academic exchanges, but is active in carrying out awareness campaigns, such as the 2022–2023 National Languages Campaign,[3] aimed at current and prospective language learners in order to increase the overall level of social awareness so greatly needed if we are to effect a drastic change in the way Australia approaches language learning.

The fifth Biennial Colloquium of LCNAU was held in November 2019 at the University of Western Australia. Convened by Nicola Fraschini and John Kinder, the colloquium took as its theme 'Exchanges: People, Knowledge, Cultures'. Over a hundred language specialists from around Australia and our region met for three days to share their experiences and problems, and to deliver insights into language teaching and learning. In light of the positive experience of the colloquium, we decided to bring together a collection

---

2 www.lcnau.org.
3 www.acicis.edu.au/lcnau-national-languages/.

of reflections on language teaching and learning in Australian universities. We wanted to take the pulse of the discipline as we entered the third decade of the twenty-first century. Our objective was to focus on the language teacher, since, in the current climate, we believe that our colleagues need to know how much excellent, world-class work is happening, what help is available, and what are the best practices to follow and to be inspired by. We aimed to compile a volume that would sample a range of issues in the field. The volume would not attempt to be 'representative' in any strict sense but rather to show, through case studies, what solutions language teachers across the country are constructing for the challenges we face. We could not hope to represent all of the languages taught in Australian universities, but we did want to cover the three areas of Indigenous, European and Asian languages.

The title of this collection, *Enabling Learning: Language Teaching for Australian Universities*, indicates that each contribution illustrates efforts by tertiary language educators to facilitate the learning of languages at the university level. The educators' endeavours recounted in this volume address a range of specific aspects of language teaching and learning at the tertiary level. The chapters offer an overview of learners from beginner to advanced level, different learning environments from traditional to online and hybrid, and different languages from Indigenous to European to East Asian. The chapters can be read in any order to gain an overall appreciation of the richness of the solutions that Australian educators consider as they try to overcome both long-term and emerging issues in the field of tertiary language instruction. Nevertheless, as editors, we have organised the volume into three parts, hoping that each part will contribute to a profound and fruitful reflection on a specific macro-topic.

The first part aims to foreground the relevance of providing better accessibility to language learning in the university context. The contributions included in this part reflect on the importance, in this regard, of policies and support at the curricular, institutional, state and national levels.

The second part includes contributions that show how innovative educational solutions can be informed by an examination of the specific characteristics of the learning environment. In particular, these contributions offer a window into the possibilities and limitations of traditional, blended and hybrid learning settings in supporting student experience and attainment.

The chapters in the third part assert the importance of intercultural competence, sustained interaction and first-hand experience in holistically boosting learners' communicative abilities and cultural understanding. This last part is particularly relevant since it reinforces the concept that language learning is much more than learning a language, an insight so often disregarded by university administrators and policy makers. Language learning is an act that includes the acquisition of all the cultural and social aspects with which every language is imbued.

Indeed, the individual chapters in the volume all contribute in different ways to demonstrating this point. The four chapters of Part 1—'Policies and Access'—analyse case studies of successful interventions aimed at increasing student access and participation, from such different perspectives as motivation, scaffolding the *ab initio* experience, macro policy and community connection.

Chapter 1 deals with the learning experience of beginner university students. In this contribution, Giuseppe D'Orazzi examines the motivational dynamics of French, German, Italian and Spanish learners, concluding that understanding diachronic changes in learners' motivation can support language educators who wish to build a learning environment that better suits student needs and provides long-term support.

Beginner learners are also the cohort discussed in Chapter 2 by Josh Brown, Manuel Delicado Cantero and Solène Inceoglu. Their contribution demonstrates the need to pay particular attention to the learner in the very first phases of their learning journey. They show how the production of ten instructional videos, which focused on developing elementary language learning skills, supported first-year students in setting realistic expectations about learning outcomes, developing learning management strategies and understanding teacher-centred vs. student-centred learning.

Chapter 3 deals with the importance of ensuring harmonious collaboration between stakeholders at many different levels if one is to sustain a successful university language program. In this contribution, Nicola Fraschini, Jo Elfving-Hwang and Yu Tao discuss the environmental background to the exponential growth in the number of Korean language learners in Western Australia. Their analysis reveals that many pieces of the puzzle, from community to national and international support, and from learner motivational profile to institutional vision, all need to be in the right place at the right time to promote growth in tertiary language student numbers.

Cathy Bow, in Chapter 4, illustrates past and current challenges in supporting the revitalisation of Aboriginal and Torres Strait Islander peoples' languages, designating access to quality training as one of the main difficulties. Bow calls for greater recognition of Indigenous languages in the Australian university curriculum in order to establish more training opportunities for linguists and language teachers. In this regard, she presents the activities of the recently established Australian Indigenous Language Institute, which, through the collaboration of a number of tertiary institutions, establishes and provides access to university courses in Indigenous languages and thus serves to increase the professionalisation of Indigenous language workers.

Under the heading 'Language Pedagogy', Part 2 ranges across flipped, hybrid and face-to-face teaching approaches. Marinella Caruso and Federica Verdina, in Chapter 5, describe the implementation and reception of the flipped learning approach to Italian language teaching. Their study highlights the many advantages that such an approach has for both teacher and student; however, their analysis also shows that the flipped learning approach must be supported by the student's understanding and acceptance of its underlying pedagogical rationale regarding independent learning and self-regulation skills.

Another online–offline hybrid form is discussed in Chapter 6, where Nicola Fraschini and Adriana Gonzales illustrate how international cross-institutional collaborations can expand opportunities for both learner and teacher through offering instruction in languages that would not be otherwise available. Their case study also details the administrative, practical and pedagogical challenges to setting up such collaborations and concludes by reflecting on lessons learned from optimising teaching and fostering learning in a cross-institutional online environment.

In Chapter 7, Mary Grace Quigley brings us back to more traditional offline environments, discussing the importance of student live interaction in promoting language learning. Focusing on intermediate learners of German, Quigley demonstrates the potential of teaching social language learning strategies to build learner engagement outside of the classroom and actively support the creation of learners' out-of-class communities of practice.

Part 3—'Intercultural Teaching'—illustrates the richness of the language learning experience for the learner, viewed as an individual and a member of the learning community. In the opening chapter, Maho Fukuno illustrates a critical aspect of the pedagogy of translation and interpretation, reflecting on the importance of the explicit teaching of translation and interpretation ethics in creating a safer environment for students of this discipline, supporting them in engaging with ethical heteroglossia, and acquiring values and ideas crucial for the contemporary global citizen.

In Chapter 9, Xiaoping Gao and Leimin Shi conduct a sociocultural theory-based analysis of online teacher–student and student–student interaction over a 13-week Chinese language course. They show that scaffolding strategies and translanguaging support online interaction, while moderate use of the learner L1 contributes to L2 development.

Finally, in Chapter 10, Anna Ivanova describes how the Australian Defence Force School of Languages (DFSL) organises Strategic Engagement (SE) courses that require learners to sustain in-country interactions in a foreign language with a foreign government, defence and industry organisations, and individuals. The courses enable learners to reach an advanced level of cultural knowledge and act as facilitators of strategic relationships and communications in non-routine military settings.

As editors, we are honoured to present this collection. The ten chapters are wide-ranging, even heterogeneous in subject, methodology and style. However, we offer them to our language teacher colleagues to highlight their efforts and their successes, and especially to celebrate the diverse and extensive contributions that Australian university educators have made to enabling student access to languages and enhancing their learning achievements.

References

Australian Curriculum, Assessment and Reporting Authority (ACARA). (n.d.) *Year 12 subject enrolments*. Retrieved on 31 July 2023 from www.acara.edu.au/reporting/national-report-on-schooling-in-australia/year-12-subject-enrolments

Brown, J. & Caruso, M. (2016). Access granted: Modern languages and issues of accessibility at university—a case study from Australia. *Language Learning in Higher Education, 6*(2), 453–471. doi.org/10.1515/cercles-2016-0025

Brown, J., Caruso, M., Arvidsson, K. & Forsberg-Lundell, F. (2019). On 'Crisis' and the pessimism of disciplinary discourse in foreign languages: An Australian perspective. *Moderna Språk, 113*(2), 40–58. doi.org/10.58221/mosp.v113i2.7549

CoEDL. (2022). *Recipients of the Patji-Dawes Language Teaching Award*. Australian Research Council Centre of Excellence for the Dynamics of Language (CoEDL). Retrieved on 17 April 2022 from www.dynamicsoflanguage.edu.au/education-and-outreach/dawes-award/

Choi, S. (2022, 3–5 February). *Future-looking Korean language education leads the way and provides quality learning in the Australian school context* [Conference presentation]. The 12th Korean Studies Association of Australasia 2021 Biennial Conference, Monash University, Melbourne, Australia.

Fraschini, N. & Tao, Y. (2023). How epistemic anxiety and curiosity link perceived value and intended efforts in the language classroom. *Annual Review of Applied Linguistics, 43*, 23–40. doi.org/10.1017/S0267190523000041

Hajek, J. (2021, 24–26 November). *The place of European languages, languages and multilingualism in Australia before and after COVID: The view from Higher Education* [Eleventh Triebel Lecture]. Languages and Cultures Network for Australian Universities (LCNAU) Sixth Biennial Colloquium (online). www.youtube.com/watch?v=KeZ5jbkFif0

Ingleson, J. (2015, 15 February). *Time for radical rethink on language policy*. Asian Studies Association of Australia. Retrieved on 17 April 2022 from asaa.asn.au/time-for-radical-rethink-on-language-policy/

Lees, O., Wijaya, S. & Renaldi, E. (2020, 5 December). Axing Asian language courses from schools and universities may leave Australia underprepared for the future. *ABC News*. www.abc.net.au/news/2020-12-05/asian-language-programs-fights-to-stay-hindi-indonesian/12934096

Lo Bianco, J. (2021). Australia needs to make languages compulsory. *Melbourne Asia Review, 7*. doi.org/10.37839/MAR2652-550X7.5

Mason, S. & Hajek, J. (2020). Language education and language ideologies in Australian print media. *Applied Linguistics, 41*(2), 215–233. doi.org/10.1093/applin/amy052

Ohashi, J. (2023). Changing one's world view: The potentially transformative power of Asian language(s) and culture(s). *Melbourne Asia Review, 13*. doi.org/10.37839/MAR2652-550X13.5

Prince, L. (2022, 7 April). *Investing in the future of Asian language literacy in Australia by learning from the past*. Asian Studies Association of Australia. Retrieved on 17 April 2022 from asaa.asn.au/55224-2/

West-Sooby, J. (2020). Engaging with the Past: Lessons from the History of Modern Languages at the University of Adelaide. In: Fornasiero, J., Reed, S.M.A., Amery, R., Bouvet, E., Enomoto, K., Xu, H.L. (eds) *Intersections in Language Planning and Policy*. Springer. doi.org/10.1007/978-3-030-50925-5_7

Part 1: Policies and access

1

The L2 learning experience as the Cinderella of the L2 motivational self system

Giuseppe D'Orazzi

Abstract

Drawing on Dörnyei's (2019) invitation to examine in more depth students' *L2 Learning Experience*, which he considers to be the 'Cinderella of the L2 Motivational Self System', this study proposes a tridimensional analysis of Dörnyei's (2009) *L2 Learning Experience* construct. *Teacher-specific Motivational Components*, *Course-specific Motivational Components* (Dörnyei 1994), and the *University Context* (based on Dörnyei's [2019] *School Context*) were used as categories of motivators to organise themes and variables emerging from research participants' responses to two questionnaires and two rounds of interviews. Students of French, German, Italian and Spanish enrolled at different Australian universities were asked to reflect on their *L2 Learning Experience* as part of a larger study on motivation and demotivation in L2 learning (D'Orazzi, 2020a). The analysis of quantitative and qualitative data allows the researcher to offer a detailed discussion of the dynamics which predominantly motivated L2 beginner students during two semesters of L2 studies. The examination of changes of motivation over time aims to cater to the interest of L2 educators who wish to understand which activities proposed within a formal learning environment foster students' motivation to learn European languages in Australia.

Keywords: L2 learning experience, L2 teaching, Australian university students' motivation, language education, European language studies

1. Introduction

In the field of applied linguistics, researchers have offered multiple definitions of second language (L2) learning motivation. Dörnyei (2020), for instance, posits that 'motivation, by definition, concerns the choice and direction of a particular action, the effort expended on it and the persistence with it' (p. 61). This chapter bases its analysis of students' experiences in the formal learning environment on this definition of motivation in the attempt to integrate the understanding of L2 learning motivation. It aims to expand on recent research on L2 learning motivation (cf. Mendoza & Phung, 2019) where effort and investment shown by L2 learners are investigated from a psychological and emotional perspective (Dewaele, 2011; Dörnyei, 2020) as well as from a sociocultural angle (Crookes & Schmidt, 1991; Ushioda, 2009).

In the recent literature on L2 learning motivation, a strong emphasis has been put on discussing the *Ideal L2 Self* and *Ought-to L2 Self*, which guide the analysis of a number of studies as presented by, for instance, Boo et al. (2015). The *Ideal L2 Self*—considered to be the learners' vision of themselves as future proficient users of an L2 and the *Ought-to L2 Self*—understood as a set of external obligations and expectations reflected on learners by people around them—make up the *L2 Motivational Self System* (L2MSS) theorised by Dörnyei (2009). A third component of Dörnyei's (2009) three-dimensional construct—the *L2 learning experience*—has not been extensively researched. The lack of attention to such an important constituent of learners' motivation led Dörnyei (2019) to label it the 'Cinderella of the L2 Motivational Self System'. In response to this gap in the literature, this study explores students' L2 learning experience with the purpose of answering two research questions:

1. How does the formal learning environment contribute to students' motivation when learning French, German, Italian and Spanish at Australian universities across two semesters?
2. Which classroom and extra-curricular activities are particularly motivating for students who have just started to learn French, German, Italian and Spanish at the tertiary level?

Students' responses to two online questionnaires and individual interviews inform the exploration of their experiences during one academic year while learning French, German, Italian and Spanish at beginner level (D'Orazzi, 2020a). Quantitative and qualitative data were collected at the Group of Eight (Go8) Australian universities[1] to give voice to a wide range of students in multiple institutions and discover which variables are more influential than others in terms of L2 learning motivation. It is hoped that the answers to the two research questions formulated for this study will support new pedagogical practices within L2 programs and research-informed L2 teaching strategies at higher university levels (see also Weinmann et al., 2021).

2. The impact of the formal learning environment on L2 learning motivation

This study accepts Dörnyei's invitation (2019) to focus on the direct impact of the classroom environment on students' motivation, and conduct new research, where the *L2 Learning Experience* theoretical construct is defined 'as a comprehensive rubric to cover the whole range of motivational influences associated with the actual process of learning an L2' (p. 21). In particular, this chapter targets a large range of classroom-related motivational influences which appear in the research conducted by You et al. (2016) but also, specifically within the Australian tertiary education landscape, by Martín et al. (2016). This study groups together multiple aspects listed by Dörnyei (2019) such as school context, syllabus and teaching materials, learning tasks, one's peers (group dynamics) and teachers. In doing so, this research is assisted by Dörnyei's (1994) ground-breaking *Three-level Framework of L2 Motivation*, which encompasses *Course-specific Motivational Components, Teacher-specific Motivational Components* and *Group-specific Motivational Components*, as reported in Figure 1.1.

---

[1] The Go8 universities are Australia's leading research-intensive universities: the University of Western Australia, Monash University, The Australian National University, the University of Adelaide, the University of Melbourne, the University of New South Wales, the University of Queensland and the University of Sydney.

Course-specific Motivational Components	Teacher-specific Motivational Components	Group-specific Motivational Components
• 'concerning the syllabus, the teaching materials, the teaching method, and the learning'	• 'concerning the teacher's personality, teaching style, feedback, and relationship with the students'	• 'concerning the dynamics of the learning'

Figure 1.1 Dörnyei's *Three-level Framework of L2 Motivation*
Source: Dörnyei (1994, p. 277).

The two categories of *Course-specific Motivational Components* and *Group-specific Motivational Components* have been merged together, since the dynamics developed in class appeared to be triggered by both the syllabus proposed by course coordinators and the interaction among students stimulated by teaching methods, materials and in-class activities. Drawing on the 'syllabus/curriculum level' theorised by Crookes and Schmidt (1991), the L2 syllabus remains a compelling force in the stimulation of motivation and in-group cohesive actions.

Studies on foreign language enjoyment (FLE) and foreign language classroom anxiety (FLCA) also shed light on the role of teachers, course planning and classroom dynamics in triggering enjoyment and, conversely, causing anxiety among students (Dewaele & MacIntyre, 2014; Fraschini & Tao, 2024). Dewaele and MacIntyre (2014) referred to the enjoyment fostered by social dynamics happening both inside and outside the L2 formal learning environment as *FLE-Social*. Li et al. (2018) delivered an analysis of how teachers' approaches and rapport-management with their students stimulate students' interests, participation and enjoyment, labelling this dynamic *FLE-Teacher* (see also Dewaele et al., 2017). The understanding of the role of teachers in the L2 learning environment is fundamental not only in terms of student motivation but also in emphasising teachers' agency within their course delivery, following Crozet and Díaz's (2020) qualitative research among L2 teachers at different Australian universities. Crozet and Díaz's exploration through the lens of teachers' identity construction and self-reflections on their agency in the academic world—teaching and researching—validates the argument that teachers hold a fundamental position in motivating and sustaining students during their L2 learning process, as strongly confirmed also by Kubanyiova (2012) (see also Irie et al., 2018).

In addition, Li et al. (2018) investigated the role of *FLE-Atmosphere*, the construct utilised to examine the enjoyment that stems from the immediate social environment created in class with interactive, engaging and interesting activities. Dörnyei's (2019) 'one's peers' component of the *L2 Learning Experience* pictures the settings created in class by students' active participation and contributions fuelling 'particular social acceptance, group cohesiveness, norms of operation and tolerance' (p. 25). The understanding of group dynamics and the internal operational norms and scripts influenced the research undertaken by Joe et al. (2017), who investigated the contribution of the 'classroom social climate' to increase student motivation. This social, inclusive and interactive atmosphere created in an L2 classroom was found to be strongly connected to students' FLE but also to their willingness to communicate within and outside the formal learning environment in several Australian universities (D'Orazzi, 2020b).

In addition to the analysis of *Teacher-specific Motivational Components* and *Course-specific Motivational Components*, this chapter encompasses a third category of motivators classified as *University Context*. This category draws upon Dörnyei's (2019) *School Context* exploring the wider university space in which students benefit from the school community and norms, including extra-curricular activities and opportunities to apply for exchange programs overseas (cf. Lasan & Rehner, 2018). The university context is strongly influenced by policies adopted by universities to favour the learning of L2s and increase students' exposure to the countries and cultures where the studied L2s are spoken—for example, exchange programs overseas (Yashima, 2002), the University of Melbourne *Breadth Subject* model and the University of Western Australia *Broadening Unit* model (Brown & Caruso, 2016) and ad-hoc L2 learning pathways such as the diploma of languages (Baldwin 2019; Brown et al. 2019).

3. The Australian university landscape

Studies on L2 learning motivation at tertiary level in Australia do not always engage with the dynamics emerging from the classroom environment. A comprehensive examination of L2 classroom dynamics in terms of motivation and demotivation was carried out by Martín et al. (2016). Their study at The Australian National University provides a multidimensional portrait of the factors that triggered students' interest in learning multiple L2s and affected their choice of continuing to pursue their L2 learning process. Martín et al. (2016) distinguished between committed students, doubters and quitters who were motivated and demotivated by a long array of variables stemming from their social environment but also from the classroom environment in which they were learning an L2 at different levels of proficiency.

The L2 classroom environment was at the centre of another study on L2 motivation in Australia. De Saint Léger and Storch (2009) emphasised the function of willingness to communicate, self-confidence and anxiety when learning French at university level. Based on their longitudinal research findings, they suggested the implementation of small-group discussions to enable students to achieve fluency and enhance their performance in a university setting. This was also considered crucial in terms of decreasing anxiety and increasing participation, which would enable affiliation orientations within the small groups to be expanded in the social context in which students were planning to use French in authentic scenarios. De Saint Léger and Storch's (2009) study resonates with the encouragement recently given by Arber et al. (2021) to rethink how languages are learnt and taught in Australia and to explore 'the complex links between languages, cultures and identities' (p. 5).

In a similar vein, more recent research conducted among learners of Italian at the University of Western Australia sheds light on the tight and pivotal links between languages, cultures and identities. Caruso and Fraschini (2021) discovered that students constructed 'multicultural' and 'mobile and linguistically competent' identities that were able to enjoy and understand Italian culture. Learners of Korean were motivated by the same factors mentioned above, with an additional desire to enjoy Korean culture in Korea and develop the intercultural communicative competence necessary for dealing with various culturally diverse scenarios (Fraschini & Caruso, 2019). A strong sense of identity also emerged among adult learners of Italian in two private schools in Sydney, who acknowledged the influential role of Italian communities in their suburbs and the general perception of Italian culture in Australia (Palmieri, 2019). Indeed, the value of the studied L2 was found to be socially constructed for learners of French (D'Orazzi, 2020c), German (D'Orazzi et al., 2022) and Italian (D'Orazzi & Hajek, 2021; 2022) across different states and territories in Australia. Students' perceptions of these languages appeared to be influenced by the value that the whole Australian society would give to the cultures and countries where these languages are spoken (D'Orazzi, 2020a; Palmieri, 2019).

4. Data collection and methodology

Data were collected principally at the Go8 Australian universities during two semesters in 2018 (prior to the COVID-19 pandemic) to provide consistency across institutions that offer all four language courses selected for this research. In two cases, Italian lessons were provided outside of the Go8 universities: the University of Queensland outsources Italian classes at Griffith University and Queensland University of Technology, while students of Italian enrolled at the University of Adelaide attend lessons at Flinders University. Responses provided by students enrolled at Griffith University, Queensland University of Technology and Flinders University were not presented in D'Orazzi (2020a), nor were three questionnaire items that were originally cut off by a Principal Components Analysis conducted to reduce the size of a very large data set (D'Orazzi, 2020a, p. 73). These three extra items are intended to enlarge the scope of this chapter and offer a more rigorous analysis of the dynamics experienced by students within their classroom environment. Out of 20 five-point Likert scale items included in the questionnaire and analysed in this chapter, 13 were inspired by Sakai and Kikuchi's study on demotivation in learning English as L2 (2009), since their analysis focuses on the dynamics experienced by students in a formal learning setting in terms of demotivation (D'Orazzi 2020d). More items were added to encompass a wider range of elements characterising students' learning experience in terms of motivation. Students had the choice of one response, from *strongly agree* (value 1) to *strongly disagree* (value 5).

All participants were *ab initio* students who received the link for the online questionnaire from their course coordinators. Overall, 31 out of 32 course coordinators agreed to forward the online questionnaire to their students. Those students who volunteered to participate in further stages of the research received a second link to complete a second questionnaire in their second semester of L2 studies at the university. A selection of students at the University of Melbourne was also interviewed after each of the two semesters in which data were collected, as explained below.

4.1. Research participants

The first questionnaire was completed by 728 participants (199 for French, 176 for German, 154 for Italian and 199 for Spanish), whereas the second questionnaire was fully filled in by 213 participants (47 for French, 57 for German, 55 for Italian and 54 for Spanish). Among these students, 37 of them (10 for French, 9 for German, 10 for Italian and 8 for Spanish) were interviewed after the first semester and 25 (6 for French, 7 for German, 6 for Italian and 6 for Spanish) were interviewed after the second semester. All interviewees' recordings were de-identified, and pseudonyms were given to ensure that their statements would remain anonymous. Table 1.1 provides a summary of the biographical features of student participants, who were all beginner learners with little or no prior exposure to the four languages considered in this study.

Table 1.1 Student participants' biographical information in both semesters

Demographic	Percentage in semester one	Percentage in semester two
Age	Below 30: 96.5% Over 31: 3.5%	Below 30: 95.3% Over 31: 4.7%
Gender	F: 72.1% M: 27.1% O: 0.8%	F: 75.6% M: 22.5% O: 1.9%
English as L1	Yes: 79.8% No: 20.2%	Yes: 85.9% No: 14.1%
English at home	Yes: 68.5% No: 31.5%	Yes: 82.2% No: 17.8%
Category	Domestic: 79% International: 21%	Domestic: 87.3% International: 12.7%
Course in study plan	Core: 32% Optional: 63.7% Other: 4.3%	Core: 47.4% Optional: 50.7% Other: 1.9%
More L2s at present	Yes: 22.8% No: 77.2%	Yes: 25.8% No: 74.2%
Prior L2 experience	Yes: 80.6% No: 19.4%	

Source: Compiled by author.

Students were mainly native English speakers, but around 20 per cent in the first semester and 14 per cent in the second semester spoke a language other than English as their first language or one of their first languages. Notably, around 20 per cent of students were learning more than one L2 at the same time and roughly 80 per cent of them had already been exposed to an L2 learning experience before starting to study French, German, Italian or Spanish at beginner level at university. Students' biographical information will be considered in the analysis of research participants' responses both to questionnaire items and interview questions.

4.2. A quantitative perspective

Mean values, standard deviations and correlations were calculated in an attempt to highlight which variables motivated students during their L2 learning experience, in line with previous studies on motivation undertaken in Australia (e.g. Palmieri, 2019; Schmidt, 2011). These statistical tools help describe students' preferences and their changes in motivation across one year of L2 studies drawing upon Fink's (2017) work. In addition, correlations contributed to the analysis of how the three categories of motivation chosen for this study were connected and to what extent they influenced each other (Pollock, 2016). The SPSS software was used to conduct statistical analysis and facilitate the visual representation of data analysis findings (Pallant, 2007).

4.3. A qualitative perspective

Following Creswell (2013), a thematic content analysis of students' narratives elicited from individual interviews was undertaken to identify the main recurrent themes related to the variables included in the two surveys. A thematic content analysis of interview narratives was chosen, since previous studies on L2 motivation at Australian universities made use of it (Campbell & Storch, 2011; Nakamura, 2016). Such an analytical tool was needed to expand on the results of quantitative data analysis previously performed by Schmidt (2014) when exploring German students' motivation in very similar settings. Students were asked to reflect on the mean values emerging from the statistical analysis to integrate their understanding and verify that the quantitative data were correctly interpreted.

5. Data analysis

Quantitative analysis of the mean values and standard deviations of the three categories of motivators suggests that students' motivation did not largely change from one semester (S1) to the other (S2) (Table 1.2).

Table 1.2 Mean (M) and standard deviation (SD) values for the three categories of motivators

Category of motivators	M S1	M S2	SD S1	SD S2
Teacher-specific Motivational Components	1.96	1.97	0.57	0.63
Course-specific Motivational Components	2.22	2.21	0.50	0.52
University Context	2.64	2.58	0.51	0.52

Source: Compiled by author.

Teacher-specific Motivational Components was found to be the strongest category of motivators with means below the value 2—corresponding to students' answer *agree* to the five-point Likert scale items included in the questionnaires. *Course-specific Motivational Components* and *University Context* recorded higher mean values, signalling a less strong agreement of students that their course and university environment were stimulating their motivation across the two semesters under analysis.

5.1. Teacher-specific Motivational Components

A closer look at *Teacher-specific Motivational Components* confirms that students enjoyed their relationship with teachers who were found to create rapport (variable 1) and make students comfortable in the classroom (variable 2), as shown by the low mean values listed in Table 1.3.

Table 1.3 Mean (M) and standard deviation (SD) values for the variables belonging to the category of motivators *Teacher-specific Motivational Components*

	Teacher-specific Motivational Components	M S1	M S2	SD S1	SD S2
1	I get along well with my teacher	1.66	1.69	0.66	0.79
2	My teacher makes me feel comfortable during lessons	1.74	1.73	0.77	0.84
3	My teacher focuses on all main language abilities (speaking, reading, listening and writing)	1.86	1.83	0.83	0.85
4	Teacher's explanations are easy to understand	1.90	1.92	0.80	0.86
5	I often have the opportunity to communicate in French/German/Italian/Spanish in class	1.98	1.95	0.81	0.87
6	My teacher focuses on translation	2.63	2.70	0.99	0.99

Source: Compiled by author.

Teachers were also praised for their ability to design their lesson around more than one skill at the same time (variable 3) and to give clear explanations (variable 4). Variable 5 also reached a generally high level of agreement, since motivated students were satisfied with the extent of opportunities available to communicate in their L2 in class. This indicates that teachers were able to create activities which would allow students to interact and develop their oral skills. Nonetheless, higher standard deviations for variables 2–5, especially in the second semester, indicate that students provided quite different responses ranging from *strongly agree* (value 1) to *strongly disagree* (value 5) depending on the specific teacher they were engaged with.

The last variable of *Teacher-specific Motivational Components* recorded higher means and higher standard deviations, which raises important questions about the use of translation drills in class but also teachers' decisions to translate lesson materials into English. Students experienced very different dynamics depending on their teachers' approaches. This is confirmed by qualitative data. Students were explicitly asked to comment on these six variables and provide plausible explanations for the results presented in Table 1.3. Students from all four cohorts highlighted that variables 1 and 2 received the highest levels of agreement because of the crucial role of their teachers in fostering motivation, as asserted by Veronica (French, S1):

> She was a lot of help in that way and made you speak and being interactive. She made it easier to learn. […] She was always asking and answering. It was very helpful in our class, definitely! I think in other classes teachers talk more and want interaction less.

Building rapport with teachers stimulated not only students' engagement but also positive emotions, which translated into a desire to learn more language content and attend lessons in good spirits. Oswine (French, S1) describes these dynamics as follows:

> I enjoyed the teaching, so I was not afraid to go to tutorials every morning.

Changes across semesters were not particularly noticeable when analysing quantitative data. Conversely, research participants commented on the low means recorded in the second semester by underlining the impact of teachers' attitudes and determination to offer students high-quality classes and opportunities to speak in class once students were able to express more concepts in their L2. Students like Kevin (German, S2) genuinely believed that teachers were active promoters of motivational forces:

> In German, I feel like the teacher wants everyone to do well. […] My teacher speaks German a lot in the class and gets us to participate a lot, so I feel that that helps a lot create motivation because we're actually speaking it. I feel all the amount of communication in the class has increased a fair bit.

The same student also extensively commented on the relatively higher standard deviations for variables 2–6, acknowledging that students might have answered differently depending on the teacher who was delivering L2 content:

> I think it depends a lot on the teacher you have because I felt that some teachers did interactive things during the lesson like with the Padlet—we had to write about a topic in German on this online page, so that the whole class could read it. I feel that this semester we did that a lot more than the previous semester. […] I feel it [students' motivation] has gone up.

A similar dynamic was experienced by Alex (Italian, S2) when identifying differences between her teacher in the first semester and her new teacher in the second semester:

> Compared to semester one teacher, he was more structured. I could see the linear progression of the course a lot more than with my other teacher. He was very accessible. I didn't feel weird asking him questions. […] My class had really good dynamics. We caught up outside class and we studied together.

Differences in students' perceptions of their teachers from a personal and professional point of view encapsulate students' learning styles and L2 aptitude. Research participants portrayed these differences quite clearly when trying to understand the wide range of responses provided to these six Likert scale items across universities and language cohorts. Cameron (Italian, S2), who changed his teacher in the second semester, posits:

> Their teaching style was a little bit different. All the things that I like they both had. […] If they both teach visually, and you are a visual learner it doesn't make a difference, but if one teacher is all about writing things down or likes to do lot of audio and the other teacher is more visual than yours and you are a visual learner, you might like the second one better.

5.2. Course-specific Motivational Components

A more diverse variety of responses is presented in Table 1.4, where students generally strongly agreed or agreed that the material used in class was useful to learn French, German, Italian or Spanish (variable 7) and liked their classmates and the relationship they developed with them (variable 8). Indeed, variables 7 and 8 recorded low mean values in semester one and slightly lower values again in semester two when students could engage with the class material and their classmates more closely.

Table 1.4 Mean (M) and standard deviation (SD) values for the variables belonging to the category of motivators *Course-specific Motivational Components*

	Course-specific Motivational Components	M S1	M S2	SD S1	SD S2
7	The material used in class is useful to learn French/German/Italian/Spanish	1.88	1.85	0.69	0.63
8	I like my classmates	1.90	1.85	0.75	0.76
9	Visual and audio materials (such as videos and DVDs) are used during lessons	2.01	2.02	0.94	0.89
10	Cultural topics covered in lessons are interesting	2.04	2.00	0.87	0.78
11	French/German/Italian/Spanish language content we study for the course is easy to understand	2.22	2.28	0.82	0.87
12	The amount of hours I need to study for tests/assessments and final exams satisfies my initial expectations	2.42	2.36	0.93	0.96
13	The pace of lessons is appropriate for learning French/German/Italian/Spanish	2.47	2.32	1.03	0.97
14	Interactive computer-based/online activities are used during lessons.	2.83	2.96	1.15	1.20

Source: Compiled by author.

Variables 9 and 10 also appear to record consensus among students over their first year of L2 studies. Students enjoyed audiovisual materials and cultural topics. A different change over time pertains to the content delivered in class (variable 11), which became less easy to understand in the second semester when more complex grammar rules were explained. In a similar vein, high means for the response *neither agree nor disagree* and relatively high standard deviations increased in the second semester for variable 14, indicating the amount of computer-based/online activities made available in class prior to the COVID-19 pandemic.

Very surprisingly, in the second semester, students declared that they took fewer hours to prepare their tests/assessments (variable 12) and that the pace of lessons was more appropriate (variable 13) compared to the first semester. This is represented by a noticeable decrease of mean values for these two variables in the second semester, despite the increase in difficulty of the L2 course experienced by many students who disagreed or strongly disagreed with the statements proposed for variables 12 and 13, as indicated by the high standard deviations.

Interview narratives helped to unpack students' responses to Likert scale items and provide a more comprehensive understanding of how *Course-specific Motivational Components* contributed to motivating research participants. Materials and activities motivated students to a very large extent, as mentioned by Grace (Spanish, S1):

> My teacher had activities lined up and conversations with different people in the class in the language. It allowed us to know people and practice and then also you have time to read and know about the culture as well very effectively.

The perception of lesson pace and workload to keep up with in an L2 course varied not only across institutions and L2 departments but also across students, depending on their prior exposure to L2 learning situations and the learning strategies applied. Angela (Italian, S1) briefly summarised these dynamics when commenting on the quantitative data analysis outcomes related to *Course-specific Motivational Components*:

> I think the pace was perfect, but you have to bear in mind that I've done another romance language before and I've a good grasp of French. I can see it in my other classmates. It was fast for people who didn't learn another language before. [...] It was great. In class, there was plenty of opportunities to practice listening, speaking and writing.

In a similar vein, students were differently motivated by the number of hours to be invested to prepare tests, assignments and exams. A large percentage of students agreed that the time spent was adequate for the reasons that Helen (Italian, S1) presented:

> I think it's very good that they do a lot of different small-work assessments [...], because it forces you to study more. If you have an assessment in week 4 and week 6, you don't do a big study in week 4 and week 6. You sort of revise more frequently than if you've only two grades a semester and it's not a big deal for the frequent assessments because they are only 10 per cent or 20 per cent. Having short goals helped my learning.

Audiovisual materials and interactive activities appeared to be used more often in the second semester than in the first semester, as mentioned by Sam who contradicts the increase of the mean for variables 9 and 14 over time (German, S2):

> It's increased the quality of interactive activities. We talk about more stuff now. I watched a movie that is old from German production, so we actually discussed a lot.

The use of more interactive online materials increased over time due to the improvement of students' proficiency in their L2 after almost one year of studies. Indeed, Olivia (German, S2) noticed how her motivation was boosted by the understanding of authentic material proposed in the L2 classroom:

> We are doing *Run Lola Run* and that's really interesting. It's a really good film, so looking at that in terms of sort of culture is really interesting. You can relate to the characters and you can see a lot of expressions and then listen to what she's saying and you connect with the character and that's more interesting. I suppose the character symbolises the culture, sort of, and not all of it, obviously.

Cultural activities motivated students even more when they needed to practise their L2 outside of the formal classroom environment. Rebecca (Spanish, S2) introduced one activity which motivated her and her classmates who could practise their L2 and observe how much language capital they acquired during two semesters of L2 studies:

> We did one project this semester which was an interview with someone else who was not from the class. That was really good because we only spoke Spanish […]. That was a good opportunity to practise my Spanish.

One more aspect that increased students' motivation over time was the improvement of the classroom atmosphere and the creation of stronger friendships among classmates. Alex (Italian, S2) emphasised how L2 classes were different from other courses since they allowed her to establish strong bonds with her peers:

> It was a really good break from my other more academic studies. It was a really good way to meet awesome people and to form friendships that you don't have a chance to do in other units. It was really fun.

5.3. University Context

Quantitative data analysis shows very heterogeneous outcomes for the variables belonging to *University Context*, which was deemed as a positive but also negative space for many student participants. Higher mean values suggest that students mostly did not agree with the variables grouped in this category of motivators. Nonetheless, relatively high standard deviations demonstrate that students held very different opinions depending on their own specific L2 learning experience (Table 1.5).

Table 1.5 Mean (M) and standard deviation (SD) values for the variables belonging to the *University Context* category of motivators

	University Context	M S1	M S2	SD S1	SD S2
15	The class size is appropriate to learn the language	2.10	2.11	0.97	0.98
16	The facilities in class are useful to stimulate my learning	2.18	2.12	0.76	0.68
17	There are lots of exchange programs overseas I can access if I learn French/German/Italian/Spanish	2.28	2.38	1.15	0.90
18	The time spent in French/German/Italian/Spanish classes is enough to learn properly	2.77	2.56	1.10	1.05
19	My university organises many activities where I can learn more on the culture of French-/German-/Italian-/Spanish-speaking countries and practise the language	2.96	2.83	0.99	1.04
20	There is substantial government financial support (e.g. scholarships) to study French/German/Italian/Spanish at university	3.34	3.39	0.86	0.86

Source: Compiled by author.

L2 class size (variable 15) and university facilities (variable 16) were normally considered adequate for an interactive and enjoyable learning experience that would allow students to acquire their desired level of L2 proficiency. The low mean for these last two variables kept students motivated during both semesters under study. Depending on the university taken into consideration—see high standard deviations—students could apply for a large number of exchange programs, as signalled by low mean values for variable 17.

Time spent in class was an issue for all those students who did not consider the number of contact hours enough to be able to learn an L2 (variable 18), despite an improvement registered in the second semester with a lower mean value.

High means and standard deviations recorded for variable 19 signal that students could not always access extra-curricular activities. This was found to be dependent on the L2 department where participants studied and on whether course coordinators highlighted the different opportunities available to students, not only to practise their L2 but also to increase exposure to the culture(s) of the countries in which the languages are spoken. Similarly, negative responses were often provided by students in both semesters when asked if there existed funds/scholarships set up to specifically enrol into L2 courses at their university (variable 20).

Qualitative data assist in completing the analysis of the *University Context* and in understanding the extent to which the variables listed in Table 1.5 motivated student participants, given their very general nature. Students confirmed that having small cohorts in class increased their motivation, as in the experiences reported below:

> *Sam (German, S1)*: For a subject that has so many people enrolled in it, the class sizes were pretty good. I felt they were small enough to be effective. We didn't have 30 students.
>
> *Francesca (Italian, S2)*: I feel the class size is a good number, maybe we have 10 or 15 people. That is a good number. It's enough to have a class conversation and to sit in different groups.

Exchange programs gave students a sense of purpose and a goal to achieve with the knowledge of their L2. Despite not having specific funds to study an L2—which justifies the high means for variable 20—students were motivated to apply for exchange programs overseas and summer courses because of different scholarships they could access. Ella (French, S1) explored how exchange programs and overseas courses increase students' motivation and how costs can be covered by scholarships and government schemes:

> I'm doing an overseas subject [course] for Italian so, I know that having something to look forward to, like visiting the country, is important. [...] When you put in your application to go overseas the university puts you automatically to receive a scholarship if you deserve it [...]. And then also something the government allows to

put the cost into your HECS[2] loan so that you don't have to pay it upfront. You can pay it whenever you earn enough. [...] So, by allowing to put it on a loan this gives more people the chance to experience other cultures and therefore people are more driven to learn other languages.

Narratives were often a space to reflect further on the responses given to survey Likert scale items, as Angela (Italian, S1) put it:

> I was really motivated because I knew I would be using Italian really really soon in my daily life when I'm going on exchange, but it's a little bit more difficult when you don't see the future when you'll be using it quite a lot, so there's no motivation to keep it up at university level. For example, the university is supporting me financially. It helps and it makes the decision easier. [...] On top of that, I know there's an Italian club as well outside the classroom.

Cultural events organised either by L2 departments or student social clubs increased students' interest whenever they had the time and possibility to attend them. As a result, students considered extra-curricular activities engaging and helpful to boost their interest in the L2 learning process itself. These activities varied largely across departments, as students repeatedly mentioned during interviews, especially in the second semester when they reported possessing a better understanding of the language after almost one year of L2 studies:

> *Peter (French, S1)*: I do think that cultural events are nice in a way they really encourage people to either learn the language or just visit the country.

> *Eike (German, S2)*: Some tutors who hold a conversation with students who want to go. You can go there and talk to her and talk to people who want to speak German this way. [...] I realised that's a good opportunity for me to speak a little bit more German.

---

2   The Higher Education Contribution Scheme is a state-managed loan which allows students to pay the Australian government for their university studies after graduation once their income hits a certain threshold.

> *Paolo (Italian, S2)*: I went to the Italian ball, which increased my motivation. It was very cool—Italian things, Italian songs. It was fun and the Italian food, which is cool. […] I went to one pass session[3] when I was in first semester. I'm lazy. I guess people go more to pass sessions and stuff. They have a Facebook page where they put the ad.

Students reflected on the importance of having more contact hours to improve their L2 proficiency levels, especially in the second semester when the workload increased, as highlighted by quantitative data analysis outcomes (variable 18). Nonetheless, a considerable number of participants were aware of the time needed to pass other core courses given the weight of an L2 course in their study plan—63.7 per cent of the research participants in semester one and 50.7 per cent in semester two chose an L2 as their optional/elective course (Table 1.1), as Veronica (French, S2) posited:

> I think that you need more contact hours to be able to learn more sufficiently, but I also think that with having most people have three other classes as well, it would be difficult to keep up to all the other classes if they have to spend so much extra time on French, because it is something you need to actively learn.

6. New directions for the field of motivation in learning European languages

Quantitative data analysis demonstrates that all three main categories of motivators identified for this study were interconnected allowing multidirectional influences. *Teacher-specific Motivational Components* recorded the strongest positive correlations with *Course-specific Motivational Components* in the first semester and even more so in the second semester, represented by the high Pearson's correlation coefficients ($r = .632$ and $.699$, respectively) presented in Table 1.6. Pearson's correlation was used because of the nature of the data (scored and not rank-ordered data) and to measure the strength of the relationship. These positive correlations suggest that teachers' actions were deeply impacted by the course syllabus and materials suggested by course coordinators and L2 department chairs. At the same level, the effectiveness of lesson plans and activities proposed in class was found to be dependent on the clarity and communicative skills of teachers who were in close contact with their students.

---

3   The Peer Assisted Study Scheme (PASS) is an internationally accredited peer-learning program that aims to support students with group study sessions led by certified student PASS leaders.

Table 1.6 Correlations between the three categories of motivators analysed in this study

Correlations in semester one			
		Teacher	**Course**
Course	Pearson Correlation	.632**	
	Sig. (2-tailed)	.000	
University	Pearson Correlation	.506**	.588**
	Sig. (2-tailed)	.000	.000

Correlations in semester two			
		Teacher	**Course**
Course	Pearson Correlation	.699**	
	Sig. (2-tailed)	.000	
University	Pearson Correlation	.497**	.586**
	Sig. (2-tailed)	.000	.000

** Correlation is significant at the 0.01 level (2-tailed)
Source: Compiled by author.

Strong and statistically significant correlations were also identified between *Teacher-specific Motivational Components* and *University Context* ($r = .506$ and $.497$ in semesters one and two, respectively) as well as between *Course-specific Motivational Components* and *University Context* ($r = .588$ and $.586$ in semesters one and two, respectively). These last correlations with *University Context* nevertheless appeared to be slightly weaker in the second semester when the correlation between *Teacher-specific Motivational Components* and *Course-specific Motivational Components* became stronger. Such a shift from one semester to the other confirms both quantitative and qualitative data analysis results, which painted the learning environment as a space in which students slowly constructed positive and close relationships with their teachers and classmates over time. Strong positive correlations between *Teacher-specific Motivational Components* and *Course-specific Motivational Components* also show that the ways teachers delivered culture-related content were as important as the lesson content itself.

In response to the first research question formulated for this study—'How does the formal learning environment contribute to students' motivation when learning French, German, Italian and Spanish at Australian universities across two semesters?'—we can confirm that teachers' ability to create communication opportunities appears to be a strong motivational component that boosted positive emotions such as enjoyment, as observed by Fraschini and Tao (2024) with students of Korean. Teachers generated engaging and inclusive learning situations while providing clear explanations and focusing on all main L2 skills (cf. Arnold, 2018; Ehrman & Dörnyei, 1998; Martín et al., 2016). Data contribute to an understanding that teachers were considered to be essential components of a motivating and engaging L2 learning experience (Kubanyiova, 2012; Irie et al., 2018). Students' narratives assist in explaining that some of their teachers were able to develop close ties with them and demonstrate their agency within the formal L2 learning environment, especially in the second semester when relationships became stronger (cf. Crozet & Díaz, 2020; Dörnyei, 2020; Fukada et al., 2020). As a result, motivated students experienced high levels of enjoyment in learning a language in a positive and highly stimulating environment (D'Orazzi, 2020b; Dörnyei & Muir, 2019; Fraschini & Tao, 2024). Favourable teacher–student and student–student dynamics confirm the compelling importance of *FLE-Teacher* and *FLE-Atmosphere* theorised by Li et al. (2018) and of the 'classroom social climate' explored by Joe et al. (2017). *Teacher-specific Motivational Components* were not always tied to motivation for those students who did not appreciate their teachers' approach and explanations. The wide range of L2 departments involved in this research ($n = 31$) indicates that teaching styles are different across teachers and departments and might not always motivate the whole class cohort (D'Orazzi, 2020d; Lamb, 2020).

Based on statistically significant and strong positive correlations, teachers' success was dependent on the material—paper-based, audio, visual and digital—used in class and the cultural topics proposed to trigger interest and boost intrinsic motivation (Crookes & Schmidt, 1991; Hanna & de Nooy, 2009; You et al., 2016). Particular attention given to concrete daily-life situations increased students' willingness to communicate and helped them acquire the communicative competence necessary to travel to countries where their L2 is spoken (Campbell & Storch, 2011; D'Orazzi & Hajek, 2021; 2022; D'Orazzi et al., 2022; Yashima, 2002). In the second semester, students declared that in spite of an increase in difficulty in keeping up with lesson content and workload (cf. de Saint Léger & Storch, 2009), they benefited from a more social and inclusive environment characterised by friendships with their classmates and a more comprehensive understanding of the material proposed by their teachers (Dewaele et al., 2017; Dörnyei & Muir, 2019). This seems to confirm the outcomes of previous longitudinal research on motivation where the formal learning environment gained more importance over other factors over a period of time (Chan et al., 2015; D'Orazzi, 2020a; Gardner et al., 2004).

Positive and engaging group and teacher–student interactions were often deemed successful thanks to the availability of appropriate space offered by those universities which also allowed classes with a maximum of 15 people—especially in the second semester when the number of students enrolled on L2 courses was smaller. Nonetheless, high standard deviations recorded for *University Context* suggest that students retained very different opinions in this regard. Not surprisingly, studies on L2 learning demotivation throw light on the demotivating role of the *University Context* on students' L2 learning experience where student cohorts are excessively large (D'Orazzi, 2020d; Thorner & Kikuchi, 2020).

Universities also motivated those students who wanted to apply for exchange programs overseas and appreciated extra-curricular activities during which they learnt more about their L2 and L2-speaking countries' cultures (Yashima, 2002). Based on qualitative data and biographical information drawn from the two surveys, *University Context* also triggered interest in learning an L2 among those students who wanted to choose an interesting optional/elective course (Table 1.1)—including breadth subjects at the University of Melbourne and broadening units at the University of Western Australia, or enrol in a diploma of languages (see also Baldwin, 2019; Brown & Caruso, 2016; Brown et al., 2019)

In regard to the second research question—'Which classroom and extracurricular activities are particularly motivating for students who have just started to learn French, German, Italian and Spanish at tertiary level?'—a range of activities were mentioned by interviewees, confirming and articulating in greater detail some of the outcomes of the quantitative data analysis. Extra-curricular activities were welcomed by motivated students who enjoyed social events in which they were invited to practise their L2 and be exposed to the cultures of the countries where their L2 is spoken. Students stated that they had attended such activities in an attempt to acquire communicative competence to be applied in real-life scenarios—that is, sociolinguistic competence (Canale & Swain, 1980; Hymes, 1972), confirming the finding by Dewaele (2004) that student participants developed greater sociolinguistic competence when they 'socialised' with French-speaking people because of 'a superior understanding of the need to express respect through pronoun choice' (p. 399). This result is closely related to the analysis offered by Lasan and Rehner (2018) of Collentine and Freed's study (2004, cited in Lasan & Rehner 2018), which explores the main features of widely accepted learning situations: *study at home*, *immersion* and *study abroad*. Lasan and Rehner (2018) criticise the flurry of research on *study at home* and *study abroad* learning situations as 'extracurricular target-language contact' opportunities against the scarce existence of studies on *immersion*, which is characterised by 'some combination of the learning and communicative contexts' (p. 633).

The study of movies and songs in class or in special events was also considered to be motivating, since it not only gave students the opportunity to test their listening and reading comprehension abilities but also helped them understand in more depth the culture of the countries in which their L2 is spoken, confirming what L2 teachers perceived in Crozet and Díaz's (2020) study. Consequently, cultural materials contributed to building students' new 'multicultural', 'mobile and linguistically competent' identities (Caruso & Fraschini, 2021; D'Orazzi et al., 2022).

Lasan and Rehner's (2018) argument that the *study abroad* learning situations have received more attention is validated by the long list of studies on L2 motivation confirming the availability of multiple exchange programs offered by universities and the positive feedback received by students who studied in hosting universities overseas (Fryer & Roger, 2018; Huang et al., 2015; Kong et al., 2018; Yashima, 2002). This is certainly the case of one research participant, Nicole (Spanish, S2), who went on an exchange program overseas and realised how studying abroad increased her motivation to interact in a Spanish-speaking social context:

> She's [my Mexican housemate] sitting there too and she's talking to a Mexican friend and she's speaking Spanish. I feel like it makes me want to keep learning because all I want is to being able to talk with her fully in Spanish and introducing me to her other friends.

Further understanding of the formal learning environment is offered by students who declared themselves to be strongly motivated by innovative and engaging forms of assessment. Some students needed to interview native speakers of the language they were studying. The use of task-based teaching approaches as a form of assessment allowed students to interact in their L2 and boost their interest in the people and cultures of the countries where their L2 would be used in daily situations—thus improving their self-esteem, engagement, motivation and autonomy (Ellis et al., 2020; Lambert, 2010). Task-based conversational activities in which students needed to show how much they had learnt increased their motivation when they realised how much they could express in their L2, especially in the second semester when their motivation and willingness to communicate increased (see also de Saint Léger & Storch, 2009). The improvement of *FLE-Social* and *FLE-Atmosphere* (D'Orazzi, 2020b; Dewaele & MacIntyre, 2014; Li et al., 2018) was often fostered by online debates and the creation of group chats via social networks in which students shared information pertaining to events and course materials, news and images of the countries in which they aimed to travel and used the language learnt at university (Hanna & de Nooy, 2009; Reinhardt, 2019).

7. Conclusions and final observations

Based on Dörnyei's (2019) critique of recent studies on motivation which do not focus on the *L2 Learning Experience*, labelled the 'Cinderella of the L2 Motivational Self System', this study has shed light on three specific motivational components by partially drawing upon an older framework theorised by Dörnyei in 1994 and a more updated understanding of the significance of the *L2 Learning Experience* (Dörnyei 2019). *Teacher-specific Motivational Components, Course-specific Motivational Components* and the *University Context* appeared to motivate students in multiple ways depending on the class activities but also on the stages of their L2 learning experience during their two first semesters studying a European language, namely French, German, Italian or Spanish, at a university in Australia. Quantitative as well as qualitative data contributed to confirming the importance of enjoyment in and outside the classroom environment, which places a greater responsibility on L2 departments to provide a larger range of immersive extra-curricular activities for their L2 students (D'Orazzi, 2020b, 2020d; Lasan & Rehner, 2018).

The dynamics experienced by students during their L2 learning experience also allowed them to construct new identities and imagine culturally diverse settings in which they could apply their L2 communicative competence acquired at university. These outcomes confirm previous studies focusing particularly on the *Ideal L2 Self*—for example, Caruso and Fraschini (2021), D'Orazzi (2020a), and D'Orazzi and Hajek (2021; 2022). New multicultural and multilingual identities were found to be triggered by the use of interactive and engaging activities in face-to-face settings, but also by the use of technology-mediated teaching practices (Hanna & de Nooy, 2009;

Henry, 2017; Reinhardt, 2019). It is hoped that the outcomes of this study might inspire L2 teachers and departments to set out new research-based strategies to increase students' motivation and engagement, as promoted by Weinmann et al. (2021), when arguing for research-based policies within the Australian L2 educational landscape. More research on this last component is strongly recommended to enable us to discover how, for example, the use of digital tools and social networks influenced students' motivation in Australia during the COVID-19 pandemic outbreak in 2020 and 2021. As Reinhard (2019) posits, 'social media, not fully explored, might offer affordances for multimodal, visual, location-based, and different forms of socio-collaborative learning' (p. 31), which might increase L2 motivation in students and fuel their desire to experience foreign cultures and develop communicative and intercultural competence.

References

Arber, R., Weinmann, M. & Blackmore, J. (Eds). (2021). *Rethinking languages education: Directions, challenges and innovations*. Taylor & Francis. doi.org/10.4324/9781315107974

Arnold, J. (2018, 26–28 November). *Affect in language learning: A map of the terrain* [Conference presentation]. Third International Conference on Language Education and Testing: Language Learning and Emotions. University of Antwerp, Belgium.

Baldwin, J. J. (2019). *Languages other than English in Australian higher education*. Springer. doi.org/10.1007/978-3-030-05795-4

Boo, Z., Dörnyei, Z. & Ryan, S. (2015). L2 motivation research 2005–2014: Understanding a publication surge and a changing landscape. *System, 55*, 145–57. doi.org/10.1016/j.system.2015.10.006

Brown, J. & Caruso, M. (2016). Access granted: Modern languages and issues of accessibility at university—a case study from Australia. *Language Learning in Higher Education, 6*(2), 453–71. doi.org/10.1515/cercles-2016-0025

Brown, J., Caruso, M., Arvidsson, K. & Forsberg-Lundell, F. (2019). On 'Crisis' and the pessimism of disciplinary discourse in foreign languages: An Australian perspective. *Moderna Språk, 113*(2), 40–58. doi.org/10.58221/mosp.v113i2.7549

Campbell, E. & Storch, N. (2011). The changing face of motivation: A study of second language learners' motivation over time. *Australian Review of Applied Linguistics, 34*(2), 166–92. doi.org/10.1075/aral.34.2.03cam

Canale, M. & Swain, M. (1980). Theoretical bases of communicative approaches to second language teaching and testing. *Applied Linguistics, 1*, 1–47. doi.org/10.1093/applin/I.1.1

Caruso, M. & Fraschini, N. (2021). A Q methodology study into vision of Italian L2 university students: An Australian perspective. *The Modern Language Journal, 105*(2), 552–68. doi.org/10.1111/modl.12713

Chan, L., Dörnyei, Z. & Henry, A. (2015). Learner archetypes and signature dynamics in the language classroom: A retrodictive qualitative modelling approach to studying L2 motivation. In Z. Dörnyei, P. D. MacIntyre & A. Henry (Eds), *Motivational dynamics in language learning* (pp. 238–59). Multilingual Matters. doi.org/10.21832/9781783092574-018

Creswell, J. W. (2013). *Research design: Qualitative, quantitative, and mixed methods approaches*. Sage.

Crookes, G. & Schmidt, R. W. (1991). Motivation: Reopening the research agenda. *Language learning, 41*(4), 469–512. doi.org/10.1111/j.1467-1770.1991.tb00690.x

Crozet, C. & Díaz, A. (2020). *Tertiary language teacher-researchers between ethics and politics: silent voices, unseized spaces.* Routledge. doi.org/10.1080/14708477.2021.1901193

D'Orazzi, G. (2020a). *Motivation and demotivation in second language learning at Australian universities* [Unpublished PhD dissertation]. University of Melbourne, Australia.

D'Orazzi, G. (2020b). Influences of willingness to communicate and foreign language enjoyment on second language learners' motivation. *Konin Language Studies, 8*(3), 263–93. doi.org/10.30438/ksj.2020.8.3.3

D'Orazzi, G. (2020c). Motivation and demotivation of French beginner university learners in Australia. *International Journal of Languages' Education and Teaching, 8*(4), 252–78. doi.org/10.29228/ijlet.46871

D'Orazzi, G. (2020d). University students' demotivation in learning second languages: The case of Australian universities. *International Journal of Literacy, Culture, and Language Education, 1*, 28–53. doi.org/10.14434/ijlcle.v1i0.31151

D'Orazzi, G. & Hajek, J. (2021). Italian language learning and student motivation at Australian universities. *Italian Studies, 76*(4), 447–65. doi.org/10.1080/00751634.2021.1923169

D'Orazzi, G. & Hajek, J. (2022). A multidimensional understanding of Italian L2 learner motivation among Australian university students. *Italica*, 99(3), 350–75.

D'Orazzi, G., Kretzenbacher, H. L. & Hajek, J. (2022). 'I imagine myself in the future speaking German'. What motivates university students in Australia to learn German over time? *German as a Foreign Language*, 2/2022, 64–90.

de Saint Léger, D. & Storch, N. (2009). Learners' perceptions and attitudes: Implications for willingness to communicate in an L2 classroom. *System, 37*(2), 269–85. doi.org/10.1016/j.system.2009.01.001

Dewaele, J. M. (2004). *Vous* or *tu*? Native and non-native speakers of French on a sociolinguistic tightrope. *International Review of Applied Linguistics in Language Teaching, 42*(4), 383–402. doi.org/10.1515/iral.2004.42.4.383

Dewaele, J. M. (2011). Reflections on the emotional and psychological aspects of foreign language learning and use. *Anglistik: International Journal of English Studies, 22*(1), 23–42.

Dewaele, J. M. & MacIntyre, P. D. (2014). The two faces of Janus? Anxiety and enjoyment in the foreign language classroom. *Studies in Second Language Learning and Teaching, 4*(2), 237–74. doi.org/10.14746/ssllt.2014.4.2.5

Dewaele, J. M., Witney, J., Saito, K. & Dewaele, L. (2017). Foreign language enjoyment and anxiety: The effect of teacher and learner variables. *Language Teaching Research, 22*(6), 676–97. doi.org/10.1177/1362168817692161

Dörnyei, Z. (1994). Motivation and motivating in the foreign language classroom. *The Modern Language Journal, 78*(3), 273–84. doi.org/10.2307/330107

Dörnyei, Z. (2009). The L2 motivational self system. In Z. Dörnyei & E. Ushioda (Eds), *Motivation, language identity and the L2 self* (pp. 9–42). Multilingual Matters. doi.org/10.21832/9781847691293-003

Dörnyei, Z. (2019). Towards a better understanding of the L2 learning experience, the Cinderella of the L2 motivational self system. *Studies in Second Language Learning and Teaching, 9*(1), 19–30. doi.org/10.14746/ssllt.2019.9.1.2

Dörnyei, Z. (2020). From integrative motivation to directed motivational currents: The evolution of the understanding of L2 motivation over three decades. In M. Lamb, K. Csizér, A. Henry & S. Ryan (Eds), *The Palgrave handbook of motivation for language learning* (pp. 39–69). Palgrave Macmillan. doi.org/10.1007/978-3-030-28380-3_3

Dörnyei, Z. & Muir, C. (2019). Creating a motivating classroom environment. In X. Gao (Ed.), *Second handbook of English language teaching* (pp. 719–36). Springer. doi.org/10.1007/978-3-319-58542-0_36-1

Ehrman, M. E. & Dörnyei, Z. (1998). *Interpersonal dynamics in second language education: The visible and invisible classroom.* Sage.

Ellis, R., Skehan, P., Li, S., Shintani, N. & Lambert, C. (2020). *Task-based language teaching: Theory and practice.* Cambridge University Press. doi.org/10.1017/9781108643689

Fink, A. (2017). *How to conduct surveys.* Sage.

Fraschini, N. & Caruso, M. (2019). 'I can see myself …': A Q methodology study on self vision of Korean language learners. *System, 87,* 102147. doi.org/10.1016/j.system.2019.102147

Fraschini, N. & Tao, Y. (2024). Emotions in online language learning: Exploratory findings from an *ab initio* Korean course. *Journal of Multilingual and Multicultural Development, 45*(5), 1305–1323. doi.org/10.1080/01434632.2021.1968875

Fryer, M. & Roger, P. (2018). Transformations in the L2 self: Changing motivation in a study abroad context. *System, 78,* 159–72. doi.org/10.1016/j.system.2018.08.005

Fukada, Y., Falout, J., Fukuda, T. & Murphey, T. (2020). Motivational group dynamics in SLA: The interpersonal interaction imperative. In M. Lamb, K. Csizér, A. Henry & S. Ryan (Eds), *The Palgrave handbook of motivation for language learning* (pp. 307–26). Palgrave Macmillan. doi.org/10.1007/978-3-030-28380-3_15

Gardner, R. C., Masgoret, A. M., Tennant, J. & Mihic, L. (2004). Integrative motivation: Changes during a year-long intermediate-level language course. *Language Learning, 54*(1), 1–34. doi.org/10.1111/j.1467-9922.2004.00247.x

Hanna, B. & de Nooy, J. (2009). *Learning language and culture via public internet discussion forums.* Palgrave Macmillan. doi.org/10.1057/9780230235823

Henry, A. (2017). L2 motivation and multilingual identities. *The Modern Language Journal, 101*(3), 548–65. doi.org/10.1111/modl.12412

Huang, H. T., Hsu, C. C. & Chen. S. W. (2015). Identification with social role obligations, possible selves, and L2 motivation in foreign language learning. *System, 51,* 28–38. doi.org/10.1016/j.system.2015.03.003

Hymes, D. (1972) On communicative competence. In J. B. Pride & J. Holmes (Eds), *Sociolinguistics* (pp. 269–93). Penguin.

Irie, K., Ryan, S. & Mercer, S. (2018). Using Q methodology to investigate pre-service EFL teachers' mindsets about teaching competences. *Studies in Second Language Learning and Teaching, 8*(3), 575–98. doi.org/10.14746/ssllt.2018.8.3.3

Joe, H. K., Hiver, P. & Al-Hoorie, A. H. (2017). Classroom social climate, self-determined motivation, willingness to communicate, and achievement: A study of structural relationships in instructed second language settings. *Learning and Individual Differences, 53*, 133–44. doi.org/10.1016/j.lindif.2016.11.005

Kong, J. H., Han, J. E., Kim, S., Park, H., Kim, Y. S. & Park, H. (2018). L2 motivational self system, international posture and competitiveness of Korean CTL and LCTL college learners: A structural equation modeling approach. *System, 72*, 178–89. doi.org/10.1016/j.system.2017.11.005

Kubanyiova, M. (2012). *Teacher development in action: Understanding language teachers' conceptual change*. Palgrave Macmillan. doi.org/10.1057/9780230348424

Lamb, M. (2020). Motivational teaching strategies. In M. Lamb, K. Csizér, A. Henry & S. Ryan (Eds), *The Palgrave handbook of motivation for language learning* (pp. 287–306). Palgrave Macmillan. doi.org/10.1007/978-3-030-28380-3_14

Lambert, C. (2010). A task-based needs analysis: Putting principles into practice. *Language Teaching Research, 14*(1), 99–112. doi.org/10.1177/1362168809346520

Lasan, I. & Rehner, K. (2018). Expressing and perceiving identity and intentions in a second language: A preliminary exploratory study of the effect of (extra)curricular contact on sociolinguistic development. *International Journal of Bilingual Education and Bilingualism, 21*(6), 632–46. doi.org/10.1080/13670050.2016.1197880

Li, C. C., Jiang, G. & Dewaele, J. M. (2018). Understanding Chinese high school students' foreign language enjoyment: Validation of the Chinese version of the foreign language enjoyment scale. *System, 76*, 183–96. doi.org/10.1016/j.system.2018.06.004

Martín, M. D., Jansen, L. & Beckmann, E. A. (2016). *The doubters' dilemma: Exploring students attrition and retention in university language and culture programs*. ANU Press. doi.org/10.22459/DD.08.2016

Mendoza, A. & Phung, H. (2019). Motivation to learn languages other than English: A critical research synthesis. *Foreign Language Annals, 52*(1), 121–40. doi.org/10.1111/flan.12380

Nakamura, T. (2016). A comparative analysis of Japanese language learners' motivation in Australia and Korea. *Innovation in Language Learning and Teaching, 12*(4), 316–29. doi.org/10.1080/17501229.2016.1213267

Pallant, J. (2007). *SPSS survival manual* (3rd ed.). Open University Press.

Palmieri, C. (2019). *Identity trajectories of adult second language learners. Learning Italian in Australia.* Multilingual Matters. doi.org/10.21832/9781788922203

Pollock, P. H. (2016). *The essentials of political analysis.* Sage.

Reinhardt, J. (2019). Social media in second and foreign language teaching and learning: Blogs, wikis, and social networking. *Language Teaching, 52*(1), 1–39. doi.org/10.1017/S0261444818000356

Sakai, H. & Kikuchi, K. (2009). An analysis of demotivators in the EFL classroom. *System, 37*(1), 57–69. doi.org/10.1016/j.system.2008.09.005

Schmidt, G. (2011). *Motives for studying German in Australia.* Peter Lang. doi.org/10.3726/978-3-653-01092-3

Schmidt, G. (2014). 'There's more to it': A qualitative study into the motivation of Australian university students to learn German. *German as a Foreign Language, 1,* 21–44. hdl.handle.net/1885/63156

Thorner, N. & Kikuchi, K. (2020). The process of demotivation in language learning: An integrative account. In M. Lamb, K. Csizér, A. Henry & S. Ryan (Eds), *The Palgrave handbook of motivation for language learning* (pp. 367–88). Palgrave Macmillan. doi.org/10.1007/978-3-030-28380-3_18

Ushioda, E. (2009). A person-in-context relational view of emergent motivation, self and identity. In Z. Dörnyei & E. Ushioda (Eds), *Motivation, language identity and the L2 self* (pp. 215–28). Multilingual Matters. doi.org/10.21832/9781847691293-012

Weinmann, M., Slavich, S. & Neilsen, R. (2021). Civic multiculturalism and the 'broken' discourses of Chinese language education. In C. Halse & K. J. Kennedy (Eds), *Multiculturalism in turbulent times* (pp. 57–75). Taylor & Francis Group.

Yashima, T. (2002). Willingness to communicate in a second language: The Japanese EFL context. *The Modern Language Journal, 86*(1), 54–66. doi.org/10.1111/1540-4781.00136

You, C. J. & Dörnyei Z. (2016). Language learning motivation in China: Results of a large-scale stratified survey. *Applied Linguistics, 37*(4), 495–519. doi.org/10.1093/applin/amu046

2

Transitioning to university: Online video resources for language students

Joshua Brown, Manuel Delicado Cantero
and Solène Inceoglu

Abstract

This chapter reports on the creation of ten online video resources for languages education aimed at current and incoming students who need more guidance on how to improve their skills in order to be successful university language learners. The videos feature footage from actual language classes and interviews with current students and staff, and focus on the main aspects of language learning: what students learn and how, how learning at university differs from high school, how to find language learning resources and so on. In this chapter, we describe the rationale for our project, the methodology we used to implement the creation of the videos, and the results of a large-scale survey conducted with language students in the School of Literature, Languages and Linguistics at The Australian National University before the release of the videos. Students' learning expectations, strategies and beliefs are discussed in line with the content of the videos. The project has strong pedagogical implications, particularly for first-year students, since it focuses on the use of video for effective instruction, teaching time management skills, setting realistic expectations for learning outcomes and teacher-centred vs. student-centred learning.

Keywords: video resources, transition, learning expectations, teaching strategies, first-year experience

1. Introduction

Current research indicates that students' expectations are a major factor in predicting academic performance in first-year university students (Baik et al., 2019; McKenzie & Schweitzer, 2010; Willans & Seary, 2018). First-year students often struggle to keep up with the workload of learning a new language and to adapt themselves to the pace of learning required for university-level work. This is not a problem with the students themselves, but rather with the expectations around studying, and the *method* of studying which is needed for success in language classes. This phenomenon is prevalent across disciplines and is not just limited to languages. Nevertheless, the sustained engagement required for language learning means many students often encounter difficulty during their first year. Two consistent problems facing many students are the mechanics of how learning is performed at university and the expectations of what to learn, and how to learn new material. This problem is particularly acute in language learning, given students' (often) unrealistic expectations of language courses (Magnan et al., 2012).

This chapter reports on the creation of ten online video resources for languages education aimed at current and incoming students who need more guidance on how to improve their skills in order to be successful university language learners. We also report the results of a large-scale survey conducted with language students in the School of Literature, Languages and Linguistics at The Australian National University (ANU) before the release of the videos. Each video discusses a particular aspect of language learning (the first video acting as an introduction), with the aim of guiding students to further resources and information about how languages are taught, and learned, at the tertiary level.[1] The topics of these ten videos are:

1. Introduction: Learning a language at university
2. Language learning resources
3. Language levels and placement test
4. Learning autonomy

---

[1] The videos are available at slll.cass.anu.edu.au/students/language-videos.

5. Making mistakes and feedback
6. Setting realistic expectations in language learning
7. Teacher-centred vs. student-centred learning
8. Techniques for language learning
9. The Common European Framework of Reference of Languages
10. Tips from language students

The rest of the chapter is structured as follows. Section 2 provides a rationale for the project and explains the reason for choosing videos as a format. Section 3 discusses the survey and methodology used for our study. Section 4 presents the videos arising from our project, how they address a specific issue in language learning, and the feedback received from our survey. Section 5 discusses our project's pedagogical implications and offers a brief conclusion.

2. Rationale for the project

Our project stems from our teaching experience and from current research indications that student expectations are a major factor in predicting academic performance among first-year Australian university students (Baik et al., 2019; McKenzie & Schweitzer, 2010; Willans & Seary, 2018). Such a claim is validated worldwide and in a variety of fields of study. To name a recent study, Hassel and Ridout (2018), in a study based on data about university psychology programs in the United Kingdom, concluded that there is still a need for better communication of expectations in order for students to achieve success.

Transitioning from high school to university is a challenge regardless of the subject matter (and beyond academic issues). The literature has characterised student attrition and student pathways as a 'wicked problem', and one that is likely to require further intervention (Beer & Lawson, 2015). To be clear, this is not an issue with the calibre of students themselves, but rather with the expectations and the *method* of studying that is necessary to succeed in first-year subjects, in our case in language classes.

In order to provide better and research-informed support to our new students and to help our colleagues better deal with their students' expectations in class, we created several reasonably short videos about key aspects of language learning. While we teach European languages, the videos were designed to be useful to colleagues teaching other languages and other subjects, who may choose to adapt the content or use some of the videos, depending on each situation.

We opted for an audiovisual format for several reasons. This format is easier to access given the prevalence of audiovisual materials in language classes and the generalised use of the technology necessary to watch these videos (e.g. access to YouTube on a mobile phone or in the library) and may provide more direct engagement to our students and allow them to watch the videos when and as many times as they want. Being a combination of audio, images and text makes the messages conveyed accessible to students with a variety of learning preferences and needs. Having a set of videos would also facilitate further distribution across other areas in our school and beyond, which could potentially motivate other colleagues to create their own transition to university materials. Videos may also be easily distributed outside of ANU (e.g. to high schools) and via social media. In addition, we saw these videos as an opportunity to involve some of our students in an activity that would help others like them in the future.

3. Survey and methodology: Students' background and language learning

Overall, the survey was designed to facilitate better understanding of the expectations and understanding of the students before watching the videos. The survey was open for two months, from September to October 2019. It was administered via Qualtrics and took approximately five minutes to complete. It was emailed to all language students at the School of Literature, Languages and Linguistics, with ethics approval from the human ethics team at ANU. We elicited 126 responses (21% response rate) across 14 questions, including both closed and open. The answers to the survey were used to design the videos, as we explain in the following section.

ANU is situated in Australia's capital, Canberra, and is part of the prestigious Group of Eight (Go8) universities—that is, the eight universities comprising Australia's leading research-intensive universities (Group of Eight, n.d.). Currently, 25 modern languages are taught at both undergraduate and graduate levels, to both *ab initio* students and those with advanced language skills. The student profile is made up of a diverse cohort, including students of different socioeconomic levels and backgrounds. Around one-third of ANU students come from Canberra, another third from the major Australian cities (mainly Sydney, Melbourne and surrounding areas), and a third are international students (*ANU Reporter*, 2021). ANU has exchange agreements with many universities around the world, and all students are encouraged to spend part of their degree overseas. In addition to being a comprehensive university, there is a strong focus on public policy research intended for use by the Australian government. Students often enrol in one or more languages, often in combination with a degree in international relations, politics, human resource management or business (ANU, 2021).

The rationale for the project's outcomes—online delivery of short videos—was driven by several factors. Firstly, we aimed to create an accessible repository from which students could easily obtain information about language programs and which could be shared through various forums, including university websites and social media. Secondly, videos can be integrated into different platforms, including school websites and the learning management systems of individual courses. Thirdly, there is currently no resource that allows new students to view an actual language class at university level, and we were keen for the project to provide realistic footage of a university-level language course, as opposed to some other potentially artificial format. Fourthly, the resource could easily be adapted across various educational institutions. In short, the innovation of the project is to present the material to students in an interesting and engaging way on topics that have never been spelled out for them before. This will allow them to form a clearer and, more importantly, realistic picture of what university learning is like, what they need to do to prepare, and which expectations to arrive with before they enrol in a tertiary language course.

4. Our videos: Procedure and discussion

We filmed ten videos in total, including eight on specific topics, one serving as a general introduction and a final one featuring students providing advice to future students.

One of the issues we regularly encounter with university language students is *how to set realistic expectations*. This was one of the questions in our survey. As Figure 2.1 shows, a majority of the students (64%) reported that they expected to improve their language skills. A sizeable minority (30%) indicated that they wanted to learn to speak like a native speaker as much as possible. Only 16 per cent chose the option that mentioned obtaining a high mark. The last 2 per cent were not sure.

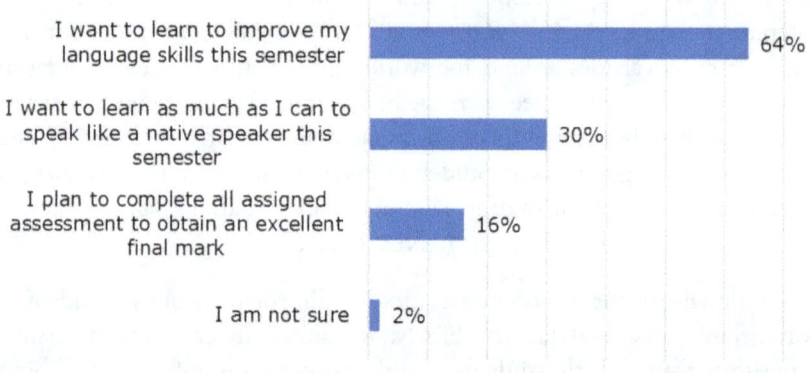

Figure 2.1 Which of the following possible expectations best captures your current expectations for your current semester as a language student?
Source: Compiled by author.

We created a video to reflect some of these ideas, especially the problems related to setting expectations that are too high for the student's level. For instance, the Common European Framework of Reference for Languages (CEFR) (Council of Europe, 2001) is a handy tool, since it helps us and our students to form an idea of the general goals of the levels so we can all work towards those goals and avoid unnecessary frustration. Another important issue has to do with the second-highest option in the survey. Setting realistic expectations also requires revisiting the goalposts. Let us exemplify this with a particular skill, pronunciation.

The literature on L2 (or L3, L4, etc.) pronunciation teaching and learning has now long highlighted the importance of incorporating explicit pronunciation teaching in our classes (Derwing & Munro, 2015; Levis, 2005). Popular pedagogical approaches, such as the communicative approach, focus on achieving communicability in the target language. While sound and well intentioned, the unintended consequence is that pronunciation has been relegated to class practice without any explicit goals or activities, even though oral tests figure prominently in language classes. The literature has also explained that, at least in part, this was a reaction to models that focused too much on pronunciation accuracy set against a native speaker model as the goal (Delicado Cantero et al., 2019; Levis, 2005; Steed & Delicado Cantero, 2018) These two extremes lead to less-than-ideal outcomes: not teaching a particularly necessary skill means that students may never know what the issues are and how to improve, and this may lead to low comprehensibility; aiming for native pronunciation sets an impossible goal that can only lead to frustration (Levis, 2005). The literature advocates for an improvement in the comprehensibility (and intelligibility) of our students in the target language, which is to be achieved slowly throughout their several years of education, not just at once or occasionally at the beginning of a course (Derwing & Munro, 2015). Thus, a new student at university needs to be aware of what they can logically expect to achieve during the semester and how to improve to be more comprehensible, not more native-like, according to their level (Steed & Delicado Cantero, 2018).

The survey aimed to explore our students' expectations of both their role as learners and our role as teachers in the classroom, and we prepared a list of questions directly targeting this topic. Typical terms associated with learners were 'practice', 'active', 'study', 'grammar' and 'regular'. Typical terms associated with teachers were 'facilitate', 'learning', 'encourage', 'feedback' and 'mistake'. One of our videos was developed with some of these ideas in mind, and addressed the concept of *learner autonomy*, defined by Holec (1981, p. 3) as 'the ability to take charge of one's own learning' and included in the CEFR (Council of Europe, 2001, p. 141). Over the past decades, teaching methodologies have stressed the benefits of learners assuming responsibility for their learning (Benson & Voller, 1997; Little, 2020). Indeed, because of the limited number of hours students spend in classrooms, it is essential for learners to develop learning strategies and autonomous practice outside the classroom (Benson, 2011). A more resourceful student is, therefore, able to continue learning at their own pace, outside the classroom, and understands that they also play an active role and that the teacher is not the sole source of learning. Such students understand that they should not rely on the teacher for everything—for instance, constant corrective feedback and direction on what needs to be studied to achieve a high mark, and so on. Some simple examples include using additional free online activities to monitor their own progress, working in groups and engaging in peer review (Scharle & Szabó, 2000). This is also linked to *student-centred teaching* (Hoidn & Klemenčič, 2020; Jones, 2007; Wright, 2011), the focus of another one of our videos.

Another video explicitly addressed *techniques for language learning* and *language learning resources*. Both topics are dealt with here, since they inform each other. Given that the pedagogy of language learning and teaching at university is often different from what students are used to in high school, the aim of creating these videos was to provide explicit guidelines for students on how best to improve their language learning, as well as where to look for up-to-date resources within and outside of the university. While techniques for language learning can vary across languages, our project identified some general approaches that students can use to improve their abilities, regardless of the language chosen, and which are informed by the literature. Tavoosy and Jelveh (2019), for example, point to the importance of factors such as responding to and repeating student answers, vocabulary checks, eliciting, modelling of target language and others.

The video on *techniques for language learning* focused on general resources, such as flashcards, word lists and language diaries, encouraging students to use words in context. It also recommends students watch content on YouTube and Netflix, make use of mobile learning technologies, and watch the same clip several times to transcribe the video. For some languages, resources such as 'news in slow Italian' or clips of slowed-down speech are readily available online. Other tips encouraged students to make use of podcasts or language exchange partners, or to copy down certain expressions with which they were unfamiliar. In terms of language learning resources, we insisted on the range of resources available in most university libraries—DVDs, grammars, subject guides for specific languages and so on—in addition to online resources and social media. Another resource pointed to community groups that meet up for language exchange, many of which can be easily found online.

In our survey we asked students to order these resources from those used most frequently to least, using 9-point Likert scale. The results can be categorised according to this usage frequency, and are reported in Table 2.1.

While students clearly make liberal use of the course textbook and a range of online media, the results point to a lack of uptake for TV and movies, library resources and podcasts. The results point to the importance of reiterating that there are a range of resources available to students that they are often unaware of. When mobile adaptive platforms are introduced into language classes, students respond positively. In a recent study, De Toni et al. (2020, p. 274) found that students considered their platform 'extremely useful', but that 'the lack of tools to meet this request [the use of technologies within and outside the classroom] is problematic'. In a section entitled 'Evaluating Language Learning Resources and Assessing Students' Use of Them', Chun et al. (2016, p. 74) point to the importance of ensuring that the effective outcomes of digital tools 'are based at least in part on students' effective use of the digital tool being investigated'. For most of the resources listed above, students are clearly aware of the presence of a range of media that can assist with their language learning. Languages also entail particular strategies for successful acquisition, given the general acknowledgment that learning strategies differ among different fields of study (Simsek & Balaban, 2010). In any case, the implication from the results presented here is the need to highlight for students the range of resources available to them. Students can receive direct benefits by adopting a range of different inputs for successful language learning.

Table 2.1 Students' reported frequency use of most used resources to least used resources

Resource	Mean	Standard deviation
Resources most used		
The course textbook	2.48	2.17
Online videos (YouTube etc.)	3.72	1.91
Your own word list / word diary / grammar list	3.78	2.24
Resources used intermittently		
TV and movies	4.2	1.89
Apps on mobile phones	4.52	2.02
Study groups	5.82	2.01
Resources least used		
Podcasts	5.85	2.4
Resources at ANU libraries or other libraries	6.96	1.88
Transcribing short videos (from YouTube etc.)	7.67	1.71

Source: Compiled by author.

The results from the survey (Figure 2.2) indicated that almost half the students (47%) had never heard of the CEFR, whereas an additional 19 per cent had heard about it but did not know what their level was. In comparison, 9 per cent of the students responded that they were not very familiar with the framework but knew what their level was, and 25 per cent reported being familiar with the framework and knowing their level. This pattern is aligned with another study in Australia in which half the students polled indicated not being familiar with the CEFR (Normand-Marconnet & Lo Bianco, 2015).

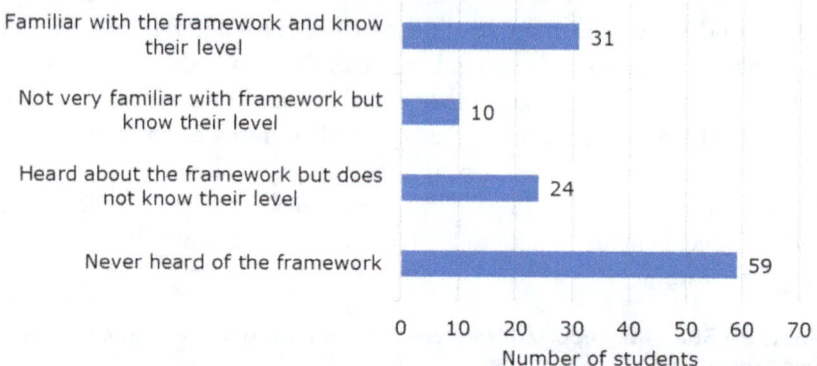

Figure 2.2 Students' familiarity with the CEFR
Source: Compiled by author.

A follow-up survey question further revealed that most of the students who reported knowing their CEFR level were at the upper-intermediate level (B2) or higher. In addition, although the majority of students not knowing their level were first- and second-year students, a surprising number of more advanced students did not seem to be familiar with their levels despite having studied in ANU language courses for several semesters (Table 2.2).

Table 2.2 Students' reported familiarity with their CEFR level

Year	Don't know	A1	A2	B1	B2	C1	C2	Total
1st	34	0	1	1	5	4	0	45
2nd	27	0	1	4	3	6	0	41
3rd	10	0	1	2	6	2	2	23
4th	6	0	1	2	4	2	0	15
5th	1	0	0	0	0	1	0	2
Total	78	0	4	9	18	15	2	126

Source: Compiled by author.

Taken together, these results point to the need to familiarise students with the CEFR, which motivated us to prepare a video on that topic. In Video 4, we drew students' attention to the fact that the framework is used all over Europe and in many parts of the world by learners, teachers, universities and employers and that understanding your language level will help you to achieve your goals, whether it's studying at the ANU, going on exchange overseas or looking for a job. We then presented a very brief overview of the six main levels of language mastery (A1 to C2) before providing examples of how the CEFR describes what language learners are able to do in reading, listening, speaking and writing. In line with the importance of developing learners' autonomy, the video emphasises that linguists and language testers estimate that each level is reached after a certain amount of guided learning hours. These hours vary across languages but, on average, learners of European languages need: 160–200 hours of study to reach A2, 350–400 hours to reach B1 and 560–650 hours to reach B2 (Knight, 2018). Clearly stating how long it approximately takes to move from one level to the next is important, because it emphasises the importance of self-directed study. At ANU, for instance, European language courses have three to four contact hours per week over the course of a 12-week semester. Yet, the courses themselves have a set total student learning time of 130 hours, and students are therefore responsible for 82 to 94 hours of independent research, reading and writing. Managing students' expectations of their proficiency is, consequently, another aspect that we deemed worthy of consideration. In Video 6, we emphasised that learning a foreign language involves a lot of continuous practice, and recommended that to make the most of their language learning experience and to be successful in the class, students are expected not only to attend classes but also: 1) come to class prepared (i.e. having done any preparatory work assigned by their instructor), 2) participate actively in the classroom activities and 3) consolidate new learning by doing homework activities.

Making errors in a foreign language is part of the learning process and reflects the interlanguage of the learners—that is, their developing system (Selinker, 1972). Accordingly, the field of second language acquisition has long been interested in the role and effectiveness of corrective feedback when it is presented orally in the classroom (Lyster et al., 2013) or in written form (Bitchener & Ferris, 2012). Yet, learners do not always notice feedback. In the survey we distributed to ANU students, we asked what they associated feedback with. Responses revealed that students mostly associated feedback with their teacher, and with corrections on both their speaking and writing. A large group of students also related feedback to assessments (also, exams, quizzes, marks, grades and assignments). At the same time, several students also mentioned peer feedback and classroom discussion. Figure 2.3 summarises in a word cloud the most common words taken from the students' answers.

ENABLING LEARNING

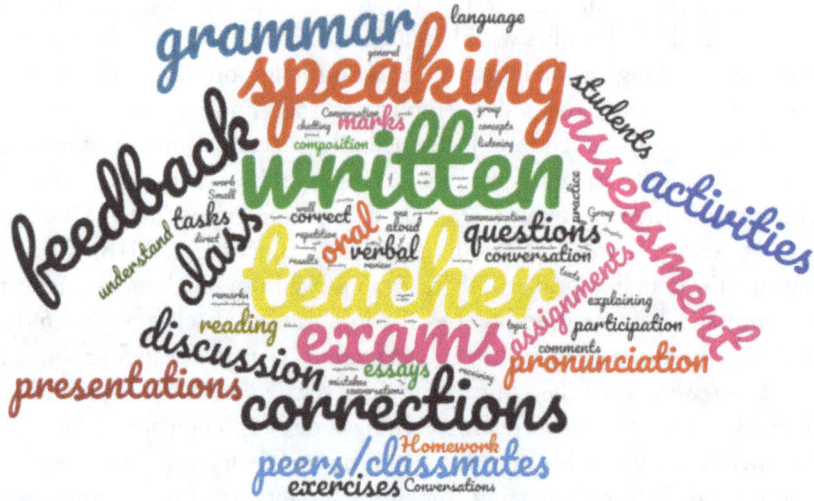

Figure 2.3 Word cloud representing the most common words associated with feedback
Source: Created by author.

In line with these results, Video 4 focused on the importance of paying attention to *corrective feedback* and provided general advice on how to deal with feedback. In particular, we emphasised that a good approach when you receive written feedback is to look at it and not just focus on the grade! Your instructor spent time reading your exam or paper and is providing you with personalised feedback so make the most of it and read it carefully. We also encouraged students to rewrite parts of an exercise or essay incorporating the feedback in order to maximise their learning development and to think of how they could incorporate that feedback for future assignments. From our teaching experience, we know that students do not always understand the feedback they receive, so we pointed out that it is important for students to let their instructors know if something is unclear and not to hesitate to ask for clarifications.

Finally, research shows that peer feedback can be beneficial for second language learning when teachers encourage students to correct their peers' errors and give them the tools to do so (Sato & Lyster, 2012). In his dual model of peer-corrected feedback, Sato (2017) suggested that to provide corrective feedback to a peer, a student must first detect the error (i.e. the gap between the error and the target-like form) in their peer's speech, then compare the error to their own interlanguage, and finally correct the error internally before providing the feedback. All together, 'these cognitive processes may contribute to restructuring and consolidation of the provider's L2 knowledge' (Sato, 2017, p. 26). Accordingly, in our video, we told students to remember that they can also provide feedback to others when they work in groups; feedback does not only come from the instructor—classmates can also help each other.

As mentioned earlier, developing good learning strategies is a crucial aspect of second language acquisition. Researchers emphasise that students who have developed learning-how-to-learn skills are not only able to use these strategies effectively in class, but also 'will be more adequately equipped to continue with language learning outside of the classroom' (Wong & Nunan, 2011, p. 144). These students can serve as great examples to other language learners. In fact, as Chamot (2001, p. 25) wrote, '[i]t may be possible to teach less successful language learners to use the strategies that characterize their more successful peers, thus helping students who are experiencing difficulty in learning a second language become better language learners'. Our last video aimed at increasing learners' motivation and development of learning strategies by hearing from *successful language peers*. Seven students representing French, Italian and Spanish volunteered to share their best language tips on video. The list below summarises their main tips:

- Integrate as many outside resources as you can into your life because it will make it so much easier to practise every day (e.g. podcasts, reading, songs, movies, YouTube tutorials in the target language). For some of these resources, it is possible to adjust the speed of speech delivery.
- Write down words you do not know on flashcards and practise before going to bed.
- Seek opportunities outside the classroom (e.g. language clubs, conversation tables).
- Be unafraid of making mistakes, 'you could be wrong or you could be right, but it's learning at the end of the day'.
- Go on exchange to immerse yourself in the culture and keep learning new things. Make friends with native speakers instead of staying in your 'comfort zone and hanging out with people who already speak English'.
- Practise your pronunciation imitating native speakers on TV while paying attention to how you shape your mouth (i.e. look at yourself in the mirror) or try using automatic speech recognition (e.g. Siri, Google's assistant, Alexa) in your target language and see if you are successful.

5. Pedagogical implications and conclusion

In this chapter, we suggested that videos could serve as a useful means to aid students during their transition to university. The video format also means that the resources can be shared easily across multiple platforms. We were careful to ensure that the videos we made remained short and to share them widely across university and professional associations, such as the Languages and Cultures Network for Australian Universities (LCNAU) and Australian Federation of Modern Languages Teachers Association. Given the range of issues and expectations that can affect students in language classes during their first year of study (but also later years), we designed our project to address several different aspects of teaching and learning. The survey we conducted allowed us to refine these topics. Following this methodology meant that we were able to target specific areas of concern expressed by students themselves, and which they found particularly difficult.

The implications arising from this project follow several directions, given the range of topics addressed by the videos. These concern the importance of ensuring language standards are met through the CEFR, the necessity of communicating to students the availability of language learning resources, language learning techniques, and other issues. Future research will be able to replicate the methodology adopted here, and individual institutions will also be able to create similar resources for their own particular circumstances and cohorts of students. The pedagogical implications also mean that there is one central resource that students from multiple languages can access for study advice and techniques to improve. Previously, resources of this nature have often been found in disparate locations, as part of general study skills websites or elicited directly from language teachers themselves. This project aimed to remedy this situation by providing a central repository for language learning resources for students in the modern university.

Acknowledgments

Our project benefited from an ANU Teaching Enhancement Grant ($2,200) specifically designed to support innovative projects that aim to improve the teaching and learning experience of students at ANU. In particular, we would like to thank Jamie Kidston and his team (Strategic Communications & Public Affairs, ANU) for their professional assistance.

References

ANU (The Australian National University). (2021). *Cohort profile and ATAR information*. The Australian National University. Retrieved on 11 November 2021 from www.anu.edu.au/study/study-options/cohort-profile-and-atar-information

ANU Reporter. (2021). ANU by numbers: domestic students. *ANU Reporter, 46*(1). Retrieved on 11 November 2021 from reporter.anu.edu.au/anu-numbers-domestic-students (site discontinued).

Baik, C., Naylor, R., Arkoudis, S. & Dabrowski, A. (2019). Examining the experiences of first-year students with low tertiary admission scores in Australian universities. *Studies in Higher Education, 44*(3), 526–38. doi.org/10.1080/03075079.2017.1383376

Beer, C. & Lawson, C. (2015). The problem of student attrition in higher education: An alternative perspective. *Journal of Further and Higher Education, 41*(6), 773–84. doi.org/10.1080/0309877X.2016.1177171

Benson, P. (2011). Language learning and teaching beyond the classroom: An introduction to the field. In P. Benson & H. Reinders (Eds), *Beyond the language classroom* (pp. 7–16). Palgrave Macmillan. doi.org/10.1057/9780230306790_2

Benson, P. & Voller, P. (1997). Introduction: Autonomy and independence in language learning. In P. Benson & P. Voller (Eds), *Autonomy and independence in language learning* (pp. 1–12). Routledge. doi.org/10.4324/9781315842172

Bitchener, J. & Ferris, D. R. (2012). *Written corrective feedback in second language acquisition and writing*. Routledge. doi.org/10.4324/9780203832400

Chamot, A. (2001). The role of learning strategies in second language acquisition. In M. P. Breen (Ed.), *Learner contributions to language learning: New directions in research* (pp. 25–43). Longman.

Chun, D., Kern, R. & Smith, B. (2016). Technology in language use, language teaching, and language learning. *The Modern Language Journal, 100*(S1), 64–80. doi.org/10.1111/modl.12302

Council of Europe. (2001). *Common European Framework of Reference for Languages: Learning, teaching, assessment*. Cambridge University Press. Retrieved on 30 August 2021 from rm.coe.int/1680459f97

Delicado Cantero, M., Steed, W. & Herrero de Haro, A. (2019). Spanish pronunciation and teacher training: Challenges and suggestions. In R. Rao (Ed.), *Key issues in the teaching of Spanish pronunciation: From description to pedagogy* (pp. 304–23). Routledge.

Derwing, T. M. & Munro, M. J. (2015). *Pronunciation fundamentals: Evidence-based perspectives for L2 teaching and research*. John Benjamins. doi.org/10.1075/lllt.42

De Toni, F., Verdina, F., Kinder, J. & Caruso, M. (2020). Adaptive and mobile learning at university: Student experience in Italian beginners' language classes. In J. Fornasiero, S. M. A. Reed, R. Amery, E. Bouvet, K. Enomoto & H. L. Xu (Eds), *Intersections in language planning and policy* (pp. 259–75). Springer. doi.org/10.1007/978-3-030-50925-5_17

Group of Eight. (n.d.) *About the Go8*. Retrived on 11 November 2021 from go8.edu.au/about/the-go8

Harris, J., Spina, N., Ehrich, L. & Smeed, J. (2013). *Literature review: Student-centred schools make the difference*. Australian Institute for Teaching and School Leadership/QUT.

Hassel, S. & Ridout, N. (2018). An investigation of first-year students' and lecturers' expectations of university education. *Frontiers in Psychology, 8*, 2218. doi.org/10.3389/fpsyg.2017.02218

Holec, H. (1981). *Autonomy in foreign language learning*. Pergamon.

Hoidn, S. & Klemenčič, M. (Eds). (2020). *The Routledge international handbook of student-centered learning and teaching in higher education*. Routledge.

Jones, L. (2007). *The student-centered classroom*. Cambridge University Press.

Knight, B. (2018). *How long does it take to learn a foreign language?* Cambridge University Press. Retrieved on 17 November 2021 from www.cambridge.org/elt/blog/wp-content/uploads/2018/10/How-long-does-it-take-to-learn-a-foreign-language.pdf

Little, D. (2020). Language learner autonomy: Rethinking language teaching. *Language Teaching, 55*(1), 64–73. doi.org/10.1017/S0261444820000488

Levis, J. M. (2005). Changing contexts and shifting paradigms in pronunciation teaching. *TESOL Quarterly, 39*(3), 369–77. doi.org/10.2307/3588485

Lyster, R., Saito, K. & Sato, M. (2013). Oral corrective feedback in second language classrooms. *Language Teaching, 46*(1), 1–40. doi.org/10.1017/S0261444812000365

Magnan, Sally S., Murphy, D., Sahakyan, N. & Kim, S. (2012). Student goals, expectations, and the standards for foreign language learning. *Foreign Language Annals, 45*(2), 170–92. doi.org/10.1111/j.1944-9720.2012.01192.x

McKenzie, K. & Schweitzer, R. (2010). Who succeeds at university? Factors predicting academic performance in first year Australian university students. *Higher Education Research & Development, 20*(1), 21–33. doi.org/10.1080/07924360120043621

Normand-Marconnet, N. & Lo Bianco, J. (2015). The Common European Framework of Reference down under: A survey of its use and non-use in Australian universities. *Language Learning in Higher Education, 5*(2), 281–307. doi.org/10.1515/cercles-2015-0014

Sato, M. (2017). Oral peer corrective feedback. Multiple theoretical perspectives. In H. Nassaji & E. Kartchava (Eds), *Corrective feedback in second language teaching and learning: Research, theory, applications, implications* (pp. 19–34). Routledge.

Sato, M. & Lyster, R. (2012). Peer interaction and corrective feedback for accuracy and fluency development. *Studies in Second Language Acquisition, 34*(4), 591–626. doi.org/10.1017/S0272263112000356

Scharle, Á. & Szabó, A. (2000). *Learner autonomy. A guide to developing learner responsibility*. Cambridge University Press.

Selinker, L. (1972). Interlanguage. *International Review of Applied Linguistics in Language Teaching, 10*(3), 209–31. doi.org/10.1515/iral.1972.10.1-4.209

Simsek, A. & Balaban, J. (2010). Learning strategies of successful and unsuccessful university students. *Contemporary Educational Technology, 1*(1), 36–45. doi.org/10.30935/cedtech/5960

Steed, W. & Delicado Cantero, M. (2018). First things first: Exploring Spanish students' attitudes toward learning pronunciation in Australia. *The Language Learning Journal, 46*(2), 103–13. doi.org/10.1080/09571736.2014.963644

Tavoosy, Y. & Jelveh, R. (2019). Language teaching strategies and techniques used to support students learning in a language other than their mother tongue. *International Journal of Learning and Teaching, 11*(2), 77–88. doi.org/10.18844/ijlt.v11i2.3831

Willans, J. & Seary, K. (2018). Why did we lose them and what could we have done? *Student Success, 9*(1), 47–60. doi.org/10.5204/ssj.v9i1.432

Wong, L. L. & Nunan, D. (2011). The learning styles and strategies of effective language learners. *System, 39*(2), 144–63. doi.org/10.1016/j.system.2011.05.004

Wright, G. B. (2011). Student-centered learning in higher education. *International Journal of Teaching and Learning in Higher Education, 23*(1), 92–97.

Appendix

Below we present the questions asked in the feedback survey used for our project.

1. Year at ANU:
    a. 1st
    b. 2nd
    c. 3rd
    d. 4th
    e. 5th
    f. 6th

2. Gender:
    a. male
    b. female
    c. prefer not to say

3. Age:

4. Language(s) studied at the ANU (multiple options):
    a. Spanish
    b. French
    c. Italian
    d. German
    e. Russian
    f. Portuguese
    g. Arabic
    h. Chinese
    i. Japanese
    j. Other [dropdown]

5. Did you study a foreign language in Year 11 and/or Year 12?
    a. Yes
    b. No

6. How familiar are you with the European Framework of Reference for Languages? [pick one]
    a.   I've never heard about it.
    b.   I've heard about it but I don't know what my level is.
    c.   I'm not very familiar with it but I know what my level is.
    d.   I'm familiar with it and I know what my level is.
    For c and d: What is your level:

7. In the language classroom, what activities do you associate with feedback?

8. What are your expectations after one semester of language learning? Which one of the following possible expectations best captures your current expectations for your current semester as a language student?
    a.   I want to learn as much as I can to speak like a native speaker this semester.
    b.   I want to learn to improve my language skills this semester.
    c.   I plan to complete all the assigned assessment to obtain an excellent final mark.
    d.   I am not sure.

9. In your opinion, what is the role of a language teacher in the classroom?

10. In your opinion, what are the three most important responsibilities of a language student in order to learn the target language?
    a.
    b.
    c.

11. Order the following resources to study languages from the one you use most frequently (1) to the one you use the least (9):
    a.   The course textbook
    b.   Online videos (YouTube etc.)
    c.   Resources at ANU libraries or other libraries
    d.   Apps on mobile phones
    e.   Study groups
    f.   TV and movies
    g.   Podcasts

    h.   Create your own word list / word diary
    i.   Transcribing short videos (from YouTube etc.)

12. When you receive written feedback on a test or essay, do you usually:
    a. just look at the final mark
    b. read the written comments
    c. think about the comments and how you can improve
    d. ask the teacher about the feedback
    e. look up the grammar point in a textbook to see how to use it properly

13. At the start of the semester, I think about the learning outcomes for the course:
    a. always
    b. sometimes
    c. I look at them, but don't know what they are / mean
    d. never

You're done! Thanks for participating in this survey.

3

Korean language education in Western Australia: Development and challenges

Nicola Fraschini, Joanna Elfving-Hwang and Yu Tao

Abstract

Korean has been one of the fastest-growing languages in terms of learner population both in Australia and in many other Western countries. Among the factors contributing to this growth, one that is probably the most frequently mentioned is the contemporary worldwide popularity of Korean pop culture. Nevertheless, this element alone is not sufficient to boost growth in language learner numbers at different levels. This chapter focuses on the case of Western Australia, presenting the background and the current state of Korean language education, and highlighting issues embedded in the Western Australian and Australian context that hinder further growth. It shows how the growth in Korean language education is sustained not only by intrinsically motivated learners, but also by the synergic collaboration of elements such as local educational policies, nationwide language policies, institutional long-term vision and committment, inter-governmental support and commercial interests.

Keywords: Korean language, Korean–Australians, Asia literacy, learner motivation

1. Introduction

This chapter focuses on the state of the Korean language education sector in Western Australia and the challenges it faces. It identifies some key drivers behind the recent growth in student numbers over the past decade and considers potential challenges for future growth. Through providing an overview and analysis of these challenges, this chapter will offer some suggestions as to how to build successful new language programs to enhance the provision of Asian languages education in Australia and particularly in regions or institutions where the teaching and learning of Asian languages have been introduced relatively recently. Korean language education offers a useful case study because of the recent mainstreaming of Korean popular culture, which has driven familiarity with and interest in Korean culture. Yet the Korean language education sector is relatively new and struggles with gaining a foothold, particularly in primary and secondary schools. So while the popularity of Korean language courses and Korean studies majors has been driven by the phenomenal popularity of Korean popular culture in its various forms, the structural challenges that constrain future development and expansion of the language education sector have meant that there is perhaps a clear limit to how much popularity alone can facilitate sustainable growth.

In this chapter, we will first give background to the development and current state of the Korean language in Western Australia, highlighting the increasing importance of the Republic of Korea (ROK) to the Western Australian economy. We will then present the results of a survey conducted with a sample ($n = 201$) of university-level Korean language learners that aimed to investigate the main motivations behind their decisions to study Korean and to illustrate what draws students to elect Koran language study at tertiary level. Finally, we will conclude with a reflection on the challenges we have experienced as educators and the lessons for the development of Korean language education going forward both in Western Australia and elsewhere in Australia. We will illustrate how the long-term success of language education is heavily dependent on institutional will and commitment to language and area studies education, as well as state and federal government policies which create the structural environment for educators to make local-level student achievement possible. We argue that ultimately, in the absence of strong state and federal government-level support, the fate of language education programs is in the hands of local institutional management, which, despite highly motivated staff and students, makes programs highly vulnerable to changes in government funding policy, institutional focus and staffing files.

2. Background

2.1. Western Australia and Republic of Korea relations in the context of language education

Unlike on the east coast of Australia, where Korean studies programs also have a significant Korean migrant community presence, the Western Australian heritage learner community is still relatively small (Shin, 2019). While in various parts of the world, Korean language education was initially established to cater to the needs of heritage learners, this has not been the case in Western Australia. For example, in regions with a strong local Korean community such as California in the United States or New South Wales in Australia, some universities introduced dual-track programs to accommodate learners beyond a beginner entry level, with most upper-level advanced courses squarely designed to cater to Korean background learners. In the past, the heritage learner stream in these areas could even be relied on to ensure that programs for *ab initio* learners were able to continue despite relatively small numbers. This is similar to what happened with Chinese or Japanese language courses in many Australian universities, including in Western Australia. However, as significant Korean migration to Western Australia has been a relatively recent development, with most migrants having arrived after the 1990s (Committee for the 50 Years History of Korean in Australia, 2008), the University of Western Australia has had to rely on beginner language learner streams to build a viable program (as described in detail in Section 2.2 below). In the past, given both the prevalence of North Korea in mainstream news and the political upheavals that dominated the representation of the Korean peninsula, numbers were very low. Moreover, since first-generation Korean speakers represent the majority of adult Koreans in Western Australia, and most 1.5- and second-generation Korean–Australians are still relatively young, the majority of Korean language learners enrolling in tertiary-level courses are domestic and international non-heritage background learners. For this reason, significant growth in student numbers only took off in the 2010s.

Table 3.1 Descriptive statistics of Korean speakers in the Australian states, 2006–2016

	NSW	Vic	QLD	SA	WA	Tas	NT	ACT	Total
Number of Korean speakers									
2006	36,630	5,983	7,411	1,503	1,920	307	63	807	54,624
2011	47,317	10,345	12,766	3,059	3,980	505	264	1,545	79,786
2016	59,876	15,545	19,602	3,583	7,134	512	370	2,383	108,999
Net increase of Korean speakers									
2006–11	10,687	4,362	5,355	1,556	2,060	198	201	738	25,162
2011–16	12,559	5,200	6,836	524	3,154	7	106	838	29,213
Net increase rate of Korean speakers									
2006–11	29.18%	72.91%	72.26%	103.53%	107.29%	64.50%	319.05%	91.45%	46.06%
2011–16	26.54%	50.27%	53.55%	17.13%	79.25%	1.39%	40.15%	54.24%	36.61%
Median age of korean speakers									
2006	30	25	24	24	26	23	31	26	28
2011	31	28	27	28	28	25	26	27	29
2016	33	29	29	30	30	30	28	29	31

Source: Australian Bureau of Statistics.

Compared to the eastern states of Australia, Western Australia has thus only recently begun to witness the emergence of a sizeable Australian–Korean community. According to Australian census data collected in August 2016, there were 7,134 Korean speakers in Western Australia, accounting for just over 6.5 per cent of Korean speakers resident in Australia (Table 3.1). While the numbers seem relatively small, they have more than tripled since 2006 when there were fewer than 2,000 Korean speakers resident in Western Australia. This represents the fastest growth in the number of background Korean speakers in all Australian states and territories over the decade between 2006 and 2016 (Table 3.1). Much of this growth has been due to Western Australia's resources sector boom, which brought major infrastructure, mining, and oil and gas projects led by large Korean companies such as Kogas, POSCO, Hanhwa and Samsung. In the same period, the general growth rate in the number of Korean speakers in the whole of Australia was just under 50 per cent.

This demographic feature of the Korean-speaking population in Western Australia has had two significant implications for Korean language education in the state. Firstly, in comparison with Australia's more populous eastern states such as New South Wales, Victoria and Queensland, the total size of the Korean-speaking community is much smaller. Moreover, among the 7,000 or so Korean speakers who live in Western Australia today, the vast majority are young professionals who have completed their tertiary education, typically in Korea, and have children still in primary or secondary school. As a result, the number of heritage learners is still very small.

Most of the non-Korean background learners of Korean have very limited prior knowledge of the Korean language, and many are motivated to learn because of their engagement with various forms of Korean popular culture, such as K-pop, K-dramas or webtoons. Despite their imagined or real familiarity with Korean culture and society through fictional representations, many have little first-hand experience of living in Korea, a situation that has been made even more acute due to the COVID-19 travel restrictions, which have prevented study abroad programs from going ahead. Given the small number of young Koreans residing in Western Australia, most students also lack adequate opportunities to come into contact with speakers of Korean before they sign up for Korean language courses or majors, and thus existing people-to-people links are less likely to play a role in motivating students to take up Korean language study.

The development of Korean language education in Western Australia thus presents us with a useful case study on how tertiary education programs in Asian languages can be designed in regions without strong migration population links (such as the United Kingdom or the Republic of Ireland). We will illustrate how neither staff and student enthusiasm for language education nor the support of external funding agencies such as the Korea Foundation or the Academy of Korean Studies is ever enough to ensure the success of a program. Instead, in planning a new program, it is important to consider the interplay between student demand, institutional structures and long-term vision, the wider political landscape determining the ideologies that inform funding structures and external support opportunities, and the need to embed Asia literacy as core to Australian educational institutions' learning goals, given that Asia's future is increasingly intertwined with Australia's success.

ROK has become an increasingly significant trading partner for Western Australia in the past two decades, and, as a result, demand for graduates with Korean language skills and cultural literacy has grown. In 2004, Western Australia established a trade office in Seoul; fast-forward to 2020–2021, when trade in consumer goods and natural resources surged to A$13.8 billion.[1] The signing of the Korea–Australia Free Trade Agreement (KAFTA) in 2014 further strengthened bilateral investment ties, as the Australian government's recognition of Korea's vital importance to Australia continued to grow (Wilson, 2018). The economic and, more recently, defence and security importance of Korea has become more relevant as both the COVID-19 pandemic and the changing security landscape in the Indo-Pacific have required middle powers such as Australia and Korea to rethink their strategic alliances and supply chains. In September 2021, a Joint Statement was released at the Australia–Republic of Korea Foreign and Defence Ministers' 2+2 Meeting in Seoul, outlining how the two countries will continue to cooperate closely on building resilient supply chains of critical minerals essential for renewable energy technologies and advanced manufacturing. This development has been driven both by existing ties and, most of all, by the realisation that global supply chain security now faces multiple potential environmental, geopolitical, societal, infrastructural and economic threats (Dalton, 2021). As of 2023, South Korea was Western Australia's third-largest trading partner, with iron ore

---

1   www.wa.gov.au/government/publications/western-australias-economy-and-international-trade#western-australia-top-10-trading-partners.

and petroleum making up more than 75 per cent of goods exported to Korea. Inward Korean corporate investment in energy, finance, property, defence and critical mineral sectors has increased the potential for Western Australian graduates to secure employment with Korean companies in Australia (Lee, 2021). For this reason, learning Korean is no longer just an option for those interested in popular culture but is now seen as a smart career choice to enhance one's curriculum vitae.

However, the main reason for the increased interest in Korean language and studies programs is still a desire to learn the Korean language in order to feel more 'immersed' in the culture of their favourite K-pop idols (Fraschini, 2020; Fraschini & Caruso, 2019; Han, 2021; Lee, 2018; Nikitina & Furuoka, 2019; Elfving-Hwang, 2021). Strong economic links with Korea, along with increasing local enthusiasm for Korean popular culture, have created a strong basis for the growth in demand for Korean language education in Western Australian tertiary institutions as well as potentially in primary and secondary schools. Yet challenges remain, due less to pedagogical challenges and more to structural issues that are difficult to solve at the local institutional level.

2.2. Tertiary Korean language education in Western Australia

In Western Australia, the Korean language is currently taught at tertiary level at two universities—UWA and Curtin University. Other Asian languages— namely, Chinese, Indonesian and Japanese—are offered in four of the state's five universities. Korean is currently taught at eight universities in Australia, and the Korean studies major programs at UWA and Curtin University are among the most recent additions to the national offerings.

Korean language courses were first introduced in Western Australia at Curtin University in 1991. Initially, this involved a Korean language stream, which was offered in the language major in the Bachelor of Arts degree program, and as part of the Graduate Diploma for Asian Languages. However, in 2010 Curtin University discontinued the program, claiming low enrolments and efficiency savings while retaining Japanese and Chinese (Lane, 2011). The following year UWA introduced a first-year Korean language course on a trial basis, driven in part by the vision of the dean of the Faculty of Arts, who saw value in strengthening Asian languages. At this point, there was also a double financial incentive to introduce Korean. Around this time, all LOTE (Language Other Than English) courses were given an additional

Commonwealth funding loading per equivalent full-time student load, and therefore Korean offered attractive financial returns if successful. The Korean government also supported the establishment of a Korean studies program at UWA with a significant grant.

With 89 students completing the pilot course in the second semester and UWA securing a A$500,000 grant to support the development of an ongoing program, there was sufficient support to commit to a new major in Korean studies. Serendipitously, in the same year, UWA's decision to reform its degree structure to make it easier for students to take a foreign language as a 'broadening' elective further made the Korean language a popular choice for students with little or no prior language learning experience. In 2012, with the support of external funding from the Korea Foundation, a permanent faculty member was appointed to develop a curriculum for the Korean studies major. The major was launched in 2014 and, due to an exponential growth in student numbers, a further appointment of a tenure-track faculty member was made in 2015.

In 2021 there was a further surge in student numbers with the introduction of a new minor program in Korean Language and Culture, which in the same year became the most popular minor across the university. Student numbers showed a strong upward trend from 2012 to 2021 (Figure 3.1).

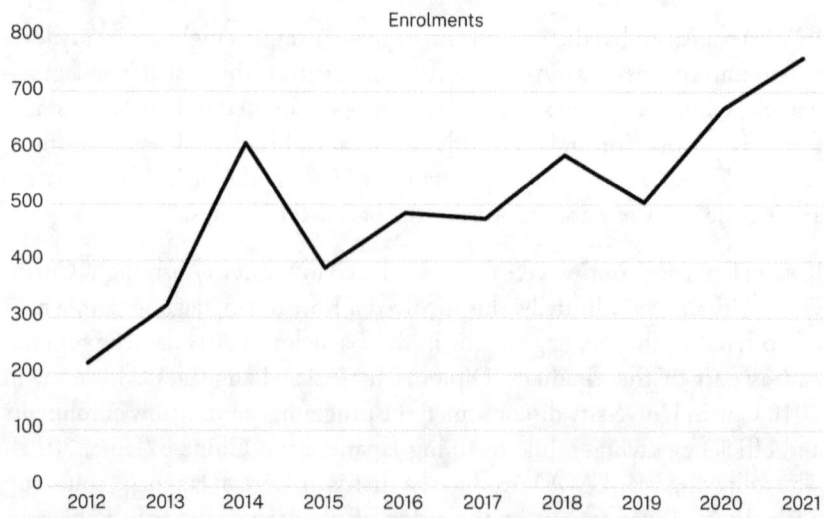

Figure 3.1 Korean studies enrolments at UWA, including studies courses with focus on Korea

Source: Compiled by author.

However, despite an impressive upward growth trend and no increase in staffing, in 2021 the program was hit with a resourcing freeze, which was attributed to a 'structural deficit' that, according to the university management, constrained funding to two full-time equivalent staff, whose contracts were transferred from teaching and research positions to 'teaching-focused' positions.

This decision was attributed in part to the financial impact of COVID-19, but the drop in fee income, despite a relatively modest drop in the number of international students, was more likely triggered by the federal government's 2020 Higher Education Support Amendment (Job-Ready Graduates and Supporting Regional and Remote Students) Bill.[2] This bill changed the funding rules to reduce student contributions to less than A$4,000 per domestic student, which has made language programs less attractive for universities to run because of the caps placed on Commonwealth-funded places, which means that universities risk running language programs at a loss once the Commonwealth funding gap has been reached.

At the same time, first-year enrolments in Korean language courses have steadily increased, showing growth of almost 50 per cent between 2015 and 2021 in the introductory first-year course. Moreover, the number of students enrolled in the second- and third-year courses has grown steadily, consolidating a positive retention rate. In other words, while the program itself demonstrated consistently strong or growing student numbers at every level, both external and internal structural resourcing decisions meant that the long-term viability of the program was being undermined through a focus on short-term profits. Meanwhile, the re-introduction of Korean at Curtin University through the establishment of a Korean studies major in 2023 confirms that the interest in Korean studies and Korean language in Western Australia is strong.

In the next section, we will discuss some of the main drivers of students' motivation to learn Korean and how these drivers can be useful in enhancing student numbers and improving retention.

---

2   The Job-Ready Graduates Bill reallocates federal university funding to priority areas, including engineering, sciences, education and languages, which the government has designated as being of strategic importance to Australia's future economic success.

3. Designing pedagogy to enhance learner motivation

3.1. Pedagogical context

Success in language learning is often driven by the degree of motivation with which students commit to the learning process, despite the obvious challenges and difficulties that learning a foreign language can pose. In order to better understand student learning needs, we deployed a survey among university students enrolled in three Korean language courses at the University of Western Australia in semester one 2016. We saw this scoping of motivations as a particularly important task, as our student cohorts follow a distinct pattern, depending on whether they choose Korean studies as their major or as an elective. While students enrolled in the major are 90 per cent domestic and 10 per cent international, the percentage of students taking the Korean language as an elective subject is well above the institutional average of 20 per cent. These students are mostly from East or Southeast Asian countries (China, Malaysia, Singapore and Indonesia). The motivations among those who take Korean language courses as electives can therefore vary, from the desire to enhance one's overall degree grade point average (GPA) through taking a course that is seen as relatively easy to achieve good grades in (Beginners' Korean) to interest in gaining a deep understanding of Korean society and culture.

Students who take Korean studies as their first major are typically driven by the latter motivation and are required to complete eight compulsory courses over three years. At the time of the data collection, the eight compulsory courses included six language courses (one per semester) and two courses on Korean Culture and Society and Contemporary Korean Society, which were taught in English and aimed to enhance the students' understanding of Korean culture, society and history, thus enhancing the employability of 'Korea-literate' graduates. The requirements of the minor program in Korean Language and Culture are completion of four language courses, or three language courses and one Korean studies course. Within the language course sequence, Korean 1 is a Level 1 course for *ab initio* learners, and students enrolled in this course typically have little or no previous experience of using the Korean language. Korean 3 is a Level 2 course for intermediate learners and Korean 5 is a Level 3 course for intermediate–advanced learners who have typically completed four Korean language courses. It should be noted that students satisfying the language proficiency requirements can enrol directly in the appropriate course as an elective regardless of their actual years in a degree program. For example, a heritage learner who just started their undergraduate program at UWA may directly enrol in Korean 3 or Korean 5 as an unattached elective, provided that they demonstrate the required level of Korean language skills in a placement test taken prior to the start of the semester.

3.2. Sample and method of data collection

The survey and the research project were approved by UWA's Human Research Ethics Committee before the commencement of the study. Participation in the survey was anonymous, and care was taken to emphasise that the students may participate in and withdraw from the survey voluntarily. By administering the survey in paper format at the end of a weekly language class, we were able to achieve a very high response rate. The survey instrument was designed with reference to the existing literature on second language motivation, learner needs analysis and learning material development (Choi, 2013; Csizér & Dörnyei, 2005; Dörnyei, 2009; Dörnyei & Chan, 2013; Donryei & Ryan, 2015; Hadfield & Dörnyei, 2013; Jee, 2015; Kwon & Lee, 2005, Son & Jeon, 2011). Specifically, the survey questionnaire consisted of two lists of statements, focusing on learner reasons for taking Korean language courses (15 items) and on their preference regarding format, typology and content of language learning materials (14 items). All items were ranked using a 5-point Likert scale. In addition, the questionnaire also collected some demographic data about learner variables, the descriptive statistics of which are reported below.

Of the 268 students enrolled in the three language courses, 201 (75%) filled in the questionnaire. Among these respondents, 163 (81.1%) students were enrolled in Korean 1, 21 (10.4%) in Korean 3 and 10 (5%) in Korean 5. The other eight (3.5%) students did not respond to all of the questions. Given the high response rate, we were also able to create a snapshot of the profile of Korean language learners at UWA from the sample's descriptive statistics (Table 3.2).

Table 3.2 Sample of Korean language learners at UWA, April 2016

	Freq. (missing)	Freq. (0)	Freq. (1)
Gender 0=female 1=male	8	146	47
New student 0=returning student 1=new (1st year) student	6	112	83
STEM 0=NOT majoring in a STEM subject 1=majoring in a STEM subject	6	102	93
Multilingual 0=NOT a multilingual speaker 1=a multilingual speaker	8	89	104
First L2 0=studying Korean NOT as a 1st L2 1=studying Korean as a 1st L2	12	165	24

Source: Compiled by author.

As illustrated in Table 3.2, female students outnumbered male students (72.6% were female, 23.4% male). This reflects the gender dynamics of Korean studies programs elsewhere, as well as other language programs at UWA. Among all students who participated in the survey, 83 (41.3%) were in their first year of study, 58 (29%) in the second year, 44 (21.9%) in the third year, and 10 (5%) had been at the university for three years or more. In other words, in the Korean studies program, the numbers of new and returning students were generally equal, with the latter slightly exceeding the former in 2016. Most of the students electing to study Korean were doing it to study for an elective (87.1%), whereas only 9 per cent of the survey participants had at the time of filling in the survey elected to study for the full Korean studies major. This is also reflective of how most students 'find' Korean studies as an area of study: they tend to 'try out' a course or two, and only commit to a full major once they feel confident enough that they will be successful in doing so. Most respondents were enrolled in a Bachelor of Science (64, 31.8%) or a Bachelor of Commerce (61, 30.3%). Other degree majors included those in the Bachelor of Arts (33, 16.41%), Engineering and Computer Sciences (24, 12%), Architecture (5, 2.5%), Medicine (4, 2%) and Law (1, 0.5%).[3] As shown in Table 3.2, almost half of the survey participants majored in a STEM subject. Furthermore, more than

---

3   An undergraduate major in education was not available at UWA at the time of the data collection.

half of the survey participants (54%) indicated that they were competent in more than one language. Therefore, only a minority of the respondents (24, or 13%) were studying Korean as their first experience of L2 learning, suggesting that Korean language study presents a less attractive option for students to explore as their first experience of foreign language learning.

3.3. Findings: Motivations to study Korean language

The survey asked students to rate 15 statements on the extent to which they agreed that the reason listed was an accurate descriptor to explain why they had chosen to study Korean. Applying factor analysis, we found that the students' rating of the 15 statements mainly reflected variations around three broad thematic variables: intrinsic interest in Korean culture and the Korean people, desire to visit or live in Korea, and enhanced employment prospects.

The first motivation was *Positive attitudes towards Korean culture and the Korean people*. This was captured in high agreement scores for statements such as 'I am interested in Korean popular culture' and 'I am interested in Korean history and traditional culture'. The second clear motivation was the *Desire to visit or live in Korea*, with high agreement levels with statements such as 'I want to travel to Korea or study in Korea' and 'I want to live in Korea in the future'. A third noticeable motivation was identified and can be summarised as *Enhanced employment prospects*, with statements such as 'I think speaking Korean will be an asset in the future' and 'I think that by learning Korean I can find a better job in the future'.

Table 3.3 Descriptive statistics of the three main learning motivations

	n	Minimum	Maximum	Mean	Standard deviation
Positive attitudes towards Korean culture and the Korean people	201	1.00	5.00	4.0174	.8637
A desire to visit or live in Korea	201	1.00	5.00	3.8458	.8544
Enhanced employment prospects	201	1.00	5.00	3.8176	.7951

Source: Compiled by author.

Using the coefficient of each statement revealed by the factor analysis process, we reconstructed each participant's score of each expressed motivation for enrolling in Korean language study, and then calculated the aggregated score for the whole cohort. As demonstrated in Table 3.3, of the three main motivations, *Positive attitudes towards Korean culture and the Korean people* was the strongest, clearly indicating that existing interest in Korean society and culture is the main motivating factor for learning Korean. On average, students assigned 4.0174 on a scale of 1 to 5 to indicate how strongly they considered *Positive attitudes towards Korean culture and the Korean people* to be a factor motivating them to sign up for a Korean language course. The other two motivations also appeared to be strong among the survey participants. On average, students assigned 3.8458 on a scale of 1 to 5 to indicate how strongly they considered *Desire to visit or live in Korea* to be a factor motivating them to sign up for a Korean language course, and 3.8176 to *Enhanced employment prospects*, suggesting that many have, through their interest in Korean culture and society, developed a desire to work and live in Korea or to seek a job that allows them to work in contexts that afford them opportunities to interact with Korean people.

From an aetiological perspective, the overarching motivation to study Korean is thus integrative and draws on existing positive perceptions towards the target language community. However, many also felt that instrumental reasons associated with sets of skills that would enable them to better perform in future careers were also important. In other words, while the main motivation was driven by emotive reasons (intrinsic motivation to learn because of attraction to another culture), students also considered the choice to be highly rational because it allowed them to imagine future selves in desirable careers. These findings were replicated in a subsequent study focusing on Korean language learner motivation and a vision study conducted on a different student cohort enrolled in the same program at a later stage (Fraschini & Caruso, 2019), suggesting that the motivations did not shift. This is an important consideration for educators because it suggests that developing clear course combinations that effectively integrate Korean studies (both linguistic and cultural training) with other major degrees such as engineering, commerce, political science and international relations are most likely to result in strong student recruitment and retention, as students can see themselves being able to apply their linguistic and cultural knowledge in future career situations.

3.4. Preference of learning activities among Korean language students

The survey also asked students to express their preference for language learning activities and material used in the classroom through rating 14 items. On a scale of 1 to 5, ranging from 'I wouldn't like it at all' to 'I would really like it', students indicated the extent to which they enjoyed each of the learning activities commonly used in second language education. We then applied a similar strategy to that used to study student motivations. Factor analysis results reveal that variations in the students' rating of the 14 items mainly reflect the variations in four underlying variables, each reflecting one broader category of learning activities. The first category can be labelled as *High-level language activities*, and includes, for example, 'academic lectures and presentations on Korea', 'workplace-related conversations' and 'professional talks'. The second category covers *Form-focused activities* such as 'grammar exercises and drills', 'vocabulary exercises', and 'short compositions practice regarding narratives and emails'. The third category focuses on *Oral language activities*, including the typical examples of 'classroom reports and presentation' and 'role-plays'. The final category comprises *Everyday language activities*, including 'conversations on everyday life topics', 'talking about Korean dramas, songs, or shows' and 'reading Korean news and newspaper articles'.

Table 3.4 Students' preference for the four main categories of learning activities

	n	Minimum	Maximum	Mean	Standard deviation
High-level language activities	201	1.00	5.00	3.0357	.9897
Form-focused activities	201	1.33	5.00	3.6766	.8919
Oral language activities	201	1.33	5.00	3.1990	.9369
Everyday language activities	201	1.67	5.00	3.9867	.7467

Source: Compiled by author.

Applying a similar strategy introduced in the last subsection, we reconstructed each participant's preference for each category of learning activities and then calculated the aggregated score for the whole cohort. As demonstrated in Table 3.4, *Everyday language activities* is the most popular category of learning activities. On average, students assigned 3.9867 on a scale of 1 to 5 to indicate how strongly they liked *Everyday language activities* during a Korean language course. This aligns with the finding where the main motivation for learning the language was to interact with Korean people and demonstrates that students actively imagine themselves in everyday situations using the Korean language. Students also demonstrated a good level of appreciation for *Form-focused activities* (grammar exercises), with an average preference score of 3.6766 on a scale of 1 to 5. The levels of enthusiasm for the other two categories of learning activities are relatively lower but remain positive on both occasions. On average, students assigned 3.1990 on a scale of 1 to 5 to indicate how strongly they liked *Oral language activities* during a Korean language course and 3.0357 to *High-level language activities*. The enthusiasm for form-focused activities points to a desire to achieve fluency and confidence in real-life situations.

Moreover, students strongly prefer the use of real-life learning materials, such as TV shows and social networking sites, to prepare themselves for situations that they see as real life in the future. However, at the same time, students do not necessarily dislike traditional learning activities that are directly associated with training in grammar, structures and vocabulary, as such training is seen as a necessary part of mastering a language. Therefore, to choose and deploy the most suitable learning activities in particular circumstances, we deemed it necessary to investigate how each category of learning activities correlates with each learning motivation.

To test this idea, we constructed four regression models to examine how each category of learning activities is correlated with the three motivations for enrolling in Korean language classes. The results are reported in Table 3.5. In each model, in addition to variables of learning motivations and learning activities, we also include a series of individual characteristics as control variables.

According to the results of Model A, other things being equal, a student in our Korean language courses who had a higher level of career-development motivation in studying the Korean language was also likely to have a higher preference for studying the Korean language through high-level language activities. This result clearly shows that students who study Korean to use it for future career development are aware not only of the need to learn how to use Korean in more formal situations and professional contexts, but also of the opportunities Korean language ability presents for them to boost their potential career options. Also, other things being equal, in comparison with their male peers, female students tend to have a higher preference for studying Korean through high-level language activities.

Table 3.5 Correlations between learning motivations and learning activities

	Preference of learning activities			
	(A) High-level language activities	(B) Form-focused activities	(C) Oral language activities	(D) Everyday language activities
Varieties of learning motivations				
Positive attitudes towards Korea and Koreans	0.069 (0.094)	0.020 (0.085)	0.221* (0.091)	0.311** (0.064)
Prospects of visiting or relocating to Korea	0.129 (0.101)	0.247** (0.091)	0.019 (0.098)	0.072 (0.068)
Desires for developing employability	0.247* (0.110)	0.050 (0.100)	0.053 (0.107)	−0.076 (0.075)
Control variables				
Gender	−0.356* (0.167)	−0.007 (0.151)	−0.287 (0.162)	−0.327** (0.113)
New student	0.177 (0.145)	−0.144 (0.131)	−0.076 (0.141)	−0.069 (0.099)
STEM	0.200 (0.144)	0.198 (0.130)	0.223 (0.140)	0.255 (0.098)
First L2	0.009 (0.222)	−0.072 (0.201)	−0.161 (0.215)	−0.207 (0.151)
Multilingual	0.015 (0.150)	0.153 (0.135)	0.079 (0.145)	0.331** (0.102)
Constant term	1.220** (0.471)	2.348** (0.425)	2.010** (0.456)	2.592** (0.320)
N. of observations	184	184	184	184
Adjust R^2	0.087	0.060	0.051	0.246

Source: Compiled by author.

According to the results of Model B, other things being equal, a student who is more strongly motivated by the prospects of visiting or living in Korea in the future is more likely to also have a higher preference for studying the Korean language through form-focused activities. Similarly, a study conducted by Fraschini and Caruso (2019) found that students who were interested in living and working in Korea, and gaining employment in a language-focused profession, such as translating, interpreting or English language teaching, were more likely to appreciate learning activities that required demonstrating a high degree of accuracy and in-depth knowledge of grammar and advanced language features.

According to the results of Model C, other things being equal, we found that students who aspire to live in Korea and are already drawn to Korean culture are also more likely to prefer to study Korean language by engaging in speaking and listening tasks, including watching Korean dramas, songs and news reports. This group was also keen to learn more about Korean culture and society. Similarly, as the results of Model D indicate, these students are also more likely to have a higher preference for studying the Korean language through activities that involve more everyday language use than discipline-specific or high-level language.

Furthermore, the results of Model D also reveal two other interesting patterns. First, other things being equal, in comparison with fellow male students, female students tend to have a higher preference for studying Korean through everyday language activities. The reason for this result probably lies in the fact that female students, more than male students, tend to express a stronger interest in consuming Korean popular culture. Second, other things being equal, in comparison with fellow students who are not multilingual speakers, students who are multilingual speakers tend to have a higher preference for studying Korean through everyday language activities. The reason for this could lie in the fact that multilingual speakers are more used to using multiple languages to communicate in everyday life and have a predisposition to learn Korean for similar purposes with less concern for obtaining a high level of accuracy. They may also be less concerned with making errors, and keener on simply achieving successful communication skills.

What all this suggests, therefore, is that most Korean language students are highly motivated by the intrinsic draw of Korean culture, with which they feel a strong affinity, as well as instrumental considerations with a view to enhancing their future employment opportunities. This dual interest provides a very strong motivational basis for developing successful programs because students are driven by an idea of a positive future self who is able to communicate and perhaps even live successfully in Korea. However, we will now turn to a discussion of how, despite the enthusiasm and motivation of high numbers of students to learn Korean language and culture, the future of Korean language education in Australian higher education is not a given. In fact, the threats to language education are less related to student interest, teaching staff or effective marketing of programs than to shifting government policies that sometimes support and sometimes undermine language education in local contexts.

4. Holding back growth: 'Asia literacy' in the national context

Lo Bianco and Slaughter (2016) have rightly observed that Australia's relationship with Asia is complex and multifaceted, and often characterised by miscomprehension and a sense of threat. Nevertheless, geographical proximity, migration and, most notably, economic ties have forced successive Australian governments to boost Australians' understanding of their neighbouring countries. The government has termed this policy-driven initiative 'Asia literacy'. However, while between 1969 and 1994 more than 40 policies, governmental white papers and policy reports pointed out the need to increase enrolments in Asian studies and Asian languages (Henderson, 2007), the government's attempts to improve Asia literacy, often framed as a neo-colonial solution to Australia's economic needs (Singh, 1995), have lacked a strategic and coordinated approach. Moreover, policies such as the latest Job-Ready Graduates Package (JRGP) in 2020 have had (perhaps unintended) negative consequences for the resourcing of programs, which has meant that even programs with large numbers of students have struggled to flourish and grow.

The National Asian Languages and Studies in Australian Schools (NALSAS) strategy introduced in 1994 focused on the importance of teaching Asian languages in Australian schools (Council of Australian Government, 1994). This national strategy was meant to implement the policy recommendations put forward in 1994 in the Rudd Report, which called for a coordinated national effort to improve Asia literacy (Henderson, 2008). The NALSAS strategy was launched and funded by the Council of Australian Government (COAG) to the tune of A$400 million in 1994 but was then discontinued in 2002—four years before the planned end date. The cost of the NALSAS strategy was justified by a promise of tangible commercial and economic returns that increased Asian language capabilities would bring to Australia (Lo Bianco, 2002). Henderson (2008, p. 190) argues that the Rudd Report and the NALSAS strategy were ground-breaking because they 'established the foundation of Asia literacy' in Australia. However, despite initial success, NALSAS did not achieve its stated aims. In his evaluation of the outcomes of the strategy, Lo Bianco (2002) notes that its main failings included the promotion of unattainable language proficiency targets, a focus on national commercial interests above the interests of Australian communities, and a lack of consideration of the needs of background speakers of Asian languages (Chinese, Japanese, Indonesian and Korean). In other words, the scope of the policy, which focused mostly on material returns, was too narrow to motivate significant numbers of language learners to learn an Asian language. Moreover, it completely failed to understand the key motivation for students to enrol in language courses, which we have discussed earlier in this chapter: the desire to interact with people from a culture in which potential learners have developed a deep interest. It is this aspect that the Australian government's policies continue to overlook and underutilise in the misguided belief that students primarily choose to study a subject because of perceived financial returns.

Again, Korean language education provides an illustration of this point. Compared to other Asian language programs, the promotion of Korean language education in schools and universities has been particularly difficult due to historically arbitrary diplomatic engagement between ROK and Australia. Moreover, it was unfortunate that just when NALSAS was being implemented, South Korea's economy was seriously hit by the 1997 Asian financial crisis. The death of the North Korean leader Kim Il-sung in 1994 and the ensuing nuclear arms testing race led by Kim Jong-Il also added to a general sense of doubt about South Korea's future as a reliable trading partner for Australia. As a result, in the 1990s very few Korean language learners chose to study Korean out of intrinsic motivational reasons, such as being drawn to Korean culture.

In 2012 the Australian government revisited the aims of the discontinued NALSAS strategy and released the *Australia in the Asian Century White Paper* (Commonwealth of Australia, 2012). The focus of the White Paper was again squarely on framing Asia education (both languages and Asian studies) as an economic necessity for Australia. The White Paper noted that for Australia to make the most of Asian markets, 'Asia literacy' was essential. Thus, the rising economic importance of Asian countries was yet again acknowledged as crucial to Australia's long-term economic future, since it was claimed that Asia was an opportunity and, at the same time, missing out on potential markets was a threat to national survival (Lo Bianco & Slaughter, 2016; Walker, 2010; Salter, 2013). Around the same time, perceptions of South Korea were changing rapidly as the country emerged as a cultural superpower. With the Korean Wave (*hallyu*) sweeping first over North and South East Asia and then spreading throughout the world, Korean popular culture has gained a global following. From internationally popular K-pop bands such as BTS, BlackPink and ATEEZ to Oscar-winning movies and record-breaking TV series on Netflix such as *Squid Game* (2021) and *Hellbound* (2021), Korean popular culture has become a recognisable brand with millions of fans worldwide. Moreover, as the cultural industries have now become Korea's largest export item, there has also been more Korean government support for Korean studies and research in Australia, as demonstrated for example by the Korean Research Centre of Western Australia, originally launched in 2020 with the support of the Academy of Korean Studies (Elfving-Hwang, 2021).

Despite these serendipitous external factors, the federal and state governments continue to miss opportunities to harness the intrinsic motivation of students who want to learn Korean. At both state and federal levels, policy and funding have not caught up with the opportunities to create clear, strong plans for language education in Australia. In fact, despite some haphazard and meagre funding to allow students to study overseas in Asia, such as the New Colombo Plan (NCP), the task of fixing the perceived lack of Asia literacy has been left to individual secondary schools, a small number of state government actors and individual tertiary institutions. As the secondary school sector is largely funded by state governments, each state and territory has, in the absence of a clear federal plan, taken a slightly different approach to funding and delivering language education. For universities, the development of Korean studies and language teaching has been left to individual departments, which devise strategies on their own using additional Commonwealth funding provided for language courses. This additional funding ended abruptly in 2021 with the rollout of the JRGP reform, which coincided with a wave of language program closures across Australia (Aspinall et al., 2020; Lees et al., 2020; Norton, 2020). Even for popular courses such as Korean studies, which have witnessed year-on-year growth, there has been a tightening of resourcing. This may have been partially caused by the challenges in pedagogy and pastoral care caused by the COVID-19 pandemic (Fraschini & Tao, 2024; Tao, 2021) and by financial pressures caused by the decrease in the number of international students. Moreover, it also meant that universities are making less money from domestic students, as student contributions have fallen and Commonwealth contributions are capped. In the next section, we will illustrate how these drivers—both cultural attractiveness of Korean popular culture and government policies—have impacted the teaching of the Korean language in Western Australian secondary and tertiary sectors, and why language learners' intrinsic motivation alone cannot guarantee the success of secondary language programs or Korean studies programs in universities.

5. Korean language education in Western Australia

In Western Australian secondary schools, Korean language education has lagged behind other Asian languages such as Chinese, Japanese and Indonesian, with only a handful of schools electing to teach Korean. After years of lobbying, in 2021 the Western Australian Department of Education announced that Korean (along with Hindi and Tamil) would be included in the state school curriculum as an examined subject valid for the Australian Tertiary Admission Rank (ATAR)[4] examinations from 2023 onwards.

Despite Korean governmental organisations (and most notably, the Korean Education Centre in Sydney) having provided considerable time, resources and fixed-term funding for schools to initiate and support the teaching of the Korean language, the uptake has been weak because Korean was not included in the state school curriculum and students, therefore, have seen very little benefit in pursuing Korean as a study subject beyond Year 10 when the curriculum becomes very busy. The Western Australian universities' admissions system awards students who complete the Year 12 ATAR examination in a recognised language additional points towards their Western Australian Certificate of Education and total ATAR score (Caruso & Brown, 2017). These extra points can often make a significant difference to whether a student gets a place in their desired university course. For this reason, languages not included in the state curriculum are not typically taught beyond Year 9. As a result, only three primary schools and one secondary school in Western Australia currently teach Korean, and so far many school administrators have been reluctant to consider introducing Korean in their schools, especially as parents are often very driven by the potential for their children to maximise their ATAR scores.

In an effort to fix the abysmal uptake in language learning at the secondary school level, in 2018 the Western Australian Department of Education introduced a policy that required all primary schools in the state to offer compulsory foreign language classes from Year 3 (seven to eight year olds) onwards. The objective of the new policy was to encourage children to study a foreign language from an early age so as to better prepare them for the globalising world. The following year the scheme was expanded to

---

4   The ATAR is a rank used to measure the academic achievement of Year 12 students across Australia, and the main criterion for university admission.

include Year 4, and in 2020 Year 5. In 2021, all primary schools in the state were expected to be learning one foreign language between Year 3 and Year 6. However, the policy has not been accompanied by an effective provision of language teacher education or strategic planning that would allow students to continue learning a language they learned in primary school and high school. This new policy, along with the introduction of Korean in the state curriculum, may ultimately build momentum for boosting the number of Korean language programs in local schools. However, since the teachers' unions in Western Australia have been warning of a huge shortage of teachers, it also means that, to date, the majority of students who study Korean language at the tertiary level in Western Australia do not typically have previous Korean language training or skills. Despite the widespread interest in learning Korean among Western Australian school- and university-age learners, opportunities to do so are very limited. In other words, one of the most pressing challenges the sector now faces is not how to attract students to study Korean, but how to put structures in place to provide strong teaching programs at primary, secondary and tertiary levels.

6. Overcoming past challenges

Due to the contextual reasons illustrated above, the development of tertiary Korean language education in Western Australia faces a range of challenges that are practical, structural and, to an extent, also ideological. While it is relatively easy to attract students to our programs, the practical challenges that relate to student retention are similar to those faced by other language programs and relate to the increasing number of 'false beginners'. These are students who have studied (in many cases, self-studied) Korean previously, but hold no formal qualification from an educational institution. While these students are often highly motivated, placing them at an appropriate level of study is challenging. In many cases, their knowledge of the Korean language and culture is normally acquired from online material, personal trips to Korea or time spent with Korean friends, and is not sufficient for them to be placed in an intermediate language class. That said, the gap between genuine and 'false beginners' can be considerable in the perception of true beginners, who are often demotivated by what they perceive as an unfair advantage. This can have a significant knock-on effect on retention rates.

Secondly, because the vast majority of the first-year cohort is enrolled in a major degree outside of the Bachelor of Arts, most take Korean language and/or Korean studies as elective courses and, in some cases, simply sign up for these courses to fulfil a graduation requirement. This group of students typically do not pursue language studies beyond the first year, and are often strategic in that they seek to enhance their overall GPA through pursuing what are considered to be 'easier' first-year courses. The minor in Korean Language and Culture introduced in 2021 at UWA is aimed in particular at capturing these students. Reports of 2021 enrolments show that this minor was the most popular among all minors available at UWA, which nurtures the hope that in the near future Korean studies courses will also be able to achieve high retention rates in intermediate and intermediate–advanced level courses. At the same time, the lack of courses offering advanced Korean severely limits the acceptance of students who already have an intermediate command of the language, such as heritage learners, and would like to proceed further in their studies. This also means that any students who have previously studied Korean in high school will be unable to enrol in the Korean studies major.

Thirdly, as the cost of running language programs no longer matches Commonwealth funding, the increase in student numbers has also led to an increase in class sizes and a reduction in contact hours. Managing large cohorts of Korean language students with limited resources makes it challenging to foster learner autonomy or to address individual student learning needs. The high uptake of Korean indicates that students are generally motivated to learn Korean as a second language; however, the large cohort size also means that the teaching staff have found it difficult to tap into the potential provided by that inherent motivation. The flipped classroom model has been particularly effective in maximising opportunities for face-to-face interactive learning. An example of this is the introduction of a weekly video clip series introducing and illustrating the main grammar points in the language classes. This allows students to learn at their own pace and also leaves more time for the use of activities in face-to-face interaction, where the instructor can follow students on a more individual basis instead of passively delivering content to the whole cohort. In the non-language courses focusing on Korean culture and society, the flipped classroom model has shifted the responsibility for learning from the lecturer to the students and allowed for student-centred and interactive modes of learning to develop in the classroom.

Finally, the biggest challenges to our programs come from shifting government funding patterns and internal university restructures, which at times work in favour of Korean studies and language programs and at other times work in the opposite direction. While staff expertise, enthusiasm and commitment are of course a large part of a successful program, the long-term success of language and area studies programs is essentially dependent on two structural key factors: adequate government (state and federal) funding structures and institutional champions who see the value of fostering a global mindset in students. Without these two, and even with external remedial funding from the Korean government, a lack of resourcing will soon become a limiting factor to program growth.

7. Concluding thoughts

This chapter has outlined some of the issues and challenges that educators face in developing Korean language education in Western Australia. We have outlined here that while a great deal of enthusiasm is shown by learners of Korean who are motivated to pursue Korean studies, structural barriers and lack of Australian state and federal funding remain some of the key issues limiting growth. While at the tertiary level, Korean language and Korean studies have benefited from the popularity of Korean TV dramas, films and music, the main drivers that have either enabled or prevented language education growth at universities have been universities' own policies, which have failed to encourage language education among students and to resource schools and departments to provide quality language education. The opposite situation can be seen in the school sector, where the state government, on the one hand, emphasises the importance of language education through policy directives that require languages other than English to be taught in primary schools, and on the other hand uses the same policy instrument to stunt the growth of language programs after Year 10 when students are perhaps at their most motivated to learn if only given the right encouragement. While teaching staff, external funding from foreign governments and positive representations of the target culture in global popular culture are, of course, important factors in building successful language programs, the case of Korean language education in Western Australia illustrates clearly the vital role that state governments, the Schools Curriculum Standard Authority and local university policies and funding decisions can play in determining the success of language education. All it takes is one policy decision, properly executed and resourced (or not), to decide whether a language subject grows—or dies out, despite the best efforts of dedicated language staff.

Acknowledgment

This study was supported by the Core University Program for Korean Studies through the Ministry of Education of the Republic of Korea and the Korean Studies Promotion Service of the Academy of Korean Studies (AKS-2022-OLU-2250005).

References

Aspinall, E. & McGregor, K. (2020). *Statement: A crisis in Asian languages*. Asian Studies Association of Australia. Retrieved on 12 January 2022 from www.asaa.asn.au/wp-content/uploads/2020/12/Statement-on-closure-of-Asian-language-programs-at-Murdoch-and-Swinburne-Universities-final.pdf

Caruso, M. & Brown, J. (2017). Continuity in foreign language education in Australia: The language bonus plan. *Australian Review of Applied Linguistics, 40*(3), 280–310. doi.org/10.1075/aral.17029.car

Choi, H. (2013). A case study of three learners of Korean as a foreign language in a US university: Their motivation to learn Korean and perceptions of Korean language classes. *Studies in Foreign Language Education, 27*(1), 261–80. doi.org/10.16933/sfle.2013.27.1.261

Committee for the 50 Years History of Koreans in Australia. (2008). *Fifty-year history of Koreans in Australia*. Jinheung.

Commonwealth of Australia. (2012). *Australia in the Asian century: White paper*. Department of the Prime Minister and Cabinet.

Council of Australian Government. (1994). *Asian languages and Australian economic future*. COAG Working Group on a National Asian Languages/Studies Strategy for Australian Schools.

Csizér, K. & Dörnyei, Z. (2005). The internal structure of language learning motivation and its relationship with language choice and learning effort. *The Modern Language Journal, 89*(1), 19–36. doi.org/10.1111/j.0026-7902.2005.00263.x

Dalton, B. (2021). Six ways to boost the Australia–Korea trade relationship. In J. Elfving-Hwang & P. Dean (Eds), *Towards deeper engagement: Prospects and reflections on the 60th anniversary of ROK–Australia diplomatic relations* (pp. 16–19). Korea Research Centre of Western Australia. hdl.handle.net/10453/163751

Dörnyei, Z. (2009). The L2 motivational self system. In Z. Dörnyei & E. Ushioda (Eds), *Motivation, language identity and the L2 self* (pp. 9–42). Multilingual Matters. doi.org/10.21832/9781847691293-003

Dörnyei, Z. & Chan, L. (2013). Motivation and vision: An analysis of future L2 self images, sensory styles, and imagery capacity across two target languages. *Language Learning, 63*(3), 437–62.

Dörnyei, Z. & Ryan, S. (2015). *The psychology of the language learner revisited*. Routledge.

Elfving-Hwang, J. (2021). Reflecting on 60 years of academic Korea expertise in Australia: (Missed) opportunities and challenges ahead. Korea Research Centre Paper Series, 1, 20–23. drive.google.com/file/d/13qivXH1XO4HBBysXe38B3OQJkBShrXRK/view

Fraschini, N. (2020). 'Because Korean is cool': Adolescent learners' vision, motivation, and the study of the Korean language. *Journal of Korean Language Education, 31* (English edition), 37–74.

Fraschini, N. & Caruso, M. (2019). 'I can see myself …': A Q methodology study on self vision of Korean Language learners. *System, 87*, 102147. doi.org/10.1016/j.system.2019.102147

Fraschini, N. & Tao, Y. (2024). Emotions in online language learning: Exploratory findings from an *ab initio* Korean course. *Journal of Multilingual and Multicultural Development, 45*(5), 1305–1323. doi.org/10.1080/01434632.2021.1968875

Hadfield, J. & Dörnyei, Z. (2013). *Motivating learning*. Pearson.

Han, Y. (2021). Motivations for learning Korean in Vietnam: L2 selves and regulatory focus perspectives. *Journal of Language, Identity and Education, 22*(6), 559–73. doi.org/10.1080/15348458.2021.1935961

Henderson, D. (2007). A strategy cut-short: The NALSAS strategy for Asian languages in Australia. *Electronic Journal of Foreign Language Teaching, 4*(1), 4–22. www.eprints.qut.edu.au/7407/

Henderson, D. (2008). Politics and policy-making for Asia literacy: The Rudd report and a national strategy in Australian education. *Asian Studies Review, 32*(2), 171–95. doi.org/10.1080/10357820802064690

Jee, M. J. (2015). A study of language learner motivation: Learners of Korean as a foreign language. *Journal of Korean Language Education, 26*(2), 213–38. doi.org/10.18209/IAKLE.2015.26.2.213

Kwon, M. K. & Lee, S. Y. (2005). Korean as a second language learners' motivation and learning achievement: From the viewpoint of adult learning. *Journal of Korean Language Education, 16*(3), 1–28.

Lane, B. (2011). Seoul revival as students embrace Korean language. *The Australian*. Retrieved on 6 October 2021 from www.theaustralian.com.au/higher-education/seoul-revival-as-students-embrace-korean-language/news-story/0809a5e961417675dd2945ced9e68566

Lee, I. (2018). Effects of contact with Korean popular culture on KFL learners' motivation. *The Korean Language in America, 22*(1), 25–45. doi.org/10.5325/korelangamer.22.1.0025

Lee, P. (2021). Integrating defence industry into the Australia–Korea security relationship. In P. J. Dean & J. Elfving-Hwang (Eds), *Black swan strategy paper: Defence and security through an Indo-Pacific lens* (pp. 22–24). UWA Defence and Security Institute.

Lees, O., Wijaya, S. & Renaldi, E. (2020, 5 December). Axing Asian language courses from schools and universities may leave Australia underprepared for the future. *ABC News*. www.abc.net.au/news/2020-12-05/asian-language-programs-fights-to-stay-hindi-indonesian/12934096

Lo Bianco, J. (2002). After NALSAS…? *Australian Language Papers, 10*(2), 7–8.

Lo Bianco, J. & Slaughter, Y. (2016). The Australian Asia project. In G. Leitner, A. Hashim & H. -G. Wolf (Eds), *Communicating with Asia: The future of English as a global language* (pp. 296–612). Cambridge University Press.

Nikitina, L. & Furuoka, F. (2019). Language learners' mental images of Korea: Insights for the teaching of culture in the language classroom. *Journal of Multilingual and Multicultural Development, 40*(9), 774–86. doi.org/10.1080/01434632.2018.1561704

Norton, A. (2020). 3 flaws in Job-Ready Graduates package will add to the turmoil in Australian higher education. *The Conversation*. Retrieved on 12 January 2022 from theconversation.com/3-flaws-in-job-ready-graduates-package-will-add-to-the-turmoil-in-australian-higher-education-147740

Reece, N. (2014). Australia after the Asian Century White Paper. *Australian Economic Review, 47*(3), 350–69. doi.org/10.1111/1467-8462.12080

Salter, P. (2013). The problem in policy: Representations of Asia literacy in Australian education for the Asian century. *Asian Studies Review, 37*(1), 3–23. doi.org/10.1080/10357823.2012.760530

Shin, S.-C. (Ed.). (2019). *Korean heritage language maintainance, learning, and development: Australian practices and perspectives.* Sotong.

Singh, G. (1995). Edward Said's critique of orientalism and Australia's 'Asia literacy' curriculum. *Journal of Curriculum Studies, 27*(6), 599–620. doi.org/10.1080/0022027950270602

Son, S. & Jeon, N. (2011). A study of language learning motivation of Korean language learners. *Journal of Korean Language Education, 22*(3), 133–52.

Tao, Y. (2021). Chinese students abroad in the time of pandemic: An Australian view. In J. Golley, L. Jaivin & S. Strange (Eds), *Crisis* (pp. 291–303). ANU Press. doi.org/10.22459/CSY.2021

Walker, D. (2010). The 'flow of Asia'—vocabularies of engagement: A cultural history. *Australian Journal of Political Science, 45*(1), 45–58. doi.org/10.1080/10361140903517700

Wilson, J. (2018). *Maturing the Korea-Australia investment relationship.* Perth USAsia Centre. perthusasia.edu.au/research-insights/publications/maturing-the-korea-australia-investment-relationship/

4

The role of universities in training Indigenous language workers: Developing an Australian Indigenous Languages Institute

Cathy Bow

Abstract

By teaching Australian Indigenous languages, universities could play a key role in maintaining strong languages, reinforcing struggling languages and reviving languages that are no longer or minimally spoken. This chapter first details the current relatively minor amount of Indigenous language teaching offered by universities. It then looks in some detail at two language courses: Bininj Kunwok, a strong language taught at Charles Darwin University (CDU) and Gamilaraay, which is being revived and is taught at the University of Sydney and The Australian National University (ANU). It then considers the factors that have helped the establishment of these courses and the challenges faced in establishing and maintaining such courses. Overseas universities have developed alternative approaches to working with Indigenous languages, and these models inspired the setting up of the AILI (Australian Indigenous Languages Institute), a partnership between CDU and ANU. Details are given of AILI courses.

Keywords: Indigenous languages, Australian Indigenous Languages Institute, language revitalisation, Gamilaraay, Bnj Kunwok

1. Introduction

The need to provide Indigenous Australians with flexible training options and career pathways for supporting the maintenance and revitalisation of Australian Indigenous languages continues to increase. A National Aboriginal and Torres Strait Islander Languages Teaching and Employment Forum in 2016 gathered experts from around the country 'to work toward a coordinated approach to the training and employment of Aboriginal and Torres Strait Islander language teachers' (First Languages Australia, 2018). At the first National Indigenous Languages Convention in 2018, training and education pathways for Indigenous language workers and linguists emerged as a key concern (Bow, 2018), with many of the Indigenous leaders and language advocates in attendance identifying a need to find appropriate ways to develop Indigenous staff. The peak body for Australian Indigenous languages, First Languages Australia, identified 'the need to professionalise the language industry, including the provision and uptake of recognised professional development opportunities through accredited courses and non-accredited courses' (First Languages Australia, 2020, p. 5). Clearly, no single solution will address the needs of all Aboriginal and Torres Strait Islander language contexts, so flexibility in both delivery and recognition of training is required.

Universities can play a pivotal role in this area, particularly since many Australian universities already offer courses in documentation and description, language teaching and learning, and teacher training. While opportunities also exist in the vocational and community sectors, currently no systematic structure exists to support and maintain long-term skills development and career progression of Indigenous Australians who will lead the next generation of Indigenous language work. Without such training, the future of Australia's Indigenous languages is likely to remain in the hands of non-Indigenous linguists, rather than decolonising the space and ensuring that the authority remains with the language owners.

An initiative known as the Australian Indigenous Languages Institute (AILI) emerged as one means to address the situation. Its tentative beginnings demonstrated a need for a coordinated approach to develop and nurture programs to support the aspirations of Indigenous language authorities.

Its aim was to create opportunities for collaboration and support across the university sector in language training. While it struggled to achieve an ambitious set of goals, much can be learned from its efforts and the challenges it encountered to inform future development in this area. This chapter expands on a previous paper which outlined the need for such training, particularly for language revitalisation (Giacon, 2020), by giving additional details about its origins and subsequent achievements.

The chapter begins by identifying three key areas for training Indigenous language workers (linguistic training, language learning and teacher training), focusing on existing opportunities and the role of the university in providing the space for this training to occur. A summary of the current training situation in Australia across these areas (Section 2) is juxtaposed with some models from North America (Section 3). A description of the AILI follows (Section 4): its goals and anticipated outcomes, a discussion of what can be learned from this initiative, its challenges and the potential for the future.

2. The current situation

> Indigenous languages are struggling for a niche within the tertiary sector. Their place is highly dependent on individuals, internal politics and the demand, or lack thereof, for knowledge of and skills in Indigenous languages outside the tertiary sector. (Amery, 2007, p. 345)

The most recent *National Indigenous Languages Report* (*NILR*, 2020) identifies only 12 Indigenous languages being transmitted to children. More encouragingly, around 120 languages are in some process of revitalisation, with renewed interest particularly in teaching and learning, drawing on existing documentation. However, Australia has no national language policy, and Indigenous languages have no official status. Only NSW has legislation that 'acknowledges that Aboriginal languages underpin Aboriginal identity and the revival and teaching of languages must accord with local community aspirations' (First Languages Australia, 2018, p. 81). The second National Indigenous Languages Survey recommended that 'the Australian Government and state and territory governments should allocate funding for the development and delivery of programs to train language workers, interpreters and language teachers' (Marmion et al., 2014, p. 47). This recommendation was reinforced in the 2020 *National Indigenous Languages*

Report, which noted that the availability of training is linked to ensuring maintenance of languages and enhancing well-being and employability of speakers. However, people surveyed for that report identified a lack of training opportunities.[1] The needs of languages undergoing processes of revitalisation differ from those where the languages are still spoken, and training can support people in both groups.

Funding is an issue for many Indigenous language groups. While some community groups are funded through philanthropic efforts, mining royalties, collaborations with universities and other sources, much of the funding for these efforts comes from the Australian government's Indigenous Languages and Arts (ILA) funding scheme. A requirement of funding under ILA has been that language centres involved in grant projects engage staff with higher education qualifications in linguistics. Currently, very few of the people filling these roles are Indigenous, and the corollary of this requirement is that the valuable work of Indigenous language workers in language centres can be undervalued. Opportunities for extending the professional knowledge of Indigenous language workers through formal studies can support the work of language centres with specialised teaching in the area of Indigenous languages and linguistics, as well as support communities which do not have recognised language centres.

In the spirit of 'don't talk about us without us', Aboriginal and Torres Strait Islander people are taking positions of leadership in all issues related to their languages, cultures, education and well-being. Universities surviving in a competitive environment where government support is being heavily reduced will continue to struggle to work together to provide such opportunities. The inclusion of Reconciliation Action Plans (Lloyd, 2018) in many universities creates a fertile environment for the development of both awareness and opportunities for Indigenous language work. However, without specific 'champions' to promote and facilitate such work (Giacon & Simpson, 2012, p. 69), it is difficult to see how the work will advance.

---

1   Of the 78 responses on this issue, 41 per cent said there were no training opportunities at all, 23 per cent said there were very few (or almost no) opportunities, and 31 per cent said there were few (or limited) opportunities. Just 5 per cent suggested the quantity of training opportunities was not limited to a small number. This was a qualitative question in the AIATSIS Survey, so responses should not be taken as representative (*NILR*, 2020, p. 67).

2.1. Linguistic training for Indigenous language workers in Australia

> The lack of opportunity for Indigenous people to access appropriate training and resources in remote and regional Australia … was clearly hindering the aspirations of Aboriginal and Torres Strait Islander peoples to develop and lead their own language projects. (Gessner et al., 2018, p. 53)

Throughout the colonial era, Indigenous people have been mostly regarded as informants for linguistic work rather than as experts in their own language. Rarely have they been able to benefit professionally from the expertise they possess. Over the last half-century, there has been a shift towards more collaborative activities in documentation and description, recognising that community members have expertise and can be experts (Czaykowska-Higgins, 2009). A push to develop more Indigenous linguists creates new opportunities for Indigenous language workers to be more actively involved in their own language work, and support the advancement of language experts who have shared their knowledge with non-Indigenous linguists without proper recognition. Appropriate training can support Indigenous linguists to develop skills in linguistic analysis, documentation and description that can further support community aspirations for language continuation. Training for speech community members allows people to engage in projects of relevance and importance in their communities, and to participate in deeper, more comprehensive projects with outsider academics (Yamada, 2014, p. 341).

Historically, the main source of training for Indigenous language workers was the School of Australian Linguistics, hosted mostly at Batchelor, outside Darwin, with some courses delivered in communities and later in Alice Springs. From the mid-1970s, the program provided language and linguistic education to over 2,000 speakers of around 100 Australian languages and dialects (Black & Breen, 2001). Offerings included units in linguistics and education, with additional practical units and electives, leading to an Associate Diploma of Australian Linguistics. Many of the students from this time were fluent in their own language but with variable academic background and capacity in English language and literacy. Much of this work supported the professional development of Aboriginal language workers employed in bilingual school programs across the Northern Territory. Through various policy changes with regard to bilingual education (Nicholls, 2005; Simpson et al., 2009), these programs reduced their involvement in both linguistics and teacher education.

In the 1990s, a series of courses were held in conjunction with the Australian Linguistics Society annual conferences with a focus on Indigenous language workers. The first Australian Linguistics Institute was held in Sydney in 1992, with further programs held biennially over the next decade. These programs drew interest and participation from all over Australia and carried a significant administrative load to organise. They were unaccredited, and figures are not currently available regarding attendance or outcomes. The initiative appears to have ceased in 2008.

The Resource Network for Linguistic Diversity (now known as Living Languages) developed a Documenting and Revitalising Indigenous Languages training program. The suite of 40 topics covers aspects of linguistics and language documentation, the use of technologies, resource development, engaging with archival materials and skill sharing. Each location negotiates its training program in consultation with staff, and the program is modified as necessary according to the participants and their needs (Gessner et al., 2018). The training supports the role of Indigenous language centres in language revitalisation and maintenance, including developing language resources, running classes, repatriating archival materials, and raising awareness about Indigenous languages (Gessner et al., 2018, p. 53). The programs were extended to vocational education and training (VET)-level accreditation (Florey, 2018) but currently no longer offer these qualifications. Further training is available through a professional development program, funded by ILA since 2014, which extends participants' knowledge and skills to running their own programs and sharing skills with others in the community and workplaces.

An overview of the landscape for linguistic training for Indigenous Australians in remote locations (Caffery, 2016) assessed the relevance of linguistic training for Indigenous Australians in northern Australia, and found that, due to the diversity of locations, attitudes, lifestyles and access to resources, standardised formal training is unlikely to provide the linguistic skills needed in any given place. Caffery found that no single solution addressed all needs, but that a combination of formal and on-the-job training is likely to be the best outcome. Beyond the skills required of all researchers, such as basic linguistic analysis, computer skills and literacy, Indigenous language researchers working independently would benefit from additional skills such as project management and applying for funding, and personal factors such as increased confidence and motivation. The importance of flexibility in training was also noted, where particular skills could be targeted to specific workplaces.

Much of the training for Indigenous language workers has been in the VET sector rather than higher education. Some excellent vocational training courses have been offered through various institutions (Amery, 2007; Carew & Woods, 2007; Cipollone, 2010; Gale, 2011, 2020; Lowe & Giacon, 2019), though across jurisdictions there is considerable variation regarding what qualifications are required for teaching languages. The requirements of the VET sector concerning regular recertification and reaccreditation also mean that the landscape is continually changing. Universities have the capacity to include skills-based training and the theoretical underpinnings to support ongoing work developing the knowledge base and skill sets required to develop career paths for Indigenous people (Giacon & Simpson, 2012). However, they would seem to be a less attractive option for Indigenous people, if proportionally lower university enrolments for Indigenous students than for non-Indigenous is a reliable signifier (Behrendt et al., 2012; Pechenkina et al., 2011), suggesting barriers or disconnection in relation to the higher education context. Creating simpler administrative paths for entry, recognition of prior achievements in the VET sector and on-the-job training, and providing sufficient support can assist people who may be hesitant to engage in university study.

This appeal from a Torres Strait Islander language advocate directly addresses Indigenous people and their needs:

> It is fundamentally important for Indigenous people to get the necessary knowledge and skills to prepare them to be effective language workers. Appropriate training will broaden your horizon and equip you with language and linguistics skills … These courses help you to appreciate language, make you understand language problems, empower you to work harder in your language maintenance efforts; they give you the opportunity to learn more about your language; they help you to know how your language works linguistically; they give you the chance to learn the appropriate linguistic terminology and they encourage you to do more for your language. (Ober, 2003, p. 13)

2.2. Training teachers of Indigenous languages

> Linguistics has largely abandoned language teaching and curricular development. Therefore, there are far fewer documentary linguists and language pedagogy specialists than the situation requires. (Dwyer et al., 2018, p. 67)

The teaching of Indigenous languages in schools is a rapidly growing field with much increased interest from schools wishing to implement an Aboriginal language program. There is a huge need for skilled and knowledgeable teachers of Australian Indigenous languages to implement and support the Framework for the Teaching of Aboriginal Languages and Torres Strait Islander Languages in the current national curriculum. This increase has largely been inspired by the emergence of language revival initiatives across the country, while also reinforced by communities of first language speakers who wish to see language included in their local school programs.

A teacher training program focused on Indigenous languages would need to operate differently to other programs, involving the trainees in development of their own language skills (Sterzuk & Fayant, 2016). It would require significant investment in staff with an extensive understanding of the challenges and needs of language revitalisation and maintenance, which extends beyond simple teacher education. Hobson outlines many of the challenges to developing strong teacher training programs in this context, including 'financial sustainability, learner distribution, linguistic diversity, program parity, standards of proficiency, community attitudes to professionalisation and learner readiness' (Hobson, 2013, p. 193). He concludes that the 'Indigenous Australian language revival movement is waiting for a university to provide an initial teacher training degree that will respond to and support its ambitions' (p. 202).

First Languages Australia has produced resources documenting professional learning opportunities in the first languages field 'to develop culturally appropriate strategies to increase career-development opportunities for people in the field of Aboriginal and Torres Strait Islander languages' (First Languages Australia, 2020, p. 2). The 2016 report highlights key actions for each state's and territory's consideration in appropriately developing and supporting Indigenous language teachers in schools, and addresses the needs of the Australian curriculum framework and a range of concerns (First Languages Australia, 2018).

Very few documentary or theoretical linguists are trained in language teaching theory or methodology (Hinton, 2010; Penfield & Tucker, 2011). Linguistic skills support the analysis of languages, and universities are ideally suited to preparing people for language teaching. Alongside teaching Indigenous languages comes the need for language resources (pedagogical dictionaries, pedagogical grammars, learners guides, alphabet books, collections of texts, language apps, etc.), all of which need sound training in language and linguistics for their preparation. Targeted teacher training supports the production of curriculum resources. There is a need for more advanced courses and high-level research to move languages, particularly those in the process of revitalisation, beyond the beginner level (Giacon, 2020). Teacher training programs need to 'treat the target language on its own terms and not as an anglicized variant' and to enable 'production of pedagogical materials that do not focus entirely on stereotypical word lists at the expense of linguistic naturalness' (Rice, 2011, p. 326).

Universities can provide teacher training to Indigenous people wanting to teach their language in schools. However, there is a lack of national regulation regarding qualifications for language teachers. Some jurisdictions allow teachers with minimal or no specific training to teach Indigenous languages in school, which affects quality of service. Tentative employment arrangements for Indigenous language teachers can lead to a lack of job stability and other disadvantages. Currently, no undergraduate programs qualify teachers to teach Indigenous languages in schools, though there are some initiatives underway. A Western Australian Aboriginal Languages Traineeship, delivered as a three-year program through the Western Australian Department of Education, can lead to a Limited Registration to Teach. The University of Sydney was working towards a Bachelor of Education program; however, concerns arose about the financial viability of the block mode delivery of programs for Indigenous students from rural and regional locations (First Languages Australia, 2018, p. 32). Postgraduate qualifications are available through the Masters of Indigenous Language Education since 2006 as a one-year, full-time program exclusively for Indigenous people from across Australia who have a teaching degree (Hobson et al., 2018). This program offers units in linguistics, education and research, but has no requirement that participants actually learn an Indigenous language. Its graduates bring a significantly improved knowledge of language and language learning to many positions associated with Indigenous languages. It does not provide a standard teaching qualification; these still need to be sought in each state or territory. International research highlights the role of universities in training teachers of Indigenous languages, with suggestions about modifications to support Aboriginal students (Hobson, 2007; Johns & Mazurkewich, 2001).

If Indigenous languages are to be taught effectively in schools, then there needs to be good backing for this not only from government education departments, but also from tertiary institutions providing programs in traditional languages and programs for teachers in teaching Indigenous languages to Indigenous children (Giacon & Simpson, 2012, p. 63).

2.3. Teaching Indigenous languages at universities in Australia

> It is a national embarrassment that it is so difficult for Australian students to study any Australian Indigenous language at tertiary level. (Simpson 2014, p. 57)

Of over 120 Indigenous languages still spoken at some level in Australia, only seven are currently available for study in Australian universities. These include four languages identified as 'strong' for having a community of first language speakers (Yolŋu Matha, Arrernte, Pitjantjatjara and Bininj Kunwok) and three in various stages of revitalisation (Kaurna, Gamilaraay and Wiradjuri). The very different language ecologies of these languages, and the institutional structures in which the programs are run, mean that these programs all have unique profiles, yet face similar challenges and opportunities. Currently, only Yolŋu Matha has a full suite of units to make up a major in a degree program; others have only one or two units. The effect of language ecologies influences the audiences for these courses. For languages in revitalisation, the target audience is largely Indigenous people with heritage connections to these languages. In some cases, the courses exclusively address that audience. For so-called 'strong' languages, the audience is largely non-Indigenous learners who may be working in a community where the language is still spoken on a daily basis. The challenges in both cases include a lack of resources (textbooks, dictionaries, reading materials), a lack of teachers (where speakers may not be educated to teach, or teachers may not be competent speakers) and a lack of students (Giacon & Simpson, 2011; Simpson, 2014; Ward, 2004, 2015; Ward & van Genabith, 2003).

The institutional structures of universities also influence these programs. Christie (2008) describes the ongoing processes of negotiation in bringing the Yolŋu studies program to fruition, which required responsible, responsive collaborative research, and ongoing accountability. The program took ten years to become stable, well supported, well documented and internationally recognised, and included negotiation with the traditional owners of the country on which it would be taught, away from Yolŋu territory (Christie, 2009). Other institutions face considerable negotiation before they can teach the language of the local area, which may not have sufficient resources (human or linguistic) to teach at the tertiary level, and may encounter a reluctance to teach a language from a different area. Opportunities for cross-institutional enrolment exist, but administrative barriers make this a difficult option, and in some cases lack of commitment from some university administrators (Amery, 2007). Online platforms such as those offered by Open Universities can facilitate such connections to single units; however, not all universities subscribe to this model.

Teaching and learning an Indigenous language is quite different from teaching and learning a world language (Amery, 2020). Including more Indigenous languages in programs alongside world or majority languages recognises their equal status with other languages taught at the university (Roy & Morgan, 2008). Currently, most of the coordinators of these language programs are non-Indigenous people working in collaboration with a community of language owners (Amery, 2016; Amery & Buckskin, 2013; Bow, 2019; Christie, 2008; Gale et al., 2020; Giacon, 2020; Hayashi, 2020; Smith et al., 2017). Equipping more Indigenous people to take charge of this work should be a priority, and would extend options beyond primary and secondary levels.

Indigenous learners have few opportunities to study their own languages at a tertiary level, and may not be motivated to learn languages from other areas. As a result, there is little modelling for prospective teachers to learn how to create appropriate courses at a higher level. However, language courses also create opportunities for people to undertake detailed analysis of their own language and to incorporate appropriate pedagogies. Some low-cost, low-tech tools can support the sharing of training programs, such as the Digital Language Shell (Bow, 2020). Few places in the world support students to study in their own Indigenous language—Hawai'i being an outstanding exception, with New Zealand offering some programs. Ngarigu academic Dr Jakelin Troy declares it a national disgrace that Indigenous learners cannot study in their own language, stating that:

> Currently there is nowhere in Australia where a student can study towards a degree in an Australian language, an Aboriginal or a Torres Strait Islander language, and obtain a Bachelor of Arts in Australian Languages/specific Australian language. This, in spite of the thousands, maybe tens of thousands (no reliable data collected yet by any education system) who study an Australian language through primary to end of secondary level … It is shameful that Australian languages are so undervalued in our Australian universities. (Troy, personal communication, 2021)

3. North American models

> Training for speech community members further levels the playing field. Not only can well-trained speech community members engage in independent projects of their own design, they can participate in deeper, more comprehensive projects with outsider academics. Ultimately, more in-depth collaboration and multiple end users' involvement in projects foster more maximally useful output. (Yamada, 2014, p. 341)

Australia can learn much from models developed in North America for training Indigenous people in teaching, documenting and learning their heritage languages. These long-standing short-term programs ('institutes') have been a great boost to First Nations people involved in language revitalisation or maintenance. Programs such as the American Indian Language Development Institute, the Canadian Indigenous Languages and Literacy Development Institute (CILLDI), the Northwest Indian Language Institute, and the Institute for Collaborative Language Research, 'all share an explicitly activist commitment to collaboration with an Indigenous community focus: working consultatively with and for a community, advocating collaborative research by modelling collaborative teaching' (Dwyer et al., 2018, p. 61). These programs are developed in response to and in collaboration with local Indigenous communities, providing training which also maintains the interconnectedness of culture, language, land and knowledgeable elders and teachers (Desmoulins et al., 2019). The combination of Indigenous and non-Indigenous trainers uses linguistic knowledge to improve curriculum and practice in the context of First Nations schools (McCarty et al., 1997). The practice serves as a means of connecting school, community and university resources to strengthen Indigenous languages. The success of these programs relies on the multiple perspectives of both instructors and participants, and the opportunities for participants to also bring back knowledge and skills to their own community (Yamada 2014).

In such programs, participants are recognised for their own expertise and contribution to language work. Even with low levels of fluency in a language, they are still experts as language owners and authorities, as rememberers or speakers, more than any non-Indigenous linguist. Language documentation not only has to serve academic goals but also community goals (Stebbins, 2012; Wilkins, 1992; Yamada, 2007), using insights from speakers about community use and identifying needs in the community.

Linguistic and teacher training is crucial for language maintenance and revitalisation, and the North American programs give good models for integrating the different elements. They offer flexibility through options for those wanting to specialise, and draw on the advantage of gathering people from different groups together for mutual learning and cost savings. Possibilities such as providing a Community Linguist Certificate, such as that offered by CILLDI (Snoek, 2011), allow for recognised accreditation for those who seek it. These programs have taken a long time to develop, with collaboration between tertiary institutes and community language groups, and they continue to refine their offerings and remain responsive to the needs of the participants, as seen in recent moves to online delivery during the COVID-19 pandemic.

4. Developing an Australian Indigenous Languages Institute

> The sad fact is that one-off courses in linguistics or second language teaching are insufficient … A scattershot approach may provide some students with enough preliminary information for successful augmentation on their own, but for most individuals, meaningful linguistic training must be coherent, consistent and reinforced over several years. (Rice, 2011, p. 327)

Gubbi Gubbi academic Kevin Lowe attended some of the training opportunities offered in North America and on return asked: 'When are Australian universities going to do something more about supporting Indigenous languages? When are they going to set up courses?' (cited in Giacon, 2020, p. 523).

The international models show how it is possible to facilitate collaboration, advocacy, Aboriginal participation and communication around the issues of teaching Indigenous languages in universities, training Indigenous teachers, fostering research in Indigenous languages and supporting Indigenous involvement. A commitment to the upskilling and professionalisation of Indigenous language workers would prevent the inevitable depletion of qualified workers in the imminent future. Pathways for careers in Indigenous language work need to be created for Indigenous language workers, who can then research, teach, advocate, and develop new programs and practices. Beyond ensuring the sustainability of language revival, maintenance and teaching in Australia, such a commitment will increase the profile of Indigenous languages nationally and internationally under the leadership and authority of Indigenous scholars.

Work in the language revival and maintenance field requires high-level learning and research into the languages as well as language teaching methodology, cultural engagement and community negotiation. Indigenous language authorities engaging in such activities will directly equip future generations of Indigenous academics to carry on this work. Without strong academic skills, the work of language revival and maintenance can be piecemeal and project-based, lacking the sustained and informed leadership of highly skilled, qualified Indigenous language professionals. Without support to achieve undergraduate qualifications, Indigenous language workers will be limited in their career pathways, and academic roles in universities will continue to be dominated by non-Indigenous people. Even for those who have already completed study through the existing training opportunities, there is a significant leap to entry into a university program, which demands challenging academic, resource and time commitments. There is a need to create opportunities for Indigenous language workers to taste formal undergraduate study and consider their future options in a safe and low-risk learning environment.

4.1. Origins of AILI

The origins of AILI are tied to a series of workshops associated with the Australian Linguistics Society (ALS) conference. In 2014, a workshop was held in Newcastle entitled 'Learning Indigenous Languages—Can Universities Help?' Around 40 people attended, with a series of speed presentations reporting on courses currently available through Australian universities. Discussion ensued about some of the current issues, including teacher qualifications and salary rates, recognition of elders in the classroom, pathways for students through primary, secondary and tertiary levels, and bureaucratic barriers. Some of the principles that emerged were that all Indigenous language courses need to be community-led to develop useful outputs, include skills transfer and promote Aboriginal cultural values.

A follow-up workshop on the same topic at the 2015 ALS conference at Western Sydney University saw the development of a working group to continue the discussion, with two focal points: training more language teachers and making more languages available at the tertiary level. The focus on the role of universities helped to separate the many issues relating to community-level language work, while not devaluing the importance of that work. The newly formed committee met online a few times during 2016, discussing issues such as cross-institutional enrolments, recognition of TAFE courses in teacher certification, and proposals for new short or accredited courses. A Facebook page was set up with the title 'Teaching Australian Languages' to enable wider discussion and sharing of ideas. At the 2016 annual general meeting of the ALS in Melbourne, the subcommittee 'Teaching Australian Indigenous Languages at University' was recognised. The Languages and Cultures Network for Australian Universities (LCNAU) conference in 2017 included a focus on Indigenous languages, and also recognised such a committee. In both formal presentations and informal meetings, the desire to develop new opportunities became more apparent, with a perception that people were interested in doing training at university in Indigenous languages and linguistics, but that there were limited courses available.

In 2016, the University of Newcastle took the lead in applying for ILA funding to establish an Indigenous Languages Institute in collaboration with other universities. The goal was to implement graduate and postgraduate study programs in Australian languages and culture, and to establish a series of short summer/winter school programs that would support initial community language planning and learning. The funding application was unsuccessful, with feedback suggesting that a future application would be more favourably viewed if a pilot program was developed as a proof of concept.

Changes in direction at the University of Newcastle led to Charles Darwin University (CDU) taking on the task of developing such a pilot, drawing on its connection to Batchelor Institute's specialised offerings in linguistics and languages designed for Indigenous students. Their three-year Bachelor of Indigenous Languages and Linguistics (BILL) has exit points after one year (Diploma of Indigenous Language Work) and two years (Associate Degree in Indigenous Languages and Linguistics). This work has now morphed into a general Bachelor of Arts program; however, a full degree can specifically address the linguistics of Indigenous languages, including some very practical units on resource development, language centre management and community language planning.

The nascent Australian Indigenous Languages Institute was created with no external funding and minimal institutional support, and was built on matching existing courses through Batchelor Institute with the presumed audience of Indigenous language workers. Basic marketing included a website (aili.cdu.edu.au) with some home-made amateur branding, and an email address and mailing list were established. A Twitter page was established to promote the programs and other topics of interest to this audience. This model relies on keen academics doing largely voluntary work outside their everyday roles.

A pilot program was run at a Summer School at the Sydney campus of CDU in January 2018. The courses were open to anyone, with any enrolled university students allowed to take them for credit; they were badged as a collaboration between CDU, BIITE and ANU, and were promoted via linguistic networks, social media, and so on. Three courses were offered (Introduction to Yolŋu Languages and Cultures, Gamilaraay 1, and Linguistics for Indigenous Languages), although in the end only the Gamilaraay course ran, with 16 students attending.

4.2. Support for travel scholarships

In 2018, a small team including Dr Kevin Lowe (University of NSW), Dr John Giacon (ANU), Greg Williams and Cathy Bow (CDU) applied for ILA funding to create ten travel scholarships to allow Indigenous students to attend training provided by the nascent AILI. The goal was to give Indigenous language workers an opportunity to experience university-level studies in Indigenous languages and linguistics, with a view to encouraging enrolment in university courses, in order for them to develop academic credentials that would enable them to lead the work of language maintenance and revival.

Existing financial support, available through funding for Indigenous people to attend universities (such as AbStudy and Away from Base), can sustain a student who enrols beyond the intensive course offerings. Academic support from language centres and academic mentors and participants would facilitate students to continue their studies at their own pace, whether this comes from their own communities, if online study is appropriate for them, or through further intensives. Even those who chose not to enrol in further studies would have an experience of study at the university level, with a cohort of other interested students, and return to their workplace with skills which can be implemented to benefit their community. Such outcomes would contribute to the professional development of the next generation of Indigenous language workers, and assist in the creation of career pathways that enable them to shape and direct the course of language work in the coming generations.

The scholarship opportunity was promoted through social media, direct emails and inclusion in newsletters of various bodies. Applicants were required to include the name and contact details of two referees, as well as a 400–500-word statement of interest, explaining their involvement in language work, their goals for language revitalisation or maintenance, and how they anticipated their community would benefit from their involvement in this course. The scholarships were particularly aimed at people with no previous university experience, in line with the goal of introducing Indigenous language workers to tertiary education. Scholarship funds covered travel between the home community and the course location, accommodation for the duration of the course, costs of meals and some local transport (per diem), course fees and materials for one of the intensive courses, and any additional course excursions or activities. On average the scholarship funds amounted to just over $2,000 per person.

The proposal was supported by a number of groups, including RNLD (Living Languages), the Centre of Excellence for the Dynamics of Language (CoEDL) and Kaurna Warra Pintyanthi at the University of Adelaide. Remote language centres from Arnhem Land, far north Queensland and northern NSW wrote letters of support acknowledging the need for such training but the lack of local capacity to offer it, and identified individuals who would greatly benefit from such an opportunity. The funding proposal was awarded over $60,000 in August 2018.

4.3. AILI programs 2019–2020

The funding boost gave momentum to the project, and made future intensive courses possible. A second Summer School was run at the Sydney campus of CDU in January 2019. Interest in scholarships was high, with 29 people applying to travel to the courses. Once again, three courses were offered: Introduction to Yolŋu Languages and Cultures, Gamilaraay 1 and Linguistics for Indigenous Languages (INL100); however, there was insufficient interest in the Yolŋu studies unit to justify flying two presenters from Darwin. John Giacon with Gamilaraay Yuwaalaraay co-teachers Priscilla Strasek, Tracey Cameron and Tanya McEwen delivered the first Gamilaraay unit with four enrolled participants. Eight students enrolled in the INL100 program, taught by Dr Nicoletta Romeo from Batchelor Institute. Five of these had received ILA travel scholarships. Classes ran from 9 am to 1 pm each day over two weeks.

In July 2019, a similar program was run, this time at the Darwin campus of CDU, called the Top End Intensive. Three units were offered, but only Linguistics for Indigenous Languages ran. This program garnered less interest overall, likely due to poor timing, as it clashed with NAIDOC Week celebrations and preceded by just a few weeks the PULiiMA Indigenous Language and Technology Conference scheduled in Darwin. In the end only four students completed the course, including three with scholarships, after two scholarship recipients had to withdraw.

With additional funds remaining, scholarship offers were extended for a third Summer School. The February 2020 event was held at CDU in Darwin, with eight people awarded travel scholarships, seven others attending with payment, and two 'support staff' from language centres. Jackie van den Bos taught and, with a high proportion of attendees using Kriol as their first language, was able to deliver some content in Kriol. To reduce costs and time away from community, the program ran for one week rather than two, with longer sessions each day (from 9 am to 3 pm), though the response from participants was that they would have preferred a slower pace over two weeks. Table 4.1 presents key figures for the three AILI events.

4. THE ROLE OF UNIVERSITIES IN TRAINING INDIGENOUS LANGUAGE WORKERS

Table 4.1 Statistics from AILI events, 2019–2020

Date, place	Units delivered	Scholarship applications	Scholarships awarded	Total course attendees	Languages represented	States represented
Jan 2019, Sydney	Gamilaraay, Intro to Linguistics	29	5	4 (Gam), 8 (Intro)	6	5
Jul 2019, Darwin	Intro to Linguistics	7	3	4	3	2
Feb 2020, Darwin	Intro to Linguistics	21	9	17	8	5
TOTAL		57	17	33	17	

Source: Compiled by author.

The initial plan was to attempt to offer a complete semester unit in a two-week intensive, but this was unrealistic. Instead, an introduction to the basics of phonetics, phonology, morphosyntax and semantics was covered, drawing largely on the languages of the participants where possible. Future options could involve the addition of some online study; however, previous feedback suggested that many Indigenous people strongly preferred face-to-face options, and in some places were limited by a lack of digital infrastructure or digital literacy.

Feedback from the participants of AILI courses was generally positive, with suggestions that the training would 'make my job a little less confusing' and that 'it was intensive linguistics, getting into the technical stuff that I need to understand!' One participant even said, 'I thought it would be more difficult! Perhaps I'm smarter than I give myself credit for' and another, 'It's fun once you get over the scary-looking terms, knowledge is power—that's what we need for ourselves and our communities: empowerment!' At least seven applications for further study were lodged either at Batchelor or other institutions.

The 2020 Summer School ended just prior to the coronavirus pandemic, which severely constrained travel opportunities. The travel scholarship funds were all spent, and all the upheaval of COVID-19 meant that further discussion about the future of the AILI was put on hold. No further funding has been sought to continue the program, and those involved have engaged in other academic activities.

5. Discussion

> AILI is an attempt to provide accessible, in-depth teaching of languages and related topics such as linguistics and revival and maintenance processes. It intends to use different modes of course delivery, including summer and winter schools, online courses and regular semester courses. It draws on the resources of a number of universities and will award tertiary qualifications. AILI assumes that universities are committed to Australian Indigenous languages and are prepared to make the considerable effort needed to teach them. (Giacon, 2020, p. 536)

While only short-lived, evidence from AILI suggests that there is a need for a university-based program to equip Indigenous language workers to document, analyse, develop and teach their own languages. AILI courses focused mostly on training in linguistic analysis, with some language learning units, but further training offered in language teaching and teacher training would be beneficial, judging by the examples from North America.

Key learnings for the Australian context include the challenge of institutionalising the programs and the value of having a permanent home for such an initiative (McCarty et al., 1997), and the need for a full-time program coordinator and secure funding. Institutions in the North American model all continue to rely substantially on volunteered time and expertise, while some suggest that 'sustainability may best be achieved by establishing charitable foundation status and cultivating donors' (Dwyer et al., 2018, p. 68).

In addition to linguistic and teacher training, computer skills could also be included in training events to support the development of resources and for administrative purposes. More advanced courses could train participants in applying for funding, running their own language programs, public speaking, and development of confidence and motivation for learners to engage in this kind of work (Caffery, 2016). In the Australian context, it should be noted that some learners require additional support in English language and literacy, particularly for participants from communities where the Indigenous languages are still in everyday use. This would also be useful for other participants who may speak English as their predominant language but lack academic literacy to engage in high-level linguistic work. Indigenous language workers—like all Indigenous people—do not form a homogeneous group, so a single solution will never be possible.

The question remains as to whether or not university is the best place to provide these kinds of training. Recognising that no one-size-fits-all approach will work for every individual or community, clearly, university will not be the right solution for everyone. What AILI provides is one piece of a larger puzzle that gives Indigenous language workers an experience of university study and encourages them to undertake further study with the appropriate support. Such training should not replace other offerings in the VET sector or specialist training from Living Languages, acknowledging that there are many different methods of knowledge transmission and not all will be appropriate in a university context (Caffery & Stafford Smith, 2016).

5.1. Challenges

Some of the challenges related to this work involve the everyday lives of participants, who may live in communities where generational trauma, food insecurity, poor housing, substance abuse and other issues may make language work a lower priority. Innovative solutions are required to deliver training to those with low literacy and for those wishing to bypass traditional text-based forms of language work. Acknowledging and appreciating the connections between language and health, caring for country, justice, education, arts and other areas may support this kind of activity, though it is unlikely to resolve the socioeconomic issues.

Funding will always be a challenge, since specific government funding initiatives are unlikely without a national Indigenous languages policy. Some community groups have access to additional funds that can support this work—for example, through mining royalties—but many do not. It is unrealistic to expect individuals to find their own funds for regular trips to a capital city to attend such training, so access to funding is crucial.

What is needed to make an activity such as AILI succeed is a significant level of support. The existing experience, based on three low-level academics working on top of their regular workloads to facilitate these events, is not sustainable. Australia simply does not have the population to support a single institution to run these events, and the models from North America show that these initiatives can only thrive once a home is found and administrative support is enabled. It would be possible to bring tutors and lecturers from different institutions together to offer courses, as has been evidenced by the ALS courses in the 1990s and beyond, but the workload for gathering people to a single location for such training is high. The Living Languages model of sending a small team of trainers to a community is more sustainable, but there are other benefits to gathering people from various communities together to share learning and experiences. One AILI participant commented specifically, 'It was good to meet different people from other communities. I felt good and happy with that other mob there.'

The need to develop highly qualified Indigenous linguists who can lead the way in the future, doing high-level research, analysis, teaching and mentoring for other Indigenous people, is a challenge for universities and for the government that could fund such positions. It may require more flexibility to engage institutions to take the task seriously, and involve more collaboration than competition for the limited funds available. Linguists are generally willing to support such activities, but the competitive nature of universities mitigates against them, even against basic outreach activities such as cross-institutional enrolment.

5.2. The future

Moves within the ALS to develop accreditation for Indigenous language workers will further support initiatives such as AILI; they will both recognise existing skills achieved through on-the-job work and facilitate training through various sources, but also support Indigenous language workers to go on to further study in units that meet their own needs. Several universities are exploring the idea of micro-credentials, where training packages with flexible structures can acknowledge and accredit such work, leading to recognised qualifications for those who desire them. Other possibilities for providing such training would be to connect with existing activities, such as reviving the workshops that used to accompany ALS conferences, or adding training components to the PULiiMA Conference, which already gathers language workers from all over the country.

Since the most recent AILI course in 2020, there has been renewed interest from several universities seeking to support more language work for Indigenous people and seeing this as a possible model. However, it has largely been identified as being owned by a local institution. Such efforts would be best suited to a ground-up movement, as a collaboration between universities and Indigenous community groups, ideally national representatives, such as First Languages Australia who have already done much valuable work in this space. Collaborative design of appropriate models of training will be slow but valuable, and would rely on sufficient administrative, academic and institutional support, as well as multidisciplinary expertise.

As the International Decade of Indigenous Languages approaches, it is incumbent on us to seek and develop new and better ways to train Indigenous people to take the lead in the future of linguistic work in Australia, as experts in their own language. Recognising the diversity of existing offerings and the importance of flexibility while supporting the aspirations of language workers and language communities will require considerable collaboration and innovation, but is certainly a task worth pursuing to ensure that control of the future of Indigenous Australian languages is in the right hands.

Acknowledgments

The work of AILI was made possible through funding from the Indigenous Languages and Arts Program (ILAO1800217). Thanks to John Giacon and Greg Williams for staying the course with AILI and for feedback on this paper, and to Kevin Lowe for the push to get started. Thanks to John, Nicoletta and Jackie for teaching the AILI courses, and to the research support team at the Northern Institute (CDU) for administrative assistance. Jane Simpson and David Nash kindly provided historical materials about the ALS's Indigenous language programs.

References

Amery, R. (2007). Aboriginal language habitat in research and tertiary education. In G. Leitner & I. G. Malcolm (Eds), *The habitat of Australia's Aboriginal languages: Past, present and future* (pp. 327–53). Mouton de Gruyter. doi.org/10.1515/9783110197846.327

Amery, R. (2016). *Warraparna Kaurna! Reclaiming an Australian language*. University of Adelaide Press. doi.org/10.20851/kaurna

Amery, R. (2020). Teaching Aboriginal languages at university: To what end? In J. Fornasiero, S. M. A. Reed, R. Amery, E. Bouvet, K. Enomoto, & H. L. Xu (Eds), *Intersections in language planning and policy: Establishing connections in languages and cultures* (pp. 475–89). Springer. doi.org/10.1007/978-3-030-50925-5_29

Amery, R. & Buckskin, V. (Jack) K. (2013). Having it both ways: Towards recognition of the Kaurna language movement within the community and within the university sector. In M. J. Norris (Ed.), *Proceedings of the 17th FEL Conference* (pp. 65–72). Foundation for Endangered Languages with Carleton University, Canada.

Behrendt, L., Larkin, S., Griew, R. & Kelly, P. (2012). *Review of higher education access and outcomes for Aboriginal and Torres Strait Islander people: Final report.* Department of Education and Training, Government of Australia.

Black, P. & Breen, G. (2001). The School of Australian Linguistics. In J. Simpson, D. Nash, M. Laughren, P. Austin & B. Alpher (Eds), *Forty years on: Ken Hale and Australian languages* (pp. 161–78). Pacific Linguistics.

Bow, C. (2018). The politics of language and technology. *Flycatcher—CDU Student Magazine, 6*, 31. researchers.cdu.edu.au/en/publications/10d8a536-1e05-4a0e-b306-99e66841f714

Bow, C. (2019). Collaboratively designing an online course to teach an Australian Indigenous language at university. *Babel, 54*(1/2), 54–60. search.informit.org/doi/pdf/10.3316/ielapa.717188768079043

Bow, C. (2020). TELL for Indigenous Australian languages. *Proceedings of the 28th International Conference on Computers in Education, 1*, 546–51. researchers.cdu.edu.au/en/publications/4efade3f-5680-42a9-b281-3d6860644e73

Caffery, J. (2016). Matching linguistic training with individual Indigenous community's needs. *The Australian Journal of Indigenous Education, 45*(2), 191–200. doi.org/10.1017/jie.2016.7

Caffery, J. & Stafford Smith, M. (2016). Linguistic and cultural factors that affect the documentation and maintenance of Australia's traditional languages. In P. K. Austin, H. Koch & J. Simpson (Eds), *Language, land and song: Studies in honour of Luise Hercus* (pp. 494–504). EL Publishing. www.elpublishing.org/PID/2033

Carew, M. & Woods, G. (2007). Angkety kalty-anthem, angketyek kalty-irrem, anwern aparlp-ilekerr (Teaching and learning language so we don't lose it): Own language work training in Central Australia. In R. Amery & J. Nash (Eds), *Warra wiltaniappendi—Strengthening languages: Proceedings of the inaugural Indigenous Languages Conference (ILC)*. University of Adelaide.

Christie, M. (2008). Yolngu studies: A case study of Aboriginal community engagement. *Gateways: International Journal of Community Research and Engagement, 1*, 31–47. doi.org/10.5130/ijcre.v1i0.526

Christie, M. (2009). Engaging with Australian Indigenous knowledge systems: Charles Darwin University and the Yolngu of Northeast Arnhem Land. *Learning Communities Journal, 7*(December), 23–35. digitalcollections.cdu.edu.au/nodes/view/4730

Cipollone, J. (2010). Aboriginal languages programs in TAFE NSW: Delivery initiatives and strategies. In J. Hobson, K. Lowe, S. Poetsch & M. Walsh (Eds), *Re-awakening languages: Theory and practice in the revitalisation of Australia's Indigenous languages* (pp. 170–80). University of Sydney. hdl.handle.net/2123/6953

Czaykowska-Higgins, E. (2009). Research models, community engagement, and linguistic fieldwork: Reflections on working within Canadian Indigenous communities. *Language Documentation & Conservation, 3*(1), 182–215. hdl.handle.net/10125/4423

Desmoulins, L., Oskineegish, M. & Jaggard, K. (2019). Imagining university/community collaborations as third spaces to support Indigenous language revitalization. *Language and Literacy, 21*(4), 45–67. doi.org/10.20360/langandlit29463

Dwyer, A., Zepeda, O., Lachler, J. & Underriner, J. (2018). Training institutes for language revitalization. In L. Hinton, L. Huss & G. Roche (Eds), *The Routledge handbook of language revitalization* (pp. 61–69). Routledge. doi.org/10.4324/9781315561271-8

First Languages Australia. (2018). *Nintiringanyi: National Aboriginal and Torres Strait Islander language teaching and employment strategy*. First Languages Australia. www.firstlanguages.org.au/nintiringanyi

First Languages Australia. (2020). *Yakilla: Training tracks*. First Languages Australia. www.firstlanguages.org.au/yakilla

Florey, M. (2018). Transforming the landscape of language revitalization work in Australia: The Documenting and Revitalising Indigenous Languages training model. In S. T. Bischoff & C. Jany (Eds), *Insights from Practices in Community-Based Research* (pp. 314–38). De Gruyter. doi.org/10.1515/9783110527018-018

Gale, M.-A. (2011). Rekindling warm embers: Teaching Aboriginal languages in the tertiary sector. *Australian Review of Applied Linguistics, 34*(3), 280–96. doi.org/10.1075/aral.34.3.02gal

Gale, M.-A. (2020). Square peg in a round hole: Reflections on teaching Aboriginal languages through the TAFE sector in South Australia. In J. Fornasiero, S. M. A. Reed, R. Amery, E. Bouvet, K. Enomoto & H. L. Xu (Eds), *Intersections in language planning and policy: Establishing connections in languages and cultures* (pp. 455–71). Springer. doi.org/10.1007/978-3-030-50925-5_28

Gale, M.-A., Bleby, D., Kulyuṟu, N. & Osborne, S. (2020). The Pitjantjatjara Yankunytjatjara Summer School: *Kulila*! *Nyawa*! *Arkala*! Framing Aboriginal language learning pedagogy within a university language intensive model. In J. Fornasiero, S. M. A. Reed, R. Amery, E. Bouvet, K. Enomoto & H. L. Xu (Eds), *Intersections in language planning and policy: Establishing connections in languages and cultures* (pp. 491–505). Springer. doi.org/10.1007/978-3-030-50925-5_30

Gessner, S., Florey, M., Slaughter, I. Y. & Hinton, L. (2018). The role of organizations in language revitalization. In L. Hinton, L. Huss & G. Roche (Eds), *The Routledge handbook of language revitalization* (pp. 51–60). Routledge.

Giacon, J. (2020). How universities can strengthen Australian Indigenous languages: The Australian Indigenous Languages Institute. In J. Fornasiero, S. M. A. Reed, R. Amery, E. Bouvet, K. Enomoto & H. L. Xu (Eds), *Intersections in language planning and policy: Establishing connections in languages and cultures* (pp. 523–39). Springer. doi.org/10.1007/978-3-030-50925-5_32

Giacon, J. & Simpson, J. (2012). Teaching Indigenous languages at universities. *Selected Proceedings of the Inaugural LCNAU Colloquium, 2011*, 61–73. open research-repository.anu.edu.au/bitstream/1885/60722/2/01_Giacon_Teaching_Indigenous_languages_2012.pdf

Hayashi, Y. (2020). Yolŋu languages in the academy: Reflecting on 20 years of tertiary teaching. In J. Fornasiero, S. M. A. Reed, R. Amery, E. Bouvet, K. Enomoto & H. L. Xu (Eds), *Intersections in language planning and policy: Establishing connections in languages and cultures* (pp. 507–21). Springer. doi.org/10.1007/978-3-030-50925-5_31

Hinton, L. (2010). Language revitalization in North America and the new direction of linguistics. *Transforming Anthropology, 18*(1), 35–41. doi.org/10.1111/j.1548-7466.2010.01068.x

Hobson, J. (2007). Training teachers for Indigenous languages education: What's happening overseas. *Warra wiltaniappendi—Strengthening languages: Proceedings of the inaugural Indigenous Languages Conference (ILC)*, 97–105. www.indigoz.com.au/hobson/HobsonILC2007.pdf

Hobson, J. (2013). Potholes in the road to an initial teacher training degree for Australian revival languages. *Selected Proceedings of the Second National LCNAU Colloquium*, 193–206. www.indigoz.com.au/hobson/LCNAU_2013_Proceedings_HOBSON.pdf

Hobson, J., Oakley, K., Jarrett, M., Jackson, M. & Wilcock, N. (2018). Bridging the gap in Indigenous Australian languages teacher education. In P. Whitinui, C. Rodriguez de France & O. McIvor (Eds), *Promising practices in Indigenous teacher education* (pp. 105–18). Springer. doi.org/10.1007/978-981-10-6400-5_8

Johns, A. & Mazurkewich, I. (2001). The role of the university in the training of Native language teachers. In L. Hinton & K. Hale (Eds), *The Green Book of language revitalization in practice* (pp. 355–366). Brill.

Lloyd, C. (2018). Reconciliation Action Plans: Origins, innovations and trends. *Journal of Australian Indigenous Issues, 21*(4), 10–45. search.informit.org/doi/pdf/10.3316/informit.143063971946912

Lowe, K. & Giacon, J. (2019). Meeting community aspirations: The current state of Aboriginal language programs in NSW. *Babel, 54*(1/2), 46–49.

Marmion, D., Obata, K. & Troy, J. (2014). *Community, identity, wellbeing: The report of the second national Indigenous languages survey*. Australian Institute of Aboriginal and Torres Strait Islander Studies. aiatsis.gov.au/publication/35167

McCarty, T. L., Watahomigie, L. J., Yamamoto, A. Y. & Zepeda, O. (1997). School-community-university collaborations: The American Indian Language Development Institute. In *Thirty year tradition of speaking from our heart* (pp. 85–104). American Indian Language Development Institute. www.aildi.arizona.edu/sites/default/files/aildi-30-year-book-01-school-community-university-collaborations.pdf

Nicholls, C. (2005). Death by a thousand cuts: Indigenous language bilingual education programmes in the Northern Territory of Australia, 1972–1998. *International Journal of Bilingual Education and Bilingualism, 8*(2–3), 160–77. doi.org/10.1080/13670050508668604

(NILR) National Indigenous Languages Report. (2020). Department of Infrastructure, Transport, Regional Development and Communications, Australian Institute for Aboriginal and Torres Strait Islander Studies and The Australian National University. www.arts.gov.au/what-we-do/indigenous-arts-and-languages/indigenous-languages-and-arts-program/national-indigenous-languages-report

Ober, D. (2003). Maintaining Australian Indigenous languages: Get serious about it, before it is too late. *Ngoonjook, 23*, 7–14.

Pechenkina, E., Kowal E. & Paradies Y. (2011). Indigenous Australian students' participation rates in higher education: Exploring the role of universities. *The Australian Journal of Indigenous Education, 40*, 59–68. doi.org/10.1375/ajie.40.59

Penfield, S. D. & Tucker, B. V. (2011). From documenting to revitalizing an endangered language: Where do applied linguists fit? *Language and Education, 25*(4), 291–305. doi.org/10.1080/09500782.2011.577219

Rice, S. (2011). Applied field linguistics: Delivering linguistic training to speakers of endangered languages. *Language and Education, 25*(4), 319–38. doi.org/10.1080/09500782.2011.577216

Roy, H. & Morgan, M. J. (2008). Indigenous languages and research universities: Reconciling world views and ideologies. *Canadian Journal of Native Education, 31*(1), 232–47. doi.org/10.14288/cjne.v31i1.196451

Simpson, J. (2014). Teaching minority Indigenous languages at Australian universities. In P. Heinrich & N. Ostler (Eds), *Proceedings of the 18th FEL Conference* (pp. 54–58). Foundation for Endangered Languages. hdl.handle.net/1885/63929

Simpson, J., Caffery, J. & McConvell, P. (2009). *Gaps in Australia's Indigenous language policy: Dismantling bilingual education in the Northern Territory.* Australian Institute of Aboriginal and Torres Strait Islander Studies. aiatsis.gov.au/publication/35378

Smith, H., Giacon, J. & McLean, B. (2017). A community development approach using free online tools for language revival in Australia. *Journal of Multilingual and Multicultural Development, 39*(6), 491–510. doi.org/10.1080/01434632.2017.1393429

Snoek, C. (2011). The Canadian Indigenous Languages and Literacy Development Institute and linguistic research. *Ethnoscripts, 13*(2), 14–26. www.ethnologie.uni-hamburg.de/pdfs/ethnoscripts-pdf/es13_2artikel.pdf

Stebbins, T. (2012). On being a linguist and doing linguistics: Negotiating ideology through performativity. *Language Documentation & Conservation, 6*, 292–317. hdl.handle.net/10125/4501

Sterzuk, A. & Fayant, R. (2016). Towards reconciliation through language planning for Indigenous languages in Canadian universities. *Current Issues in Language Planning, 17*(3–4), 332–50. doi.org/10.1080/14664208.2016.1201239

Ward, M. (2004). The additional uses of CALL in the endangered language context. *ReCALL, 16*(2), 345–59. doi.org/10.1017/S0958344004000722

Ward. M. (2015). CALL and less commonly taught languages: Challenges and opportunities. In F. Helm, L. Bradley, M. Guarda & S. Thouësny (Eds), *Critical CALL—Proceedings of the 2015 EUROCALL Conference, Padova, Italy* (pp. 549–552). Research-publishing.net. doi.org/10.14705/rpnet.2015.000391

Ward, M. & van Genabith, J. (2003). CALL for endangered languages: Challenges and rewards. *CALL Journal 16*(2–3), 233–58.

Wilkins, D. (1992). Linguistic research under aboriginal control: A personal account of fieldwork in central Australia. *Australian Journal of Linguistics, 12*(1), 171–200. doi.org/10.1080/07268609208599475

Yamada, R.-M. (2007). Collaborative linguistic fieldwork: Practical application of the empowerment model. *Language Documentation & Conservation, 1*(2), 257–82. hdl.handle.net/10125/1717

Yamada, R.-M. (2014). Training in the community-collaborative context: A case study. *Language Documentation & Conservation, 8*, 326–44. hdl.handle.net/10125/24611

Part 2: Language pedagogy

5

Flipping the classroom in beginner Italian: Implications for teaching and learning

Marinella Caruso and Federica Verdina

Abstract

This study analyses the implementation of the flipped classroom approach in a university beginner Italian language course and its implications for teaching pedagogy. The flipped classroom was designed around the specific needs of language education and the benefits of an inductive, student-centred approach that promotes interactive learning. The approach followed a cycle of in-class preparatory discovery of the language contents, post-class/pre-class explicit delivery of contents (video lessons), in-class interaction and practice, and post-class reinforcement (online activities). Students watched instructional videos to prepare for in-class practice and carried out post-class activities as reinforcement and/or formative feedback. While adopting a highly flexible content delivery, this structure emphasised the students' responsibility in completing pre-class activities to be able to engage in in-class interaction.

The format was adopted in a 12-week semester unit at the end of which an anonymous survey on Qualtrics evaluated the students' experience with the new approach. An important outcome was in the area of accountability. In language learning, it is crucial that students understand the importance of regular work outside the classroom. In the flipped model adopted, independent learning is naturally promoted, and students acknowledged that in our survey.

By having to complete pre- and post-class activities as an integral part of the course, students learned the benefits of regular practice as a key strategy of language learning, contributing therefore to their self-regulation skills. The flipped approach was assessed by students as one that offers many advantages over the traditional approach. However, our analysis shows that for it to be embraced it is crucial that students understand its underlying pedagogy.

Keywords: flipped classroom, Italian L2, independent learning, interactive learning

1. Introduction

When the University of Western Australia was forced to move to remote teaching in 2020 at the start of the COVID-19 pandemic, having a flipped course on offer, which was originally designed to be long-term and coherent, was a great bonus. The design of the unit supported continuity of teaching and learning, making the transition to fully online learning smooth and rapid for both teachers and students, and allowing for learning objectives to continue to be met. A fundamental pillar of the flipped approach is, in fact, a component of online asynchronous content delivery. Later in the year, when social distancing restrictions eased, most of the students chose to return to our original flipped modality. This shows that no matter the circumstances or nature of students' needs, in-class learning continues to be highly valued. The flipped course for beginner Italian discussed in this study was designed precisely for its ability to combine the flexibility and adaptability of online delivery with the affordance and effectiveness of in-class interactive learning and feedback.

The choice to move to the flipped learning approach was essentially guided by the following three factors: 1) the practicality of moving the lecture from the classroom to the online space in order to meet current students' schedules and study habits; 2) the wish to offer more effective learning through flexibility, individualisation and interactivity; 3) the wish to promote independent learning. Flipped learning is now a widespread teaching approach, employed in a large number of disciplines and contexts, from kindergarten to higher education, and is supported by a growing body of empirical investigations, scoping reviews and meta-analyses (see e.g. Strelan et al., 2020a). These studies have analysed various perspectives of flipped learning and identified key determinants of a successful flipped classroom. However, no investigations, to our knowledge, have yet considered the implementation of the flipped classroom in Italian beginner university courses, particularly in connection with the issues of accountability and independent learning. We have conceptualised the flipped approach as a:

> set of pedagogical approaches that (1) move most information-transmission teaching out of class; (2) use class time for learning activities that are active and social; and (3) require students to complete pre- and/or post-class activities to fully benefit from in-class work. (Abeysekera & Dawson, 2015, p. 3)

In our study, we examine students' experience of the flipped classroom—what they valued and why—with a special focus on whether this approach encourages students to develop agency and autonomy in learning.

This chapter on the implementation of a flipped beginner Italian language university course contributes to the conceptualisation of the flipped approach by exploring a new context and new data and provides pedagogical recommendations for future successful implementations of the flipped language classroom in higher education. It is particularly relevant for language educators who, as they had never done before the 2020 crisis, are reflecting on effective pedagogies in order to develop student-centred environments that promote active learning. While we share the view that 'foreign language programs still need to undergo restructuring if they are to remain players in higher education' (Moreno & Malovrh, 2020, p. 260) and that technology plays an important role in this process, it is also important to remember that 'technology can only become effective and useful in language teaching and learning environments in hands of competent teachers' (Basal & Aytan, 2014, p. 3), emphasising teachers' agency and role.

This chapter is organised as follows: Section 2 critically reviews the literature on the flipped approach; in Section 3, we present the design of our flipped model; in Sections 4 and 5, we present the research undertaken on students' experience with the flipped classroom; results are discussed in Section 6; and conclusions and recommendations are drawn in Section 7.

2. Flipped learning

2.1. Definitions

While no single definitive model exists, scholars have identified the essence of a flipped approach in two main elements: a) the redistribution of learning spaces and b) the 'conception of the teaching sequence' (Sailer & Sailer, 2020, p. 2). As first stated by the Flipped Learning Network (2014, p. 1):

> Flipped Learning is a pedagogical approach in which direct instruction moves from the group learning space to the individual learning space, and the resulting group space is transformed into a dynamic, interactive learning environment where the educator guides students as they apply concepts and engage creatively in the subject matter.

In this sense, flipped learning transforms pedagogical practices 'by switching the knowledge dissemination phases, which are typically performed in class, with knowledge application phases, which are typically performed individually out-of-class' (Sailer & Sailer, 2020, p. 1). More specifically, in a flipped classroom, explicit instruction is delivered online so that space in class is freed up to engage students in active learning, guide them, scaffold their learning processes and provide useful feedback (Jaramillo, 2019; Sailer & Sailer, 2020). In terms of teaching sequence, the moment of explicit instruction precedes the moment of in-class activities and is traditionally referred to as pre-class engagement. The definition given by the Academy of Active Learning Arts and Sciences (2021) also underscores the redistribution and sequence of the learning space:

> the flipped approach *inverts* the traditional classroom model by introducing course concepts *before* class, allowing educators to use class time to guide each student through active, practical, innovative applications of the course principles. (our emphasis)

2.2. Flipped learning and performance

Since the early implementation of the flipped approach in courses from different disciplines, several investigations have been undertaken, including a number of meta-analyses (Låg & Sæle, 2019; O'Flaherty & Phillips, 2015; Strelan et al., 2020a). One major concern of scholars has been whether the flipped approach leads to improved performance (Gasparini, 2020; Hung,

2015; Låg & Sæle, 2019, Murillo-Zamorano et al., 2019; Tadayonifar & Entezari, 2020; Yang et al., 2018). While O'Flaherty and Phillips (2015) first called for stronger evidence in evaluating student outcomes, the more recent meta-analysis by Strelan et al. (2020a), based on 198 studies, reports a moderate positive effect on student performance, supporting the effectiveness of the flipped approach across all disciplines, and particularly in humanities, where the effect was found to be strong. Tellingly, the effect size of 0.5 identified by the authors is not only comparable to that associated with pedagogies that strongly rely on feedback and on the use of technologies, but '*twice as large* as the effect sizes due to class size, teacher personality, programmed, discovery based or individualised instruction, and technologies such as clickers and one-on-one laptops' (p. 16, our emphasis). In relation to impact on performance, this meta-analysis also reveals that a measure of pre-class engagement affects student outcomes positively.

2.3. Scaffolding and cognitive load

The students' positive assessment of the flipped approach and the improved performance noted by some studies have been explained in connection with a number of factors. In their study on Chinese L2 at university, Sit and Guo (2019) found that the delivery of instruction via videos with captions allowed for effective scaffolding of language acquisition. Applying cognitive load theory, Tonkin et al. (2019) found that the implementation of pre-class instructional videos was beneficial in managing German grammar acquisition, as it allowed students to process information at their own learning pace. The use of pre-class explicit grammar instruction has also been found to impact positively on metacognitive awareness and deeper learning: 'studying the grammatical structures prior to class might have promoted consciousness-raising, enabling students to notice the use of structures and process the knowledge deeper' (Jaramillo, 2019, p. 44). Based on qualitative data, the study of Shih and Huang (2020) on EFL (English as a foreign language) confirms the positive impact of the flipped classroom on metacognitive development. The authors found that through the use of online videos students were encouraged to make a more active use of metacognitive strategies 'to monitor and evaluate their learning process and product' (p. 10), while at the same time, their 'knowledge of themselves as learners and their knowledge of their strategy use were raised' (p. 10).

2.4. Motivation, interactive learning and inductive teaching

Several other benefits of the flipped approach identified in the literature are in the areas of student motivation (Abeysekera & Dawson, 2014; Chuang et al., 2018, Sergis et al., 2018), student satisfaction (Strelan et al., 2020b), accountability and ownership of learning (Shyr & Chen, 2018; Chivata & Oviedo, 2018), and engagement and attendance (Shih & Huang, 2018). Models of the flipped classroom are constantly reviewed and adapted, as in the case described by Andujar and Nadif (2022), where the EFL course was designed to target students with disabilities through the creation of videos with captions and subtitles.

In the area of motivation, Sergis et al. (2018) demonstrate that the flipped approach correlates with high levels of psychological need satisfaction, defined, following self-determination theory, in terms of needs for autonomy, relatedness and competence (Ryan & Deci, 2000). As the authors explain, when a student-centred approach is emphasised, students invest more time on self-directed learning (need for autonomy) and collaborative activities (need for relatedness) and feel more confident about engaging in the learning process (need for competence). As their needs are satisfied, their motivation increases. In their quantitative investigation of EFL, Chuang et al. (2016) explored students' individual traits (beliefs, self-efficacy and motivation) in relation to outcomes of the flipped classroom and concluded that students with higher instrumental motivations benefited most from the flipped classroom (displaying external regulating scheme as a strategy to achieve their goals). They also discovered a direct effect of beliefs on learning outcomes.

Another study in the area of second language learning and, specifically, on the development of writing abilities in Italian is Gasparini (2020). The author found that the flipped classroom was not only perceived positively by the students, but also led to improved attendance and improved performance, thanks to the opportunity for more interactive and collaborative learning and greater feedback during class activities. Similarly, Moreno and Malovrh's (2020) comparative study of face-to-face vs. flipped approaches in beginner Spanish showed that the students from the flipped classroom progressed either in the same way or outperformed the control group in the areas of speaking and listening due to the increased opportunity for in-class practice. Providing further insights into the relationship between flipped learning and language skills, Tadayonifar and Entezari (2020) found evidence that flipped classrooms affected learning skills differently, with speaking skills showing the greatest amount of improvement.

With regard to the teaching of grammar, Cerezo et al. (2016) show that the flipped classroom and an inductive approach to grammar teaching can go hand in hand. They investigated the learning of Spanish grammatical structures (the verb *gustar*) and their findings revealed that students who were taught the grammatical structures via an inductive approach outperformed the control group students on almost all productive post-tests and also experienced greater retention. In addition, they found that the guided induction group were more aware of the Spanish structures and more capable of retaining recently acquired knowledge. These findings are particularly relevant for our study, which combines the flipped approach with inductive teaching.

2.5. Independent learning

Another important research finding for this project is in the area of 'self-regulation', which is in fact understudied and which our project aims to address. As effectively expressed by Jaramillo (2019, p. 54):

> the nature of the flipped approach requires students to be persistent, committed, and able to strategically organize their time, set their goals, and manage the freedom to study by themselves. In other words, students are to develop agency and self-regulation behaviors to benefit from the flipped model.

Taking responsibility for one's own learning is central to the interpretation of learner autonomy (Macasking & Taylor, 2010), and recent evidence suggests that a flipped model is perceived as one that promotes autonomy because (among other factors) it relies on students making choices about their learning process, pace and materials (Tsai, 2021). However, the development of self-regulated behaviour can be challenging. The inability to engage with the flipped methodology is addressed in the study of Garcìa Medina (2017, as referred to in Andujar & Nadif, 2022), who found that some students (specifically those over the age of 40) struggled to complete their pre-class activities. To foster independent learning within a flipped classroom, goal setting and peer feedback are discussed as valuable strategies in Shyr and Chen's (2018) study.

Finally, strictly connected to the issue of self-regulation, learner training is the focus of Tecedor and Perez's study (2019) on Spanish in a university setting. Through a large-scale survey, the authors identified the following predictors of satisfaction with flipped instruction: elementary course, earlier experience with flipped approach and understanding how the platform works. Difficulties encountered by students included not being able to get feedback while on the online platform, not understanding the feedback, accommodating their expectations and taking responsibilities. The authors emphasise the importance of training students (in an ongoing way) to understand the philosophy behind the flipped model, which can be achieved, for example, by giving them lists of best practices and studying behaviours or helping them connect online tasks with in-class activities. The importance of explaining and consistently monitoring students' understanding of the structure and benefits of the approach are also identified in Zhang and Zou's summary (2022) of state-of-the-art technologies used in language education in the last few years 'in case some students do not understand the meaning of the approach or cannot regulate themselves to keep up with the learning pace' (p. 21).

The connection between the flipped approach and issues of agency and accountability has important implications for the role of the teacher in the flipped approach. When students are actively engaged with their own learning, the teacher becomes 'a guide' (Andujar & Nadif, 2022, p. 1138). Indeed, Basal (2015) considers the teacher's function of guiding the student to be 'the most important element for securing desired outcomes' (p. 34). Before teachers even begin engaging with students in the classroom, however, we know they play a crucial role in the restructuring and innovating of courses through technology. As convincingly articulated by Warschauer and Meskill (2000, p. 316):

> the key to successful use of technology in language teaching lies not in hardware or software but in 'humanware'—our human capacity as teachers to plan, design and implement effective educational activity.

In the next section, we discuss the design of our flipped course for beginner Italian.

3. Research questions

The aim of this research was to understand how students responded to our flipped course and what language educators can learn in terms of future implementations of the flipped model. Our two main research questions were:

1. How did students perceive their experience with the flipped Italian beginner course?
2. Did students feel the approach promoted independent learning?

The first question implies issues of satisfaction, enjoyment, perception of usefulness and effectiveness. The second question covers the area of accountability and self-regulation. In addressing our questions we aim to offer an investigation of students' perceptions in relation to computer literacy, completion of the online tasks, understanding of the underlying pedagogy and other factors that were believed to be influential in shaping these perceptions.

4. Course design

Theoretically, our course design is framed within a cognitive model of language processing (cf. Ellis & Wulff, 2019). It combines an inductive approach to language learning with explicit grammatical instruction and emphasises active, independent learning.

Without changing the essence of the flipped model, and supported by scholarly works in the field, we designed a course that follows a cycle of four main learning phases (Figure 5.1).

As illustrated in Figure 5.1, our dialogic model guides learning through scaffolding within a sequence of coordinated activities. In their first class, the one-hour Tutorial 1, students are introduced to vocabulary and grammatical structures. Following an inductive instruction approach, in this first class, students are guided to become aware of the input, challenged to think and trained in the various levels of metacognition/cognitive processes, like noticing, patterning, categorising, inferring, making hypotheses, rule formulation and activation of prior knowledge. The next step in the cycle consists of explicit instruction via videos, which is then followed by the two-hour class, Tutorial 2, devoted to active learning, problem-solving and overall language practice. The weekly cycle concludes with out-of-class online consolidation activities and revision, also referred to as 'post-class activities'.

ENABLING LEARNING

Figure 5.1 Flipped model
Source: Created by author.

The main online content of the course, the so-called 'pre-class component of Tutorial 2', consists of 25 video lessons, which cover the grammar topics of the course. Each video is linked to a quiz aimed at verifying understanding of the topic. The video lessons were designed and created by one of the authors and are usually about five minutes in length and never more than 15 minutes long. The videos (two to three per week) were made available after the first tutorial (on Tuesday afternoon) and had to be watched before the second tutorial (on Thursday). Following Chuang et al. (2016), we integrated a quiz in each video as a strategy to 'regulate the viewing of the videos and ensure necessary exposure to new course materials before attending face-to-face class meetings' (p. 58). For the consolidation phase, after the second tutorial, there was also a total of 22 online activities (referred to as 'e-tivities', mainly quizzes with unlimited attempts), which covered listening, reading, writing and grammar practice.

Altogether, this online content counted towards 10 per cent of the final mark. Marks were given for completing the online activities but not on the basis of performance, and students received immediate feedback on every quiz. The benefit of assigning some grades for the completion of pre-class activities is now supported by existing studies finding that 'whether there is a measure of pre-class engagement in a flipped classroom affects student outcomes' (Strelan et al., 2020b, p. 297). This, as we discuss further, did play a role in students' positive experience with the course.

Finally, and very importantly, we planned our in-class interactive activities so we could focus on those areas that students usually find more challenging (O'Flaherty & Philips, 2015), such as productive tasks like speaking. This also favoured the provision of feedback, a key determinant of students' learning (Caruso et al., 2019; Ellis, 2017; Nassaji & Kartchava, 2017).

The structure of the course was fully explained in an introductory video recorded by the course coordinator and made available on the LMS (learning management system) before the start of the course. In the second semester unit, guided by the literature (Moranksi & Kim, 2016; Jaramillo, 2019; Tecedor & Perez, 2019) and by our semester one feedback, we designed, in addition to the video, a single introductory lecture in the first week, to offer further orientation on the understanding of the flipped approach.

5. Methodology

5.1. Setting and participants

At the University of Western Australia, Italian language courses were introduced in 1929, and now Italian is one of eight modern languages taught there. Italian can be studied as part of a major (first or second), as a minor or an elective.[1] Italian is also offered at the postgraduate level and within the Diploma of Languages. Students can start at beginner, intermediate or near-native level and can enrol in Italian in their first, second or third year of university study. Italian attracts students from a variety of linguistic and cultural backgrounds, including students of Italian background and international students. Around 300 students enrol in Italian classes every year, with an overall majority of beginner students enrolled in a Bachelor of Science. The first course in the beginner sequence (ITAL1401) is offered in both the first and second semesters. The implementation of the flipped approach was originally prompted not only by a wish to innovate

---

1 At the time of carrying out the research, students from all faculties could also study an Italian course as a 'broadening unit'—that is, courses related, broadly speaking, to multicultural and global understanding.

and improve our courses, but also by the decreasing attendance at lectures, the increasing number of non–Italian major students interested in greater flexibility, and by the university itself promoting new directions in teaching.

Participation in this study was voluntary and was sought in class. Our semester one course included 94 students, while semester two had 54 enrolled students. They were all invited to participate in the study by completing an anonymous survey (cf. 5.2 below). A total of 76 students completed the survey (51.4%). The demographics of the study participants are summarised in Table 5.1.

Table 5.1 Demographics of participants (summary)

	Semester one	Semester two
Number of participants	55 (59% of enrolled students)	21 (40% of enrolled students)
Age	67% 18–24 10% 45–54 9% 55–64 5% 65 and older	67% 18–24 19% 25–34 14% above 45 (3 students)
Gender	73% F, 25% M, 2% no answer	62% F, 38% M
Degree of enrolment	45% Bachelor of Arts 24% Bachelor of Science	52% Bachelor of Science 19% Bachelor of Arts
Italian as major	24%	0%
Italian as broadening unit	65%	90%
Enrolment level	75% first year 11% third year 9% second year	57% first year 24% third year 14% second year
Declared computer literacy	53% advanced	81% advanced

Source: Compiled by author.

5.2. Research instrument and procedures

To evaluate the student's experience with the flipped approach, an anonymous survey was run on Qualtrics at the end of each semester (Appendix). The link to the survey was made available via the course LMS page. The survey included 25 multiple-choice questions covering, in the first part, the students' demographics and study background, and, in the second part, their learning experience. We investigated access and use of the online resources, engagement with the material and the course, possible technical difficulties, as well as the students' perceptions of their experience in terms of enjoyment, effectiveness for learning and accountability. The questions eliciting the students' perceptions of the flipped approach were designed as a 5-point Likert scale, from Strongly Agree (5) to Strongly Disagree (1). The survey also included a final open question, 'Did you get what you expected from a flipped classroom experience? What would you want more/less of? (e.g. too much/little online content; or too much/little face-to-face time)', which allowed us to collect valuable qualitative data.

The quantitative data were analysed statistically through SPSS, with the significance level set at the standard of 0.05. Chi-square and regression tests were used to identify relationships between variables. The comments to the open question were analysed using the NVivo software package, with the aim of identifying emerging common themes.

Before presenting the results, it is important to consider that the participants from the two semesters differ with regard to some of their demographics. For example, in semester two, only 19 per cent of students were enrolled in an arts degree as opposed to 45 per cent in semester one ($p = 0.017$, based on chi-square test). Furthermore, in contrast with semester one, semester two did not include any students who wished to major in Italian ($p = 0.024$; $p < 0.05$). For these reasons, to analyse data from both semesters at once (and thus create a larger sample size), we used ordinal logistic regression or binary logistic regression where possible, with 'semester' as a control variable. This adjusts for potential differences between semesters.

6. Results and discussion

In the sections that follow we present and discuss the quantitative data pertaining to the students' perception of the flipped approach with respect to three main areas: enjoyment/satisfaction, effectiveness and accountability. We then turn to the qualitative data to provide further insights.

6.1. Enjoyment and overall satisfaction

The measure of enjoyment in relation to the flipped approach can be first drawn from the responses to the survey questions Q19a—'I enjoyed not having to come to a weekly lecture in this course and being able to access unit content via the Video Lessons', and Q19b—'I enjoyed the flexibility of content delivery in this course', as presented in Table 5.2.

Table 5.2 Enjoyment

		SA (5)	A (4)	N (3)	D (2)	SD (1)	Mean	SD
Q19a. I enjoyed not having to come to a weekly lecture	Sem 1	22 (44%)	12 (24%)	11 (22%)	2 (2.4%)	3 (6%)	3.96	1.17
	Sem 2	13 (61.9%)	6 (28.6%)	2 (9.5%)	–	–	4.52	0.66
Q19b. I enjoyed the flexibility of content delivery	Sem 1	29 (55.8%)	18 (34%)	3 (5.8%)	1 (1.9%)	1 (1.9%)	4.40	0.84
	Sem 2	14 (66.67%)	5 (23.8)	1 (4.8%)	1 4.8%)	–	4.52	0.79

Source: Compiled by author.

Students clearly appreciated the flexibility of the flipped approach (SA+A = 90%, in both semesters), and most also enjoyed the fact that the lecture had been replaced with online video lessons, although the extent of agreement with Q19a varies between semesters. The relationships shown in Table 5.3 help us gain more insights into these results. For example, the analysis shows that the likelihood of agreement on question 19a decreases with age—in other words, the older the student is, the less likely it is that they enjoyed not going to a lecture. Furthermore, there is an association between enjoying not having to go to a lecture and computer literacy. The odds ratio (2.5, $p = 0.003$) indicates that the more advanced students are in their computer literacy, the more likely they are to be satisfied with the online delivery. These findings have important implications in terms of ensuring support for all students who may be lacking digital literacy.

Table 5.3 Factors related to students enjoying not having to go to weekly face-to-face lectures

Dependent variable: Q19a. I enjoyed not having to go to a weekly lecture (5-point Likert scale)	
Q2-Age (ten-year brackets)	odds ratio 0.554, p-value <0.001
Q9-Computer literacy (5-point scale, 'poor' to 'expert')	odds ratio 2.5, p-value = 0.003

Notes: The independent variables were each tested separately using ordinal logistic regression. 'Semester' was used as a control variable in each case.

Source: Compiled by author.

The analysis identified two further significant relationships in the area of enjoyment. As shown in Table 5.4, enjoyment of flexible content delivery is associated with both the completion of the video lessons, and the completion of the post-class online activities (odds ratio = 2.659, *p*-value = 0.024). Completion of the online content of the course clearly goes hand in hand with an appreciation of the flexibility allowed by the flipped approach, suggesting that students may be prompted into action by engaging with materials that are delivered online.

Table 5.4 Relationship between enjoyment of flexibility of content and completion of online content

Dependent variable: Q19b. I enjoyed the flexibility of content delivery (5-point Likert scale)	
Q14 — Completion of video lessons (4-point scale, 'never' to 'always')	odds ratio = 3.344, *p*-value = 0.05
Q16 — Completion of online activities (3-point scale, 'always', 'more than half', 'less than half')	odds ratio = 2.659, *p*-value = 0.024

Note: The independent variables were each tested separately using ordinal logistic regression. 'Semester' was used as a control variable in each case.
Source: Compiled by author.

The results of the survey show that the great majority of students appreciated the flexibility of the course as well as not having to attend the weekly lecture, although age and computer literacy influenced the level of satisfaction. Moreover, the appreciation of the flipped structure of the course is closely related to student engagement in the course, as demonstrated by the higher level of completion of online video lessons and post-class consolidation activities among students who enjoyed the flexibility of content delivery. This is an important finding, as student satisfaction has a positive effect on student performance, motivation and retention and, more broadly, on the success of the course (Strelen et al., 2020b).

6.2. Effectiveness

The perceptions of the effectiveness of the approach and the usefulness of the online materials emerge from the responses to the questions from Table 5.5, which are all very positive.

Table 5.5 Students' perceptions of the effectiveness of the flipped approach

		SA (5)	A (4)	N (3)	D (2)	SD (1)	Mean	SD
Q19c. The video lessons were useful in my learning experience in ITAL1401	Sem 1	38 (73.1%)	11 (21.2%)	2 (3.9%)	1 (1.9%)	–	4.65	0.65
	Sem 2	14 (66.7%)	6 (28.6%)	1 (4.8%)	–	–	4.62	0.58
Q19d. Being able to watch the video lessons at my own pace was useful for my learning	Sem 1	39 (75%)	10 (19.2%)	2 (3.9%)	–	1 (1.9%)	4.65	0.73
	Sem 2	16 (76.2%)	5 (23.8%)	–	–	–	4.76	0.43
Q19e. Completing the video lessons allowed me to be well-prepared for Tutorial 2	Sem 1	26 (50%)	18 (34.6)	6 (11.5%)	1 (1.9%)	1 (1.9%)	4.29	0.88
	Sem 2	13 (61.9%)	6 (28.6%)	1 (4.8%)	1 (4.8%)	–	4.48	0.79
Q19f. The weekly online activities helped me keep up with the work	Sem 1	27 (51.9%)	18 (34.7%)	2 (3.9%)	4 (7.7%)	1 (1.9%)	4.27	0.98
	Sem 2	14 (66.7%)	5 (23.8%)	1 (4.8%)	1 (4.8%)	–	4.52	0.79
Q19g. The weekly online activities taught me the importance of regular practice	Sem 1	31 (59.6%)	12 (23.1%)	6 (11.6%)	2 (3.9%)	1 (1.9)	4.35	0.96
	Sem 2	13 (61.9%)	5 (23.8%)	1 (4.8%)	2 (9.5%)	–	4.38	0.95
Q19i. The weekly e-tivities were useful in my learning experience	Sem 1	30 (57.7%)	15 (28.9%)	4 (7.7%)	2 (3.9%)	1 (1.9%)	4.37	0.92
	Sem 2	13 (61.9%)	8 (38.1%)	–	–	–	4.62	0.49
Q19k. Overall the flipped approach was effective for my learning of Italian	Sem 1	24 (46.2%)	18 (34.6%)	7 (13.5%)	2 (3.9%)	1 (1.9%)	4.19	0.94
	Sem 2	15 (71.4%)	3 (14.3%)	3 (14.3%)	–	–	4.57	0.73

Source: Compiled by author.

As Table 5.5 illustrates, agreement on all these statements was very high. Combining the responses for SA with those for A, we obtain an agreement rate of 81–100 per cent, with an overall higher agreement for semester two. Students from both semesters particularly appreciated the video lessons (Sem. 1—SA 73.1%, A 21.15%; Sem. 2%—SA 66.7%, A 28.6) and being able to watch them at their own pace (Sem. 1—SA 75%, A 19.2%; Sem. 2—SA 76.2%, A 23.8), confirming the findings of earlier research on the benefits of flexible learning modes of delivery (cf. Strelan et al., 2020a, 2020b; Drennan et al., 2005).

The analysis has also identified some significant relationships. All of the statements relating to the effectiveness of the approach are associated with the completion of the online materials, as illustrated in Table 5.6, with some relationships significant at a 0.1 per cent level.

Table 5.6 Overall effectiveness and completion of online content

Dependent variables (all measured by 5-point Likert scale)	Q14 Completion of video lessons (4-point scale, 'never' to 'always')	Q16 Completion of online activities (3-point scale, 'always', 'more than half', 'less than half')
Q19c. The video lessons were useful in my learning experience in ITAL1401	odds ratio = 7.936, p-value <0.001	odds ratio = N/A, p-value = 0.001
Q19d. Being able to watch the video lessons at my own pace (pausing and rewinding as I pleased) was useful for my learning	odds ratio = 4.310, p-value = 0.004	odds ratio = 4.169, p-value = 0.004
Q19e. Completing the video lessons allowed me to be well prepared for Tutorial 2	odds ratio = 3.593, p-value = 0.003	odds ratio = 3.264, p-value = 0.006
Q19f. The weekly online activities helped me keep up with the work	odds ratio = 4.339, p-value = 0.001	odds ratio = 4.891, p-value <0.001
Q19g. The weekly online activities taught me the importance of regular practice for language learning	odds ratio = 2.663, p-value = 0.023	odds ratio = 2.802, p-value = 0.016
Q19h. I was motivated to complete the weekly online activities because they counted towards the assessment	odds ratio = 4.701, p-value <0.001	odds ratio = 3.357, p-value = 0.005
Q19i. The weekly e-tivities were useful in my learning experience in ITAL1401	odds ratio = 4.196, p-value = 0.002	odds ratio = 4.429, p-value = 0.021
Q19k. Overall the flipped approach was effective for my learning of Italian	odds ratio = 4.843, p-value <0.001	odds ratio = 2.656, p-value = 0.021

Notes: The independent variables were each tested separately using ordinal logistic regression. 'Semester' was used as a control variable in each case.

Source: Compiled by author.

The results above provide evidence that students perceived the flipped approach as effective for their learning, confirming research on the benefits that such an approach has on cognitive load management (Tonkin et al., 2019). Moreover, student responses indicate that by having to complete pre- and post-class activities as an integral part of the course, they learned the benefits of regular practice as a key strategy of language learning, contributing therefore to their self-regulation skills (cf. Jaramillo, 2019).

In addition, the motivation to engage with online activities deriving from having a grade associated with their completion is strongly associated with actually completing the task (Q19h, $p < 0.001$). One student commented in the survey open question, 'Having marks allocated to the quizzes helped me to keep on top of the content before class', further clarifying the benefit of the online content for managing the course workload, and of having a measure of online engagement for learners' motivation. These findings support the findings of previous research on the positive effect of assessing pre-class engagement (Strelan et al., 2020b), but also the well-established view on the power of assessment in prompting action—the so-called 'hidden curriculum' (Snyder, 1971). Finally, the statement 'I was motivated to complete the weekly online activities because they counted towards the assessment' is also associated with watching the introductory video (odds ratio = 0.088, p-value = 0.043), which emphasises the importance of preparing students for the experience with the flipped classroom (Tecedor & Perez, 2019).

6.3. Accountability

One particular area of interest in this project was how the course pedagogy impacted on students' accountability. The large majority of the students from our sample demonstrate positive perceptions towards being made accountable through the flipped teaching, with an overall agreement rate for 'The flipped approach in this course made me feel I had greater responsibility for my learning' of 81 per cent and 90 per cent (SA + A) in semester one and semester two, respectively.

In a similar fashion to previous associations, the rate of agreement about the effect of the flipped approach on accountability is also related to the completion of the online content (Table 5.7), supporting the close relationship between engaging with online content and feeling responsible for their own learning.

Table 5.7 Flipped approach and accountability

Dependent variable: Q19j. The flipped approach in this course made me feel I had greater responsibility for my learning (5-point Likert scale)	
Q12. How many tutorials of ITAL1401 have you attended during the semester? (3-point scale; 'Less than half', 'More than half', 'All or almost all')	odds ratio = 3.702, p-value = 0.050
Q14. Completion of video lessons (4-point scale, 'never' to 'always')	odds ratio = 2.857, p-value = 0.015
Q16. Completion of online activities (3-point scale, 'always', 'more than half', 'less than half')	odds ratio = 2.517, p-value = 0.029

Notes: The independent variables were each tested separately using ordinal logistic regression. 'Semester' was used as a control variable in each case.
Source: Compiled by author.

Unsurprisingly, a significant association was also found between the students' perceptions of their increased responsibility and their attendance at in-class tutorials. While the relationship may not be causative, it suggests that accountability encompasses the recognition that engaging in face-to-face activity is important for the learning process. This result adds to previous findings on how the flipped classroom can lead to improved attendance (Gasparini, 2020). Moreover, we found that the agreement on statement Q19j is significantly higher (p = 0.026) among students from semester two than among students from semester one. This finding may be explained with reference to the demographics of the different cohorts, with the younger age group of semester two possibly needing a more scaffolded and monitored approach to learning (cf. Shyr & Chen, 2018).

6.4. Interactivity, clarity, learning at your own pace and balance: Insights from students' comments

A total of 47 comments were elicited through the final survey question, 'Did you get what you expected from a flipped classroom experience? What would you want more/less of? (e.g. too much/little online content; too much/little face-to-face time)'. Although they did not provide a large qualitative data sample, the comments were analysed and coded using NVivo, which identified some clear themes in connection to the areas of satisfaction and effectiveness. Apart from a few general responses ('It was great', 'I enjoyed the flipped classroom', 'I thought it was really good',

'I really enjoyed it'), a number of comments link the students' enjoyment of the flipped classroom to the increased opportunity for active learning, as in the examples below.[2]

> The flipped classroom experience was great! I thought it was nice to get three hours of small group tutorials a week, in many of my other first-year units there is very little interaction outside of lectures.

> I enjoyed that we focused a lot on speaking, my other languages don't do that.

> Enabled more face-to-face in tutorial time.

Other comments specifically point to the quality of the online content:

> Federica's online videos (and all the other online content) themselves were well presented, clear and, I'm sure, useful to my learning experience.

> The recorded lectures were very clear and made it easy to understand the concepts.

> I enjoyed how there were informative slides behind the teacher, that the teacher taught slowly so I could keep up and how she translated everything into English.

> As well, I found the tutorial videos really entertaining and easy to follow. Thanks!

Some students emphasised the opportunity for learning at their own pace and for revising:

> I had no expectations coming into the unit, as I had never done a course with flipped learning. I quickly grew to love the content delivery. You can learn at your own pace, and always go back to the videos if more help is needed later down the line/for revision.

> I really enjoyed the flipped experience, particularly because I could access the post-tutorial activities very easily for revision.

---

2   All comments are quoted in their original form.

Another theme that emerges strongly in the data, partly prompted by the survey question, is the balance between online and face-to-face activities, as exemplified by the comments below. Although the majority of comments suggest that students were satisfied with the amount of online content, not every student agreed:

> There was always enough online activities, but never so many that I had difficulty finding time to complete them.

> I thought the online/classroom balance was basically perfect, so I don't think much should change (if at all!).

> At times too much online content.

The only negative comment in the data showing clear resistance to the flipped approach was:

> I disliked how much the course relied on students watching videos online. Why should I study Italian at university when I could just watch youtube videos on grammar, or do duolingo for free?

This comment addresses the very question of why to adopt the flipped classroom at university. We discuss this aspect in the next and final section.

6.5. Understanding and embracing the pedagogy

Although the students' evaluation of the flipped classroom is largely positive, some comments emphasise the importance of ensuring a clear understanding of its pedagogy. For example, the first two comments below reveal dissatisfaction with the sequencing of the content:

> Yes, although would have enjoyed watched (sic) videos before Tutorial 1 to get some prior learning of the new content in advance.

> I liked the online videos, but maybe instead of two video lessons a week, maybe one video lesson post tutorial 1, and then a face-to-face lecture.

As discussed earlier (Section 2), the sequence of the content is a pillar of the flipped pedagogy and it is crucial that students understand the place of the pre-class engagement in the teaching cycle and that 'flipped learning is not simply adding lecture videos outside the classroom' (Basal, 2015, p. 34). The next comment is also useful in identifying possible elements of dissatisfaction, as it reveals the implications that information gaps (in this case not knowing about the quizzes integrated in the videos) can have for engagement with a flipped course:

> Since I didn't start the class in week 1, I did not know about the integrated quizzes before a few weeks later, thought it was just the videos. Make it more clear that it is a test there, not just 'click to launch', to me that just sounds like I'm launching the video:)

Finally, it is important to consider that many studies on computer-assisted language learning have identified a correlation between computer literacy and satisfaction (Zhang & Zou, 2022). Since our data show that computer literacy is associated with age ($p = 0.017$; $p < 0.05$), it is reasonable to infer that age may be a variable of satisfaction, with older learners less inclined to embrace the flipped pedagogy. Although the negative comments above cannot be linked in any way to age or computer literacy (but cf. Section 6.1 on the association between enjoyment and age), it is possible that for mature students, as indicated by Murillo-Zamorano et al. (2019, p. 2), the digital and audiovisual component of the flipped course does not generate the same 'emotional connection' as for generation Z, to whom the flipped approach appeals the most. Our findings, however, suggest that this lack of engagement among older students could certainly be due to lack of prior experience with digital educational designs rather than age in itself. Traditionally, higher education attracts many mature students to Italian courses, due to the appeal of Italian cultural heritage (Palmieri, 2018; Caruso & Fraschini, 2021). These students need support to engage successfully with their course.

7. Conclusion

Our data reveal that the students' experience with flipping was overwhelmingly positive. The students' perceptions of the teaching approach employed in the beginner Italian course not only support future implementation of the flipped pedagogy, but also yield important evidence on the benefits of flipping the language classroom. The analysis discovered positive associations between flexible content delivery on the one hand, and student satisfaction, their ability to develop knowledge at their own pace, and their recognition of regular practice as an effective strategy in language learning on the other.

The evaluation of our flipped approach was slightly more positive in semester two, possibly due to some extra steps taken in promoting students' understanding of the flipped pedagogy, like the addition of a face-to-face lecture in Week 1. Following from the findings of the first survey, in particular the qualitative data, an orientation lecture was introduced at the start of semester two. This may have facilitated a better understanding of the underlying principles of the approach, particularly the place of the online content and the teaching sequence. Compared to semester one, a smaller cohort of students, more advanced computer literacy and a higher rate of digital natives may also explain the difference in evaluation.

A key outcome for us was in the area of accountability. In language learning, it is crucial that students understand the importance of regular work outside the classroom. In a flipped model, where practice in class is so intertwined with pre-class explicit instruction (delivered online), independent learning is not only naturally promoted but also becomes structural, or, in other words, a fundamental element of the approach.

Based on our findings, the main recommendations for educators interested in implementing a flipped language classroom are as follows: 1) introduce a measure of online pre-class engagement, for example via online quizzes; 2) invest in explaining to learners the pedagogy of the flipped approach, particularly in connection with self-regulation, and in monitoring their understanding; 3) develop a plan for supporting students with technology literacy where required. While flipping the language classroom requires considerable commitment and organisation from educators, our findings demonstrate that the approach will have an invaluable positive impact on students' learning experiences.

Acknowledgment

We are grateful to Dr Louis Marshall for his assistance with the statistical analysis.

References

Abeysekera, L. & Dawson, P. (2015). Motivation and cognitive load in the flipped classroom: Definition, rationale and a call for research. *Higher Education Research & Development, 34*(1), 1–14. doi.org/10.1080/07294360.2014.934336

Academy of Active Learning Arts and Sciences. (2021). *Updated definition of Flipped Learning.* www.aalasinternational.org/updated-definition-of-flipped-learning/

Andujar, A. & Nadif, F. Z. (2022). Evaluating an inclusive blended learning environment in EFL: A flipped approach. *Computer Assisted Language Learning, 35*(5–6), 1138–67. doi.org/10.1080/09588221.2020.1774613

Basal, A. & Aytan, T. (2014, 13–14 November). *Using Web 2.0 tools in English language teaching* [Conference presentation]. International Conference ICT for Language Learning, 7th Edition. Florence, Italy. conference.pixel-online.net/files/ict4ll/ed0007/FP/1314-ICL807-FP-ICT4LL7.pdf

Basal, A. (2015). The implementation of a flipped classroom in foreign language teaching. *Turkish Online Journal of Distance Education, 16*(4), 28–37.

Caruso, M. & Fraschini, N. (2021). A Q methodology study into vision of Italian L2 university students: An Australian perspective. *The Modern Language Journal, 105*(2), 552–68. doi.org/10.1111/modl.12713

Cerezo, L., Caras, A. & Leow, R. P. (2016). The effectiveness of guided induction versus deductive instruction on the development of complex Spanish *gustar* structures: An analysis of learning outcomes and processes. *Studies in Second Language Acquisition, 38*(2), 265–91. doi.org/10.1017/S0272263116000139

Chivata, Y. P. & Oviedo, R. C. (2018). EFL students' perceptions of activeness during the implementation of flipped learning approach at a Colombian university. *Gist Education and Learning Research Journal, 17*(1), 81–105. doi.org/10.26817/16925777.436

Chuang, H. H., Weng, C. Y. & Chen, C. H. (2018). Which students benefit most from a flipped classroom approach to language learning? *British Journal of Educational Technology, 49*(1), 56–68. doi.org/10.1111/bjet.12530

Drennan, J., Kennedy, J. & Pisarski, A. (2005). Factors affecting student attitudes towards flexible online learning in management education. *The Journal of Educational Research, 98*(6), 331–38. doi.org/10.3200/JOER.98.6.331-338

Ellis, N. C. & Wulff, S. (2019). Cognitive approaches to second language acquisition. In J. W. Schwieter & A. Benati (Eds), *The Cambridge handbook of language learning* (pp. 41–61). Cambridge University Press. doi.org/10.1017/9781108333603.003

Ellis, R. (2017). Oral corrective feedback in L2 classrooms: What we know so far. In H. Nassaji & E. Kartchava (Eds), *Corrective feedback in second language teaching and learning* (pp. 3–18). Routledge.

Flipped Learning Network (FLN). (2014). *The four pillars of F-L-I-P™*. www.flippedlearning.org/definition-of-flipped-learning/

Gasparini, S. (2020). Design and assessment of flipped instruction: A study of student learning and perceptions in higher education. *Form@re—Open Journal per la Formazione in Rete, 20*(1), 220–36. doi.org/10.13128/form-8233

Hung, H.-T. (2015). Flipping the classroom for English language learners to foster active learning. *Computer Assisted Language Learning, 28*(1), 81–96. doi.org/10.1080/09588221.2014.967701

Jaramillo, N. V. (2019). Evaluating a flipped intermediate Spanish course through students and instructor's perceptions. *The JALT CALL Journal, 15*(2), 41–62. doi.org/10.29140/jaltcall.v15n2.172

Låg, T. & Sæle, R. G. (2019). Does the flipped classroom improve student learning and satisfaction? A systematic review and meta-analysis. *AERA Open, 5*(3), 1–17. doi.org/10.1177/2332858419870489

Macaskill, A. & Taylor, E. (2010). The development of a brief measure of learner autonomy in university students. *Studies in Higher Education, 35*(3), 351–59. doi.org/10.1080/03075070903502703

Moranski, K. & Kim, F. (2016). 'Flipping' lessons in a multi-section Spanish course: Implications for assigning explicit grammar instruction outside of the classroom. *The Modern Language Journal, 100*(4), 830–52. doi.org/10.1111/modl.12366

Moreno, N. & Malovrh, P. A. (2020). Restructuring a beginner language program: A quantitative analysis of face-to-face versus flipped-blended Spanish instruction. *Hispania, 103*(2), 259–74. doi.org/10.1353/hpn.2020.0036

Murillo-Zamorano, L. R., Sánchez, J. Á. L. & Godoy-Caballero, A. L. (2019). How the flipped classroom affects knowledge, skills, and engagement in higher education: Effects on students' satisfaction. *Computers & Education, 141*, 103608. doi.org/10.1016/j.compedu.2019.103608

Nassaji, H. & Kartchava, E. (Eds). (2017). *Corrective feedback in second language teaching and learning: Research, theory, applications, implications*. Routledge. doi.org/10.4324/9781315621432

O'Flaherty, J. & Phillips, C. (2015). The use of flipped classrooms in higher education: A scoping review. *The Internet and Higher Education, 25*, 85–95. doi.org/10.1016/j.iheduc.2015.02.002

Palmieri, C. (2018). *Identity trajectories of adult second language learners: Learning Italian in Australia*. Multilingual Matters. doi.org/10.21832/PALMIE2197

Ryan, R. M. & Deci, E. L. (2000). Self-determination theory and the facilitation of intrinsic motivation, social development, and well-being. *American Psychologist, 55*(1), 68–78. doi.org/10.1037//0003-066x.55.1.68

Sailer, M. & Sailer, M. (2021). Gamification of in-class activities in flipped classroom lectures. *British Journal of Educational Technology, 52*(1), 75–90. doi.org/10.1111/bjet.12948

Sergis, S., Sampson, D. G. & Pelliccione, L. (2018). Investigating the impact of Flipped Classroom on students' learning experiences: A Self-Determination Theory approach. *Computers in Human Behavior, 78*(1), 368–78. doi.org/10.1016/j.chb.2017.08.011

Shih, H.-c. J. & Huang, S.-h. C. (2020). EFL learners' metacognitive development in flipped learning: a comparative study. *Interactive Learning Environments, 30*(8), 1448–60, doi.org/10.1080/10494820.2020.1728343

Shyr, W. J. & Chen, C. H. (2018). Designing a technology-enhanced flipped learning system to facilitate students' self-regulation and performance. *Journal of Computer assisted learning, 34*(1), 53–62. doi.org/10.1111/jcal.12213

Sit, H. H.-w. & Guo, S. (2019). An exploration of design principles to enhance students' L2 acquisition in a flipped class. In A. W.-b. Tso (Ed.), *Digital humanities and new ways of teaching* (pp. 111–31). Springer. doi.org/10.1007/978-981-13-1277-9_7

Snyder, B. R. (1971). *The hidden curriculum*. Knopf.

Strelan, P., Osborn, A. & Palmer, E. (2020a). The flipped classroom: A meta-analysis of effects on student performance across disciplines and education levels. *Educational Research Review, 30*, 100314. doi.org/10.1016/j.edurev.2020.100314

Strelan, P., Osborn, A. & Palmer, E. (2020b). Student satisfaction with courses and instructors in a flipped classroom: A meta-analysis. *Journal of Computer Assisted Learning, 36*(3), 295–314. doi.org/10.1111/jcal.12421

Tadayonifar, M. & Entezari, M. (2020). Does flipped learning affect language skills and learning styles differently? *E-Learning and Digital Media, 17*(4), 324–40. doi.org/10.1177/2042753020931776

Tecedor, M. & Perez, A. (2019). Perspectives on flipped L2 classes: Implications for learner training. *Computer Assisted Language Learning, 34*(4), 506–27. doi.org/10.1080/09588221.2019.1626439

Tonkin, K., Page S. & Forsey M. (2019). Managing cognitive load with a flipped language class: An ethnographic study of the student experience. *Foreign Language Annals, 52*(3), 551–75. doi.org/10.1111/flan.12412

Tsai, Y. R. (2021). Promotion of learner autonomy within the framework of a flipped EFL instructional model: Perception and perspectives. *Computer Assisted Language Learning, 34*(7), 979–1011. doi.org/10.1080/09588221.2019.1650779

Warschauer, M. & Meskill, C. (2000). Technology and second language teaching. In J. W. Rosenthal (Ed.), *Handbook of undergraduate second language education*, (pp. 303–18). Routledge.

Yang, J., Yin, C. & Wang, W. (2018). Flipping the classroom in teaching Chinese as a foreign language. *Language Learning & Technology, 22*(1), 16–26. doi.org/10125/44575

Zhang, R. & Zou, D. (2022). Types, purposes, and effectiveness of state-of-the-art technologies for second and foreign language learning. *Computer Assisted Language Learning, 35*(4), 696–742. doi.org/10.1080/09588221.2020.1744666

Appendix

Survey

Q1 Please select your gender.
- a. Male
- b. Female
- c. Prefer not to answer

Q2 Please select your age range.
- a. Under 18
- b. 18–24
- c. 25–34
- d. 35–44
- e. 45–54
- f. 55–64
- g. 65 or older

Q3 Which degree are you enrolled in?
- a. Bachelor of Arts
- b. Bachelor of Commerce
- c. Bachelor of Design

    d. Bachelor of Science
    e. Bachelor of Philosophy
    f. Other. Please specify

Q4 I am a
    a. First-year student
    b. Second-year student
    c. Third-year student
    d. Other. Please specify

Q5 Which of the following best describes your situation?
    a. I am majoring in Italian Studies
    b. I am taking ITAL1401 as a broadening/elective unit
    c. I am not sure yet
    d. Other. Please specify

Q6 How many languages other than Italian and English do you speak?
    a. 0
    b. 1
    c. 2
    d. 3 or more

Q7 Did you study Italian at high school?
    a. No
    b. Yes, only in Year 7
    c. Yes, till Year 8
    d. Yes, till Year 9
    e. Yes, till Year 10
    f. Yes, till Year 11
    g. Other. Please specify

Q8 Did you live in Italy for more than three months?
    a. No
    b. Yes. Please specify when

Q9 I rate my computer literacy as
   a. Expert
   b. Advanced
   c. Intermediate
   d. Basic
   e. Poor

Q10 Did you start the course in week 1?
   a. Yes
   b. No

Q11 Before starting the course, did you watch the introductory video prepared by the unit coordinator to introduce the unit?
   a. Yes
   b. No, I never watched it
   c. No, but I watched it after starting the semester

Q12 How many tutorials of ITAL1401 have you attended during the semester?
   a. All or almost all
   b. More than half
   c. Less than half

Q13 I have accessed the online materials through (you can select more than one choice).
   a. my desktop computer
   b. my laptop
   c. my smartphone
   d. my tablet
   e. the computers in the library
   f. all of the above
   g. Other. Please specify

Q14 I have completed the Video Lessons & integrated quizzes before Tutorial 2.

    a. Always
    b. More than half
    c. Less than half
    d. Never

Q15 If you have NOT completed the Video Lessons & integrated quizzes BEFORE Tutorial 2, please tell us why. You can select more than one option.

    a. I forgot
    b. I have experienced technical problems with the videos
    c. I am not a tech-savvy
    d. I thought I could still be prepared for Tutorial 2
    e. I thought I could get a good final mark for the whole unit anyway
    f. I did not have time
    g. I already knew the topic
    h. Other
    i. Not applicable

Q16 I have completed the Post-Tutorial 2 activities regularly (before the following week).

    a. Always
    b. More than half
    c. Less than half
    d. Never

Q17 If you have NOT completed the Post-Tutorial 2 activities regularly, please tell us why. You can select more than one option.

    a. I forgot
    b. I have experienced technical problems
    c. I am not a tech-savvy
    d. I thought I could get a good final mark for the whole unit anyway
    e. I did not have time
    f. I didn't enjoy them
    g. I didn't find them useful
    h. Other
    i. Not applicable

Q18 Please indicate whether you agree or disagree with the following statements.
   a. It was easy to access the videos lessons and integrated quizzes
   b. It was easy to access the Post-Tutorial 2 activities

Q19 Please indicate whether you agree or disagree with the following statements.
   a. I enjoyed not having to come to a weekly lecture in this course and being able to access unit content via the Video Lessons
   b. I enjoyed the flexibility of content delivery in this course
   c. The Video Lessons were useful in my learning experience in ITAL1401
   d. Being able to watch the Video Lessons at my own pace (pausing and rewinding as I pleased) was useful for my learning
   e. Completing the Video Lessons allowed me to be well prepared for my Tutorial 2
   f. The weekly online activities helped me to keep up with the work
   g. The weekly online activities taught me the importance of regular practice for learning Italian
   h. I was motivated to complete the weekly online activities because they counted towards the assessment
   i. The weekly online activities were useful in my learning experience of ITAL1401
   j. The flipped approach in this course made me feel I had greater responsibility for my learning
   k. Overall the flipped approach was effective for my learning of Italian

Q20 Please indicate whether you agree with the following statements. During the TUTORIALS …
   a. I was able to practice my language skills through interaction with the teacher
   b. I was able to practice my language skills through interaction with other students
   c. I feel that enough time was dedicated to using the new weekly language structures
   d. I feel that enough time was dedicated to learning new vocabulary
   e. I feel that enough time was dedicated to pair/group interaction

Q21 Which of the following language skills would you have liked to practice more during the tutorials? You can select more than one skill.

a. Speaking
b. Writing
c. Vocabulary
d. Reading
e. Grammar
f. Listening

Q22 Did you encounter any technical difficulties with watching the Video Lessons or submitting the integrated quizzes? You can select more than one option.

a. None
b. It took a long time for the videos to play
c. My Internet at home is not good
d. I could not access the Video Lessons from my tablet
e. I could not submit the quiz from my smartphone
f. Other

Q23 Did you encounter any technical difficulties with completing the online Post-Tutorial 2 activities? You can select more than one option.

a. None
b. Videos took a long time to play
c. My Internet at home is not good
d. I could not do the activities on my smartphone
e. I could not do the activities on my tablet
f. I didn't have the software required for some activities
g. Other

Q24 Please provide further details on the technical issues you have experienced, if applicable.

Q25 Did you get what you expected from a flipped classroom experience? What would you want more/less of? (e.g. too much/little online content; or too much/little face-to-face time …)

6

Administrative and pedagogical considerations for collaborative online Korean courses: A case study

Nicola Fraschini and Adrienne Gonzales

Abstract

This chapter addresses issues and solutions pertaining to pre-COVID-19 online language teaching by presenting a case study in the development and implementation of a cross-institutional, cross-continental hybrid Korean language course. In March 2019 the University of Denver (DU) and the University of Western Australia (UWA) launched a hybrid Korean language course, taught from Western Australia for DU students. This case study offers a unique perspective on the processes, challenges and solutions for successfully implementing a collaboration that promotes access to less commonly taught languages by leveraging available technology and institutional collaborations. Firstly, we review literature relevant to online language learning and teaching. Then, we describe the administrative, organisational and technical details of the pilot course design. Drawing from the teacher's self-reflective journal, we uncover and analyse themes in the teacher experience that provide insight into and considerations for synchronous online Korean language teaching. Finally, we offer additional thoughts for post-pandemic practices.

Keywords: Korean language, online teaching, international collaboration, teacher's perspective, COVID-19

1. Introduction

Language teaching and learning have for many years taken advantage of increased access to tools and innovative shifts in methodologies that have allowed for constantly evolving educational approaches. Principles and practices that are known by many names, such as technology-enhanced language learning (TELL), computer-assisted language learning (CALL) and others, have shifted the way teachers and learners access and engage with linguistic and cultural content and expand their multicultural and multilingual competencies. Once serving as a supplement to traditional face-to-face language instruction, advancements in tools and technologies now offer entire shifts in instructional delivery modalities, expanding the reach of the classroom across the globe. Remote online teaching has been employed to shorten physical distances and create learning opportunities that would have otherwise been prevented by geographical or institutional constraints (Blake, 2005; Guo & Möllering, 2016).

While affordances for both teaching and learning are often at the forefront of discussions about language learning technology, it is critical to also consider the impact on institutional and administrative policies, since these can play a role in who teaches, when and how. Policy changes and institutional support for innovations and collaborations can have important implications for course offerings, program development and student retention.

This chapter addresses issues and solutions pertaining to online language teaching by presenting a case study in the development and implementation of a cross-institutional, cross-continental hybrid Korean language course. In March 2019, the University of Denver (DU) and the University of Western Australia (UWA) launched a hybrid Korean language course, taught from Western Australia for DU students. This case study offers a unique perspective on the processes, challenges and solutions for successfully implementing a collaboration that promotes access to less commonly taught languages by leveraging available technology and institutional collaborations. This project contributes to the literature on distance foreign language teaching by focusing on the cross-institutional teaching of an Asian language (White, 2014). We review some of the literature relevant to synchronous online language learning in the following sections. Then, we describe the design and set-up of the pilot course. Drawing from the teacher's self-reflection journal, we uncover and analyse themes in the teaching experience that provide insight into and considerations for synchronous online Korean language teaching. We conclude by offering additional thoughts on online foreign language teaching in a post-pandemic era.

2. Online synchronous language teaching

Student–student and teacher–student interaction in online and computer-based foreign language teaching has been popular since the late 1990s. In the early stages, online interaction was limited mainly to written communication (Hampel, 2006), in either asynchronous forms such as emails (Peterson, 1997), blogs and wikis (Thorne & Payne, 2005) or synchronous forms such as text-chat (Tudini, 2003). With regards to oral forms of communication, despite Levy and Stockwell's early observation that 'the value of conferencing in language learning is indisputable' (2006, p. 94), its introduction in classroom practices a few decades ago was constrained by hardware affordability, software quality and connectivity availability.

Now, thanks to advances in software, hardware and the internet, the language teaching field has evolved from costly conferencing classes conducted through a camera and a phone line (Azuma, 2010) to cost-effective and accessible online synchronous instruction. Online language learning activities conducted in a remote synchronous setting have been implemented in several formats. Collaborative wikis and teleconferencing activities, for example, are considered effective multimedia tools to support student learning and intercultural competence (Blake, 2017; Freiermuth & Huang, 2021; Lenkaitis, 2020; Lim & Lee, 2015; Wang, 2015). Besides peer-to-peer exchanges, one-to-one teacher and learner interaction in a format similar to private tutoring was also considered effective (Kozar, 2015, 2016).

Before the online teaching revolution brought about by the COVID-19 pandemic, work on online synchronous language teaching focused on the challenges created by the online environment (Lee, 2015; Yu, 2018) and on the use of the hardware, in particular the webcam, by both teachers and students (Codreanu & Combe Celik, 2013; Kozlova & Zundel, 2013; Guichon & Wigham, 2016; Guo & Möllering, 2016). Other studies comparing instruction in offline and online settings demonstrated that online courses taught as teacher-to-class video conferencing, if carefully designed, can deliver results comparable to traditional offline courses (Blake, 2017; Blake & Shiri, 2012; Enkin & Mejias-Bikandi, 2017;

Moneypenny & Aldrich, 2016; Peterson, 2021). Gacs et al., (2020) found that classes conducted suddenly online because of an emergency situation, as was the case during the pandemic in 2020, were not comparable to their face-to-face counterparts because of the impossibility of applying a carefully planned design. The authors concluded that crisis-prompted remote teaching is generally of lower quality, carries testing security issues, difficulty with accessibility and connectivity, and may not fulfil equivalent learning outcomes.

A carefully designed and planned online class does not try to reproduce online the face-to-face environment (Gacs et al., 2020). Instead, it takes advantage of the unique features of the virtual environment to enable student learning. González-Lloret (2020) argued that through collaborative technology-enabled tasks, it is possible to recreate also in the online environment the type of output and interaction needed to effectively learn a language, concluding that technology in the online language classroom opens possibilities previously unavailable in the traditional face-to-face setting. Payne (2020) advised grading online activities depending on their cognitive load to make teaching effective in the virtual classroom, because synchronous communication has a different cognitive load than asynchronous communication and therefore a pre-recorded online video lecture will have a cognitive load lower than a live video chat in the L2.

The careful design of activities is essential to address also the emotional side of the online language learning experience. Even if Pichette's (2009) research did not find any significant differences in the level of foreign language anxiety among online and offline language learners of all levels, in a study conducted during the pandemic, Resnik and Dewaele (2021) found that the online environment weakens language learner positive and negative emotions due to the difficulty in establishing social bonds. In another study conducted during the pandemic among online university students of Korean, Fraschini and Tao (2024) found that the level of enjoyment was consistently higher than the level of anxiety, and that perceived teacher friendliness and increased Korean language use in the virtual classroom were positively correlated to positive emotions. Russel (2020), discussing anxiety in online language learning, concluded that the remote environment could be manipulated to lower speaking anxiety in language learners.

While there is some previous work on video conferencing-mediated instruction and online language teacher training (e.g. Hampel & Stickler, 2005), in the field of Korean as a foreign language, the majority of the research is focused on the students, their needs and their perceptions of the learning experience, with limited consideration of the teacher experience (Choi, 2017; Choi et al., 2018; Lee, 2015; Lim & Lee, 2015; Lim & Pyun, 2016; Seo & Bang, 2019). This chapter aims to shed light on the teacher perspective by discussing the course design and implementation and analysing the reflective teaching journal of the instructor of a semester-long hybrid course. As illustrated above, considerations such as the teacher's role in planning for course design and set-up, in adjusting the cognitive load of activities and in shaping students' affective response, are important in developing a better understanding of the teacher's experience and point of view. In the following section, we describe the administrative and curricular components that create the foundation and framework for this course.

3. Course design

3.1. Background

At the initiation of the partnership with UWA, DU's Department of Languages and Literatures offered several credit-bearing options for language study (Arabic, Chinese, French, German, Hebrew, Italian, Latin, Japanese, Spanish and Russian). In recent years, despite a decline in overall enrolments in the study of languages other than English, the United States has seen a dramatic increase in Korean language enrolments (Looney & Lusin, 2019). This trend was reflected in student requests for Korean language instruction at DU. To meet this growing demand for Korean and other less commonly taught languages, the Center for World Languages and Cultures (CWLC) developed a Directed Independent Language Study program to allow students to pursue self-study in languages of academic, professional or personal interest. With increased interest, the CWLC began to leverage its international strategic partnerships to develop instructor-led language courses. After a successful pilot course for online Swedish language through Lund University, the CWLC began to explore options to offer Korean to DU students through UWA.

Embarking on an international collaboration involving curriculum matching, credit transfers, and the sharing and exchanging of resources is a complicated endeavour, and the development of the course described in this contribution was made possible by institutional policies and large-scale initiatives that encouraged and supported this type of work. DU's ten-year strategic plan, *Impact 2025*, committed to *Discovery and Design in an Age of Collaboration*. *International Impact* was one strategic initiative intended to support this transformative direction, and the Office of Internationalization at DU prioritised institutional partnerships with universities and increased opportunities for internationalisation on campus. UWA's status as a strategic partner institution, and an existing memorandum of understanding with DU, helped facilitate this project from an administrative and logistical perspective.

3.2. Administrative and curricular considerations

From a curricular perspective, even though the effectiveness of online and hybrid teaching modalities had been demonstrated with appropriate design and implementation (e.g. Goertler, 2011; Meskill & Anthony, 2015), there remained some resistance among the DU faculty to full acceptance and support for the creation of new online language learning opportunities, even in cases where it broadened access to less commonly taught languages otherwise not offered at the institution. In order to receive the necessary approvals to move forward with this project and create a credit-bearing option for DU students to study Korean remotely through UWA, DU and UWA developed underlying policies to ensure academic rigour and include the program in the DU curriculum:

1. The course content in DU's Korean: Beginning Level 1 would match the Level 1 entry unit of the UWA Korean language program (KORE1401).
2. DU's Korean: Beginning Level 1 would be given the course prefix INTZ, indicating that the course was offered through the Office of Internationalization, rather than the academic Department of Languages and Literatures.
3. DU's Korean: Beginning Level 1 would count as elective credit and would not count towards the common curriculum foreign language requirement.
4. For students who elected to study abroad at UWA and continue the Korean language course sequence in person, the second Level 1 Korean language unit of the UWA program (KORE1402) would transfer back to DU and fulfil the common curriculum foreign language requirement.
5. Students who desired to continue their Korean language studies after completion of Korean: Beginning Level 1 could continue to do so at DU through the Directed Independent Language Study program. In this case, credits earned would continue to count as elective credits

only and would not fulfil the common curriculum foreign language requirement, which might incur competition for enrolments with other language programs.

In addition to these curricular considerations, there were logistical challenges for offering a cross-global course via synchronous online delivery. Course meetings were carefully scheduled to accommodate the 14-hour time difference, while ensuring that the meeting times would not deter interested students. Minimum enrolment for language courses at DU is typically set at eight students. However, since this was a pilot program, the institution was committed to running the course with lower enrolment. The final enrolment in the course was nine students, which was considered very strong and promising for longer-term viability, particularly since it was only offered as elective credit. The demonstrated success of the course would create possible opportunities for further curricular integration in the future, allowing students to apply the course credits towards relevant degree programs such as Asian studies, international studies and so on.

To ensure the employment of best pedagogical practices that would set students up for success, we designed a hybrid course solution that would provide learners with multiple modalities for input and engagement with the class content. Collaborative activities were conducted in the online classes through breakout rooms, and opportunities to engage in spoken interactions with peers and instructors were made available through the design of the face-to-face sessions.

Because this collaboration was supported by an institution-level partnership, funding was made available for the course coordinator to travel from UWA to DU for the first week of term to orient students to the course, meet with and train the teaching assistant (TA), connect with the on-site support staff, and get an overall feel for the institution. The initial establishment of a face-to-face connection was helpful for this pilot course, since it allowed the course coordinator to establish a social connection with the students, an element otherwise missing in the online language learning environment (Resnik & Dewaele, 2021).

For the duration of the ten-week academic quarter, the course met for two hours, twice per week. The first session of the week was a synchronous online lecture delivered by the instructor. These sessions covered the main grammar points and related exercises, both written and oral. The second session of the week was an in-person meeting, facilitated by the TA. The TA-led sessions provided opportunities for reinforcement through more spoken interaction and activities, such as role-plays, reading and listening.

For this course, various course materials were made available to students. The main textbook adopted for the course was *Sogang Korean 1A* (Kim et al., 2008), published by the Sogang University Korean Language Education Centre. To supplement the course text, the instructor uploaded video clips containing concise explanations of grammar points, a PDF workbook for classroom activities, grammar notes and homework exercises with answer keys to the learning management system (LMS) in advance of online and in-person sessions. Online sessions were automatically recorded and shared with students for review purposes.

As an additional resource for students taking Korean: Beginning Level 1, the CWLC hired an undergraduate native speaker of Korean to serve as a peer tutor. CWLC tutors' primary role is to leverage their position as peer experts to help students become more self-sufficient and confident language learners. Critical to this, as Williams (2011) states, is regular and frequent training to prepare peer-educators to serve in this capacity. Drawing from various established tools and practices (e.g. Leons, 2013; Paige et. al., 2002; Thot, 1999; Wood & Tanner, 2012), the CWLC tutors complete training modules that focus on tutoring best practices, strategies for working with language learners, the L2 writing process, facilitating L2 conversations and working with learning differences. The underlying philosophy communicated through the training is that tutors encourage fellow students by modelling and sharing best practices in language learning. The additional support and guidance were an important addition to help keep students engaged throughout their remote learning experience.

Finally, because this was a new course delivery modality for students, CWLC staff were also available on-site to assist students in navigating the course, facilitate communication with the various instructional staff and connect with the appropriate study abroad advisers for possible continued study.

3.3. Software and hardware set-up

The video conferencing platform Zoom was used to deliver the course. This platform was preferred among other options for its audiovisual quality and stability and for allowing breakout rooms, a function used to create sub-meetings within a primary meeting. This feature was considered essential to the running of communicative language activities, since it enables students to interact with peers also in the online environment.

The venue chosen for delivery of the online classes was a video conference room equipped with a Polycom system. This venue was preferred thanks to its hardware, which offers audio and video quality exceeding that of the more widely available desktop devices. Additionally, the venue offered the possibility of using a physical whiteboard showing background slides without the need to continuously switch from a screen-sharing view to another. Besides the Polycom system, other pieces of hardware used by the instructor included two laptops. One laptop was connected to the beam projector to display the PowerPoint slides, while the second laptop was connected to the video conference system as the meeting host. While these options use a significant number of resources, they allow for a PowerPoint presentation, the use of the breakout room function by the host and the use of high-quality audiovisual equipment such as the Polycom system. The students were able to see at the same time both the slides and the instructor as if they were together in a physical classroom. The instructor experienced no significant technical issues, and the students did not complain about or report technical problems such as poor connection or audiovisual quality.

The nine students enrolled in the course took the weekly online class from different locations. Most of them were at home, while others were in a room in the university library or in a shared space in their dormitory. One student always connected with a smartphone, while the others used laptops.

4. Analysis of the reflective journal

The instructor's teaching journal was intended to foster self-reflection about the main lessons learned in conducting the synchronous online sessions in the ten-week hybrid course. Journal entries, written in the first person, constitute a form of narrative inquiry. Self-narratives in applied linguistics have been used not only to offer a window on identity and beliefs (Norton & Early, 2011, Nunan & Choi, 2010) but also, in the case of teachers' narratives, to provide an understanding of teachers' experiences from their own perspective and serve as a tool for the study of teachers' reality, educational practices and professional life (Barkhuizen et al., 2014). The teaching journal analysed here consists of a total of eight entries, one for each online session taught. Week 1, which was taught entirely in person, and Week 9 (public holiday) do not have entries. Each journal entry was written on the same day as the corresponding class.

A qualitative analysis of the journal entries was conducted by coding recurrent themes (Auerbach & Silverstein, 2003) and highlighted three main topics: students' participation and feedback, breakout room activities, and managing activities and class time. These three topics were further confirmed by a quantitative analysis conducted with Voyant Tools, which illustrated how the words 'students' (54 repetitions), 'class' (46 repetitions), 'online' (22 repetitions), 'time' (21 repetitions) and 'breakout' (20 repetitions) were among the most frequently used in the journal.

4.1. Student interaction and feedback

The instructor observed the students' behaviour to be different compared to traditional offline teaching settings. The Zoom gallery mode was used to allow students and the instructor to see each other simultaneously, recreating an environment similar to the physical classroom. However, the students could not talk with each other, although they could speak out loud when asking a question. The instructor observed that in the virtual environment created by the Zoom meeting, the students could not support each other's learning and scaffold their peers to comprehension through small private student-to-student talks. In a language classroom, this is a considerable limitation, since two students from the same language background, in a traditional class, often ask and answer quick questions to each other in their mother language without interrupting the flow of the lesson. The result is that the virtual classroom was primarily focused on the teacher, as the only actor with whom students could communicate by asking questions or by replying when called out.

The instructor perceived that the online environment and the audio and video set-up had a significant impact on retaining students' attention. Compared to traditional settings, the instructor observed that students demonstrated considerable attention during all classes, which was surprising considering that the lessons were conducted in the evenings from 6 pm to 8 pm. One of the possible reasons for this high level of attention is to be found in the online environment, which does not allow the learners to understand when the instructor is looking at them and thus creates a sort of panopticon environment. Even though all students always had their webcams on for the entire duration of each class, they were unable to establish eye contact with the instructor, since they did not know at which specific individual the instructor was looking. The lack of clear visual communication clues directed to the teacher, such as gestures or certain facial and body expressions used in the physical classroom but not picked up on camera, limited opportunities for feedback. This means that feedback, both from instructor to students and from students to instructor, about, for example, the pace of the lesson, was severely limited by the constraints of the online meeting environment.

Additionally, the instructor's feedback on student writing was severely limited by the online environment. Although the instructor could see that students were writing on their notepads and on the exercise booklet, it was not possible to check, for example, the spelling of what they were writing. This represents a further point of difference from the physical classroom, where the instructor can walk around, check what students are writing and give them individual and personalised feedback. Despite the weekly written homework submissions, an issue related to insufficient feedback on writing became evident after the mid-term test, when the students demonstrated they had achieved speaking skills that were more advanced than their writing skills. The issue of feedback on writing in online environments becomes more crucial in the context of languages with non-Latin script. This challenge is further amplified by the layout of the Korean keyboard. Students would need to memorise the position of the Korean letters, but this would be a difficult task for true beginner learners. This issue prevented the students from sharing their writing with the teacher in an effective manner during the classes.

4.2. Time

Another recurrent issue encountered in the online classes was that of time management. The lack of visual cues allowing the instructor to understand the level of students' comprehension perceptibly slowed down the teaching pace as the instructor increased the number of repeated explanations. Consequently, the instructor often spoke more slowly than usual to make sure students were understanding. The instructor also perceived a small delay between audio and video, resulting in the instructor's voice being delivered to the students slightly later than the image. The delay was apparent from students' often-slow reactions to the instructor's prompts. The repetition and slower-than-usual talk negatively affected the amount of time that could be spent on activities, and, overall, less content was covered in the online classes compared to face-to-face classes dealing with the same material. The need to adjust expectations is common to any online language teaching situation (Gacs et al., 2020), and the instructor realised soon that only 90–95 per cent of the planned activities could be conducted in the virtual classroom. This lesson was considered when adjusting the syllabus for the same course conducted fully online in 2020 and 2021.

4.3. Breakout rooms

Without breakout room activities, students would not have engaged with each other verbally, and the overall online class would have turned into a lecture. Breakout room activities were also fundamental in allowing students to interact and establish social bonds (Resnik & Dewaele, 2021). The instructor randomly allocated two to three students to each breakout room. Students in a room could interact more among themselves.

The main advantages of conducting activities by dividing the students into small breakout rooms are increasing peer scaffolding and enhancing active participation. Students, in particular those sharing the same language background, used the time in the small-group breakout room for comprehension checks and peer scaffolding in their mother language. Breakout rooms enhanced peer feedback and participation, with students proving to be more active in the breakout rooms than in the main meeting room, where most of them remained silent. The use of the breakout rooms facilitated communication and increased opportunities for meaningful oral interaction.

From the instructor's point of view, the use of breakout rooms is not without drawbacks. For example, the instructor has considerably reduced control over what happens in every single room. Additionally, if the instructor is engaged with students in a particular room, it is not possible to give appropriate feedback to students in other rooms. The difference with traditional student pair work in an offline setting is that, by checking all rooms before concluding a task, the time spent on the activity is significantly longer compared to the same activity conducted in a face-to-face setting, which further affects the issue of time management discussed above.

5. Post-pandemic considerations

The pilot hybrid course was run during the DU Spring Quarter, from April to June of 2019, with the intention of offering the course again the following academic year. In the shift from a hybrid to a fully online course modality due to the COVID-19 pandemic, additional issues arose, prompting the need for quick adjustments regarding assessment, writing and course materials. Typing and online assessment became considerable issues, due to a characteristic of the Korean language, which is written with an alphabetic non-Latin script. A third issue—the lack of appropriate e-textbooks—is to be discussed instead within a broader consideration of online language education.

The Korean language is written with a non-Latin script of 24 basic letters. While learners of Chinese and Japanese can type on a keyboard using the Latin alphabet for how a word is pronounced and are then able to select the appropriate character, this is not possible for learners of Korean, since Korean has its own keyboard layout. Unfortunately, learners of Korean in English-speaking countries do not have the layout visible on their keyboards, requiring the use of virtual keyboards on their screens, which are time-consuming and impractical for those just beginning to learn the script itself. This issue can be addressed by restructuring the low-level curriculum to include typing among the learner objectives and providing the students with appropriate software to practise typing in Korean gradually.[1]

Following the consideration that online education should not try to replicate the face-to-face classroom environment (Gacs et al., 2020), online testing should avoid replicating a paper-based piece of assessment on a screen. In line with the concerns about typing in the Korean language, all language assessments for the successive DU and UWA Korean language courses were designed through the respective LMS, but they could not include any type of open-ended item. The level of difficulty of the tests developed during the COVID-19 period and deployed on the LMS was considerably lower than the tests assigned to the previous cohorts. As with paper-based tests, the construction of quality online tests necessitates a bank of assessment items that can be graded for difficulty depending on the variation of the multiple-choice format.

---

1 Such software, developed in 2021 by the first author, is freely available online at keykorea.vercel.app.

The last consideration of teaching in an online environment concerns the textbook. While, for other languages, e-books may already exist, none of the university-level Korean language textbooks available for English-speaking students were available in this format at the time the course was set up. Gacs et al. (2020) noted that online language teaching is particularly time-consuming, as the development of online classes requires a considerable amount of input. The development of foreign language e-books designed not as a file transposition of a traditional book but as online learning tools on their own terms would represent a significant advantage for teachers.

6. Conclusion

The planning and preparation for the hybrid Korean course and subsequent analysis of the teacher's reflective journal facilitated preparation for the shift to fully online course delivery in 2020. The COVID-19 pandemic forced educators all over the world to look for solutions to address their online teaching needs effectively (Hodges et al., 2020), and today remote language teaching is seen as a necessity rather than a complement to the face-to-face classroom. Now considered a core teaching competency, experience in designing online language courses has become a requirement for recent language-related academic appointments in Australia—for example, those posted in 2021 in Korean and Japanese studies at the University of Sydney.

Leveraging the available technologies along with the new and widespread acceptance of the affordances of online teaching and learning, we are now better prepared than ever to work collaboratively across the globe to offer access to educational experiences beyond the offerings of a single institution. However, there is still work to be done and improvements to be made. Notwithstanding the advantages of synchronous online learning, this contribution has also shown the need to be aware of its constraints. The first limitation is represented by feedback availability, which is not personalised and whose provision is limited in the online environment. A further limitation of the online environment is the lack of depth of teacher–student and student–student relationships compared with those built in traditional offline classrooms, which can lead to less enjoyable classes (Resnik & Dewaele, 2021). In the online environment, the teacher and students cannot interact before or after the class, since all participants disconnect as soon as the lesson is finished. The only opportunity that students have to ask individual and personal questions is through emails, and this makes it challenging for teachers to understand the students, their needs and their difficulties. Online office hours, or online peer-tutoring of the kind offered by DU, could provide other ways of overcoming the lack of feedback. Reflections and experiences like those presented in this chapter can contribute to the further optimisation of online teaching solutions and to the broadening of cross-institutional collaborations to boost and expand the study of foreign languages.

References

Auerbach, C. & Silverstein, L. B. (2003). *Qualitative data*. NYU Press.

Azuma, S. (2010). Business Japanese through internet-based videoconferencing. *Global Business Languages, 8*(10). docs.lib.purdue.edu/gbl/vol8/iss1/10

Barkhuizen, G., Benson, P. & Chik, A. (2014). *Narrative inquiry in language teaching and learning research*. Routledge.

Blake, R. (2005). Bimodal CMC: The glue of language learning at a distance. *CALICO Journal, 22*(3), 497–511. doi.org/10.1558/CJ.V22I3.497-511

Blake, R. (2017). Distance education for second and foreign language learning. In S. Thorne & S. May (Eds), *Language, education and technology. Encyclopedia of language and education* (3rd ed.). Springer.

Blake, R. J. & Shiri, S. (2012). Online Arabic language learning: What happens after? *L2 Journal, 4*(2), 230–46. doi.org/10.5070/L24212462

Choi, E. J., Han, H. R. & Seo J. M. (2018). A basic study to develop real-time video Korean curriculum: Focusing on female-marriage immigrants in Cyber University. *Journal of Korean Language Education, 29*(2), 181–208.

Choi, M. H. (2017). The efficacy of videoconferencing on the development of L2 Korean learners' reading and listening skills. *Multimedia-Assisted Language Learning, 20*(4), 44–65.

Codreanu, T. & Combe Celik, C. (2013). Effects of webcams on multimodal interactive learning. *ReCALL, 25*(1), 30–47. doi.org/10.1017/S0958344012000249

Enkin, E. & Mejías-Bikandi, E. (2017). The effectiveness of online teaching in an advanced Spanish language course. *International Journal of Applied Linguistics, 27*(1), 176–97. doi.org/10.1111/ijal.12112

Fraschini, N. & Tao, Y. (2024). Emotions in online language learning: Exploratory findings from an *ab initio* Korean course. *Journal of Multilingual and Multicultural Development, 45*(5), 1305–1323. doi.org/10.1080/01434632.2021.1968875

Freiermuth, M. R. & Huang, H. C. (2021). Zooming across cultures: Can a telecollaborative video exchange between language learning partners further the development of intercultural competences? *Foreign Language Annals, 54*(1), 185–206. doi.org/10.1111/flan.12504

Gacs, A., Goertler, S. & Spasova, S. (2020). Planned online language education versus crisis-prompted online language teaching: Lessons for the future. *Foreign Language Annals, 53*(2), 380–92. doi.org/10.1111/flan.12460

Goertler, S. (2011). Hybrid and open/online learning: Adapting to a changing world of language teaching. In N. Arnold & L. Ducate (Eds), *Present and future promises of CALL: From theory and research to new directions in language teaching* (pp. 471–501). CALICO.

González-Lloret, M. (2020). Collaborative tasks for online language teaching. *Foreign Language Annals, 53*(2), 260–69. doi.org/10.1111/flan.12466

Guo, S. & Möllering, M. (2016). The implementation of task-based teaching in an online Chinese class through web conferencing. *System, 62*, 26–38. doi.org/10.1016/j.system.2016.07.003

Guichon, N. & Wigham, C. R. (2016). A semiotic perspective on web conferencing-supported language teaching. *ReCALL, 28*(1), 62–82. doi.org/10.1017/S0958344015000178

Hampel, R. (2006). Rethinking task design for the digital age: A framework for language teaching and learning in a synchronous online environment. *ReCALL, 18*(1), 105–121. doi.org/10.1017/S0958344006000711

Hampel, R. & Stickler, U. (2005). New skills for new classrooms: Training tutors to teach languages online. *Computer Assisted Language Learning, 18*(4), 311–326. doi.org/10.1080/09588220500335455

Hodges, C., Moore, S., Lockee, B., Trust, T. & Bond A. (2020, March 27). The difference between emergency remote teaching and online learning. *Educause Review*. www.er.educause.edu/%20articles/2020/3/the-difference-between-emergency-remote-teaching-and-online-learning

Kim, S. H., Kim, H. J., Kim, J. A. & Kim, B. K. (2008). *Sogang Korean 1A*. Sogang University Institute for Continuing Education.

Kozar, O. (2015). Language education via audio/video conferencing (LEVAC): A discursive investigation. *Linguistics and Education, 31*, 86–100. doi.org/10.1016/j.linged.2015.05.007

Kozar, O. (2016). Teachers' reaction to silence and teachers' wait time in video and audio conferencing English lessons: Do webcams make a difference? *System, 62*, 53–62. doi.org/10.1016/j.system.2016.07.002

Kozlova, I. & Zundel, E. (2013). Synchronous online language teaching: Strategies to support learner development. In C. Meskill (Ed.), *Online teaching and learning: Sociocultural perspectives* (pp. 99–116). Bloomsbury Academic.

Lee, Y. H. (2015). A case study on real-time distance video Korean education—Based on the KF Global E-school: Sookmyung Womens' Univ.-Kuwait Univ. Korean Language Program. *The Donam Language and Literature, 28*, 413–37. doi.org/10.17056/donam.2015.28..413

Lenkaitis, C. A. (2020). Technology as a mediating tool: videoconferencing, L2 learning, and learner autonomy. *Computer Assisted Language Learning, 33*(5/6), 483–509. doi.org/10.1080/09588221.2019.1572018

Leons, E. (2013, August). Diverse and differently abled: Understanding the learning journey. *The Language Educator*, 32–34.

Levy, M. & Stockwell, G. (2006). *CALL dimensions: Options and issues in computer-assisted language learning*. Lawrence Erlbaum Associates.

Lim, B. J. & Lee, H. J. (2015). Videoconferencing for Korean language education: Synchronous online interactions between learners of Korean and English beyond the classroom. *Journal of Korean Language Education, 26*, 1–28. doi.org/10.18209/iakle.2015.26..1

Lim, B. J. & Pyun, D. O. (2019). Korean foreign language learning: Video conferencing with native speakers. In Information Resources Management Association (Ed.), *Computer-assisted language learning: Concepts, methodologies, tools, and applications* (pp. 1123–46). IGI Global. doi.org/10.4018/978-1-5225-7663-1.ch054

Looney, D. & Lusin N. (2019). Enrollments in languages other than English in United States institutions of higher education, summer 2016 and fall 2016: Final report. Modern Language Association. www.mla.org/content/download/110154/2406932/2016-Enrollments-Final-Report.pdf

Meskill, C. & Anthony, N. (2015). *Teaching language online*. Multilingual Matters. doi.org/10.21832/9781783093786

Moneypenny D. B. & Aldrich, R. S. (2016). Online and face-to-face language learning: A comparative analysis of oral proficiency in introductory Spanish. *The Journal of Educators Online, 13*, 105–74. doi.org/10.9743/JEO.2016.2.2

Norton, B. & Early, M. (2011). Researcher identity, narrative enquiry, and language teaching research. *TESOL Quarterly, 45*(3), 415–39. doi.org/10.5054/tq.2011.261161

Nunan, D. & Choi, J. (Eds). (2010). *Language and culture: Reflective narratives and the emergence of identity.* Routledge.

Paige, R. M., Cohen, A. D., Kappler, B., Chi, J. C. & Lassegard, J. P. (2002). *Maximising study abroad: A students' guide to strategies for language and culture learning and use.* University of Minnesota Center for Advanced Research on Language Acquisition. www.carla.umn.edu/maxsa/guides.html

Payne, J. S. (2020). Developing L2 productive language skills online and the strategic use of instructional tools. *Foreign Language Annals, 53*(2), 243–49. doi.org/10.1111/flan.12457

Peterson, J. (2021). Speaking ability progress of language learners in online and face-to-face courses. *Foreign Language Annals, 54*(1), 27–49. doi.org/10.1111/flan.12511

Peterson, M. (1997). Language teaching and networking. *System, 25*(1), 29–37. doi.org/10.1016/S0346-251X(96)00058-9

Pichette. F. (2009). Second language anxiety and distance language learning. *Foreign Language Annals, 42*(1), 77–93. doi.org/10.1111/j.1944-9720.2009.01009.x

Resnik, P. & Dewaele, J.–M. (2021). Learner emotions, autonomy and trait emotional intelligence in 'in-person' versus emergency remote English foreign language teaching in Europe. *Applied Linguistics Review, 14*(3). doi.org/10.1515/applirev-2020-0096

Russel, V. (2020). Language anxiety and the online learner. *Foreign Language Annals, 53*(2), 338–52. doi.org/10.1111/flan.12461

Seo, J. S. & Bang, S. W. (2019). A case study of Korean tutoring using video conferencing. *Bilingual Education, 74*, 213–37. doi.org/10.17296/KORBIL.2019..74.213

Thorne, S. L. & Payne, J. S. (2005). Evolutionary trajectories, internet-mediated expression, and language education. *CALICO Journal, 22*(3), 371–97. doi.org/10.1558/cj.v22i3.371-397

Thot, I. D. (1999). *How to tutor a student in a foreign language*. Santa Monica College. www.eric.ed.gov/?id=ED433898

Tudini, V. (2003). Using native speakers in chat. *Language Learning and Technology, 7*(3), 141–59. doi.org/10125/25218

Wang, Y. C. (2015). Promoting collaborative writing through wikis: A new approach for advancing innovative and active learning in an ESP context. *Computer Assisted Language Learning and Teaching, 28*(6), 499–512. doi.org/10.1080/09588221.2014.881386

White, C. (2014). The distance learning of foreign languages: A research agenda. *Language Teaching, 47*(4), 538–553. doi.org/10.1017/S0261444814000196

Williams, L. B. (2011). The future of peer education: Broadening the landscape. *New Directions for Student Services, 133*, 97–100. doi.org/10.1002/ss.388

Wood, W. B. & Tanner, K. D. (2012). The role of the lecturer as tutor: doing what effective tutors do in a large lecture class. *CBE—Life Sciences Education, 11*(1), 3–9. doi.org/10.1187/cbe.11-12-0110

Yu, L. T. (2018). Native English-speaking teachers' perspectives on using videoconferencing in learning English by Taiwanese elementary-school students. *JALT CALL Journal, 14*(1), 61–76. doi.org/10.29140/JALTCALL.V14N1.224

7

Connections between learners' communities of practice and their use of social language learning strategies: A case study

Mary Grace Quigley

Abstract

There are many strategies that can be taught and employed to foster language learning. This chapter takes social language learning strategies—that is, those directly linked to engaged interaction—as its focus. Previous literature demonstrates a positive relationship between the use of language learning strategies and language proficiency development. Less well explored is the connection between the strategies that learners employ outside the classroom and their creation of L2-speaking communities of practice. This chapter examines learners' pre-existing strategies for creating communities of practice in which German is used. Additionally, within the context of a case study, this chapter investigates the potentials of teaching social language learning strategies to encourage learner engagement outside of the classroom. The case study described involved intermediate learners of German at an Australian university. Interview and questionnaire data provide insights into learners' out-of-class communities of practice and the strategies that they use, along with the potentials of social strategy instruction in the language classroom.

Keywords: communities of practice, learning strategies, learner engagement, action research

1. Introduction

Language learning is a multifaceted process that in some cases involves a great deal of rote, grammatically focused learning, depending on the language learning context. Many strategies applicable to this type of learning are commonly taught as a part of schooling. Along with the potential for a focus on language form, however, language learning is always accompanied by an aspect of social learning. This chapter takes social language learning strategies—or strategies for structuring and approaching the social elements of language learning—as its focus, and looks firstly at how learners of German at an Australian tertiary institution use these strategies. Aligning with a focus on social learning, this chapter investigates the connections between learners' communities of practice, the discourses attached to them and learners' use of a range of social strategies available to them. Finally, this chapter reports the initial findings of an action research experiment involving the teaching of social language learning strategies.

2. Theoretical background

Language learning strategies constitute a wide-ranging field in terms of the types of strategies that exist for learners and the areas of language learning on which they focus. This section firstly provides an overview of language learning strategies and clarifies specifically what is meant in this study by social language learning strategies. To better describe and understand the social aspects of language learning, this study also draws on the theoretical construct of communities of practice. Communities of practice are helpful when looking at how language(s) and discourses are embedded in the practices of the everyday lives of language learners (Norton, 2013). They are particularly relevant when investigating learners' out-of-class language use within a foreign language learning environment. Previous literature has tended to focus on either strategy teaching (e.g. Cohen, 2014; Lai, 2019) or learners' L2-speaking communities of practice (e.g. Kurata, 2010;

Norton, 2013; Yoshida, 2013; Kayi-Aydar, 2014). After giving an overview of previous research and theory in these areas, this section outlines the motivations for researching learners' social strategies and communities of practice in combination with one another.

2.1. Social language learning strategies

Language learning strategies broadly can be understood as any conscious actions taken by the learner which have an intended positive effect on learning, such as making learning easier, more efficient, more enjoyable or more personally relevant (Oxford, 1990; 2017; White, 2008; Cohen, 2014). Strategies often involve the use of techniques to help learners memorise, comprehend, produce, gain access to or organise information about a language they are learning (O'Malley & Chamot, 1990). Strategies have great potential to be personalised according to learners' individual needs and goals and have a direct connection to learner autonomy (Cotterall & Reinders, 2004). Strategies give learners the power to shape their own learning according to their individual requirements (Cotterall & Reinders, 2004; Cohen, 2014).

Previous research has demonstrated that the use of language learning strategies is associated with positive language learning outcomes (e.g. O'Malley & Chamot, 1990; Oxford, 1990; Chamot, 2007; Chen, 2007; Lee & Oxford, 2008; Kao & Oxford, 2014). However, learners' strategy use has been shown to be significantly more effective when combined with explicit classroom strategy instruction (Chamot, 2001; Oxford, 2008). When learners are not given guidance on how to select strategies that align with their personal learning goals, their strategy-related decisions are often made 'in a desperate way' (Oxford, 2008, p. 51). Studies investigating the effectiveness of language learners' strategy use in combination with directed classroom strategy instruction have revealed that the teaching of strategies can be an effective way to help learners select and employ strategies that are of the greatest benefit to their learning (e.g. Nakatani, 2005; Brown, 2007; Chamot, 2007; 2009; Chen, 2007; Gunning & Oxford, 2014).

There are many strategies for language learning which correlate more broadly with strategies for a range of forms of learning, beyond the learning of languages. A group of strategies that are highly relevant to the learning of an L2 are social language learning strategies, which are the focus of this chapter. Social strategies, as they have been termed by Oxford (1990) and

O'Malley and Chamot (1990), are actions taken by learners which help them to use and engage with the L2 in a naturalistic, meaning-focused and, as such, social way. They are strategies which aid learners in using the L2 to express their own thoughts, personalities and ideas in ways that are meaningful to them. Social strategies encompass actions that learners can take during interactions in the L2 to make language use easier and more comfortable. This might include planning conversation topics in advance, taking deep breaths to keep calm while speaking, or momentarily switching to the L1. They can also help learners to create and discover opportunities to engage with the L2—for example, by finding another L2 learner to practise speaking or writing with in a comfortable environment such as over a coffee or through the exchange of messages on social media.

Within the strategy typologies suggested by previous researchers, social strategies have usually been limited to those that help learners to speak in the L2. However, language is in and of itself social (Norton, 2013; De Fina, 2015). The use of language, be it receptive (reading or listening), or productive (speaking or writing), is a social act. When learners engage with and comprehend a text such as a podcast, a newspaper article or a novel, they position themselves socially in relation to that text. They interpret the ideas put forward and establish their own opinions in relation to those expressed in the text (Canagarajah, 2013; Joseph, 2016; Preece, 2016). Language use is social beyond instances of face-to-face speech. Therefore, social strategies within this study represent a broad range of actions that learners can use to foster naturalistic language use and meaningful engagement with the L2.

This broader understanding of social strategies is motivated by recent studies of out-of-class learning, which have shown that significant language learning gains can be made through forms of naturalistic, social engagement beyond spoken interaction. Sockett (2014) found that L1 French speakers were able improve their English language competency through 'online informal learning', involving primarily receptive activities such as watching television and listening to music. Further, Cole and Vanderplank (2016) found that learners of English in Brazil who engaged in meaning-focused activities in English, many of which were online, were able to make greater language gains than classroom learners of English. Along with these studies, there is an increasing amount of literature on the importance of out-of-class learning (e.g. Benson & Reinders 2011; Lai et al., 2015; Bernales, 2016; Lee & Hsieh, 2019), which emphasises the value of autonomous, meaning-focused activities. Huang and Benson (2013) additionally discuss the importance of engaging with personally meaningful material outside of class to foster both L2 development and learner autonomy. Learners' social engagement with the L2, whether receptive or productive in nature, can significantly contribute to their ability to communicate using the L2. Teaching social language learning strategies offers learners a way to structure their approach to out-of-class naturalistic learning.

Social strategies stand in a mutually supportive relationship with cognitive and metacognitive language learning strategies—that is, those for learning language structure. Knowledge of language structure contributes to the ability to use the L2 socially. Strategies for learning and memorising language structures tend to be the most intuitive and familiar to learners because they correspond with many other facets of learning. In contrast, social strategies are often underestimated or forgotten. There is great potential for learners to benefit from classroom activities that motivate them to use these strategies.

2.2. Understanding learners' communities of practice

Both in investigating how learners engage with the L2 outside of class and in exploring the possibilities of suggesting strategies to further this type of language use, the construct of communities of practice is a useful one. Communities of practice can assist in understanding learners' out-of-class social groups and the discourses attached to them. Communities of practice can be understood as a kind of 'small culture' (Holliday, 1999), which, in contrast to a 'large culture', such as national culture, represent shared practices between smaller groups of people, such as a classroom group, or a group of friends. Within the language classroom, for example, many communities of practice exist, overlapping with one another. They are created through shared practices and the knowledge of those habitual practices, which is shared between members (Lave & Wenger, 1991; Eckert & McConnell-Ginet, 1992; Wenger, 1998; van Lier, 2004). Language practices play a key role in the creation and maintenance of communities of practice. When learners engage with meaningful L2 texts, they are engaging in L2 discourse, which is attached to certain communities of practice. This might be expressed as particular registers, vocabularies or certain types of media associated with a particular social group (Gee, 1990; van Lier, 2011).

The important role played by learners' communities of practice in determining their naturalistic engagement with the L2 has been established through the research of Norton (1995, 2000, 2013). Norton's research investigated English language learners' socially motivated reasons for choosing not to use English outside of class, despite being highly motivated to learn. Norton developed the construct of 'investment' to describe scenarios in which learners' social investment in particular communities of practice might clash with their motivation to learn the L2, causing them to make language use choices that do not align with their language learning motivations. Such a clash of investments can also be observed in Kurata's (2010) research looking at learners of Japanese at an Australian university. Her research found that, despite being motivated to practise Japanese and making efforts to find Japanese L1 speakers, learners were ultimately more invested in their social relationships with those speakers than in pursuing their language learning, choosing to speak mainly in English during social encounters with the Japanese L1 speakers. This shows that language use habits quickly form within learners' communities of practice and that, if they do not consciously reflect on language learning goals, learners are unlikely to direct social situations towards language learning opportunities.

Both Kurata's and Norton's research has highlighted the important role played by learners' investment and their everyday communities of practice in determining their willingness to engage with the L2. The decision to use the L2 or another available language involves consideration of the social situation, the habits associated with the relevant communities of practice, and learners' investment in a range of social factors such as friendships or the desire to portray oneself a certain way. Social language learning strategies can help learners to be more aware of their own habits surrounding choices to use the L2 or another language. They can also help to make learners more aware of the language learning potential of their out-of-class environments. The present study therefore sets out to investigate learners' communities of practice and how these interact with learners' use of social language learning strategies. Furthermore, this study examines the potential of explicit teaching of social language learning strategies as a way to encourage learners to increase their use of the L2 as part of their communities of practice outside of the classroom.

3. Research design

3.1 Research questions

The research reported in this chapter is guided by two research questions. Research question 1 focuses on learners' social strategy use and communities of practice outside of the classroom. Research question 2 investigates the potential of explicit instruction of social language learning strategies.

> *Research question 1*: To what extent do learners use social strategies to facilitate using the L2 as part of their participation in communities of practice? How does this relate to their investment in learning the L2?

> *Research question 2*: What is the potential for the explicit instruction of social language learning strategies to influence learners' out-of-class activities and the use of the L2 in their communities of practice?

3.2. Ethical considerations

This project was conducted with approval from the University of Adelaide's Human Research Ethics Committee (HREC H-2019-026). A participant information sheet was provided to every participant and each participant was free to opt into or out of all aspects of the data collection process. All names of participants used in this chapter are pseudonyms and all participant data have been deidentified.

3.3. Participants

The participants of this project were 37 undergraduate learners of German at an Australian university. These learners were enrolled in two B1-level (as defined by the Common European Framework of Reference for Languages [Council of Europe, 2019]) language classes, both of which were taught by the researcher. The majority were aged between 18 and 24 years. At the B1 level, learners begin to be able to engage with and comprehend texts and media that are more closely aligned with what they engaged with in the L1. Learners were assigned to one of two groups, a control ($n = 14$) and an experimental group ($n = 15$), respectively, for the purposes of a strategy teaching experiment, detailed in the next section.

3.4. Teaching social strategies

This project involved an action research element in which a seven-week strategy teaching experiment was carried out. The class groups were not aware of which group they had been assigned to. The experimental group participated in a weekly 10–15-minute strategy teaching session. The control group did not participate in any such strategy sessions. Each session had a different focus, often connected to the previous session. Students were free to choose their preferred language, English or German, during the strategy sessions; however, they were encouraged to speak German. A summary of the focus of the individual strategy teaching sessions and the associated activities is provided in Table 7.1.

Table 7.1 Summary of strategy teaching sessions and activities

Session 1	Gathering knowledge of strategies and sharing ideas about types of social strategies students already use.
Session 2	Discussion of how to find and choose appropriate materials to read as well as how to go about reading. Homework task: finding a text to read and reporting progress next week.
Session 3	Reflections on initial attempts at finding material to read, discussion of strategies used so far. Homework task: continue reading.
Session 4	Discussion of experiences attempting to read, learners bring a chosen text with them to show each other and discuss.
Session 5	Discussion of how learners find opportunities to use German outside of class, learners encouraged to see each other as a resource to practise speaking and writing. Homework task: finding someone to speak German with for ten minutes.
Session 6	Reflection on speaking homework task, discussion of social strategies for speaking. Homework task: finding someone to speak German with for ten minutes and try to incorporate strategies.
Session 7	Reflection on homework task. Discussion of strategies for managing emotions related to language learning.

Source: Compiled by author.

3.5. Data collection: A mixed methods approach

Language learning is understood within this research project to be a complex process involving many aspects of learners' identities and lives, extending far beyond the walls of the classroom, into their everyday lives (van Lier, 2007; De Fina, 2015). Accordingly, this research uses a mixed methods approach (see Creswell, 2003) for data collection. Using a range of instruments and data collection methodologies allows for a range of perspectives and focuses within the data, as well as cross referencing of results (Dörnyei, 2007; Flick, 2011). The sources of data for this project are outlined below.

3.6. Questionnaire

Two questionnaires were used in this research. The first questionnaire was completed by 37 participants belonging to both the experimental and control groups in the third week of semester, prior to the strategy teaching sessions. A second questionnaire was completed by 29 participants after the conclusion of the strategy teaching sessions in the tenth week of semester. Both questionnaires were identical, with the exception of a section of questions on biographical data and learning motivation that was included in the first questionnaire only, and a section of questions in which learners reflected on their learning and strategy use throughout the semester, which was added to the second. The questionnaires were structured according to the guidelines for questionnaires on language learning provided by Dörnyei (2003). They included both Likert scale items, to allow for generalisations across the group, and open-ended questions in which learners could elaborate on their responses.

In line with the case study nature of this research project, both questionnaires have been analysed using descriptive statistics. Each questionnaire item has been analysed as an individual variable and, additionally, some variables have been combined with other similarly themed variables to create a factor. Learners' responses to certain thematic factors are also represented in terms of the average answer given for each variable across the group.

3.7. Interviews

After the conclusion of the strategy teaching sessions, and the completion of the second questionnaire, a total of 25 semi-structured interviews were carried out with learners from both experimental and control groups. Excerpts from 5 of those 25 interviews are presented in this chapter. These have been selected on the basis that they are representative of common themes across a number of interviews. Interviews took approximately 30 minutes and were conducted one-on-one with the researcher. They have been transcribed according to the guidelines provided by Brosius et al. (2016). Transcription conventions are outlined in Table 7.2.

Table 7.2 Interview transcription conventions

//	overlapping speech
/	unfinished sentence
[...]	omitted speech
[ ]	additional information
( )	extra auditory sounds or movements, e.g. laughing or gestures
CAPSLOCK	emphasis
Italics	midsentence code-switching
(...)	pause, full stops indicate number of seconds
I:	utterances by the interviewer
R:	utterances by the respondent

Source: Brosius et al. (2016).

Interviews were approached as socially situated interactions in which the researcher also plays a role (Deppermann, 2013). The interviews aimed to gather data on individual learners' German-speaking communities of practice outside of the classroom. They also investigated the social motivations for learners' choices to create or resist opportunities for practising German outside of class. Interview analysis was carried out using thematic coding (Guest et al., 2012). Learners in the experimental group are indicated with a star (*).

4. Results and discussion

4.1. Learners' investment in German-speaking communities of practice

Learners' choices related to their use of the L2 outside of class are closely tied to their social investment in choosing to learn a language at university. As part of interviews and the initial questionnaire, information about learners' investment in language learning and their L2 communities of practice was gathered. The questionnaire gathered general data about learners' reasons for choosing to learn German and about the kinds of activities they engaged in using the L2 outside of class. The interviews allowed students to provide greater detail about how these choices and activities fitted in within their social lives. Within the interviews, learners were questioned regarding their views of language learning and why it is important to them. Many learners discussed being invested in learning German as symbolic knowledge. In Interview excerpt 1, Tessa describes language learning in general as something she perceives as being socially important because of its potential to broaden one's thinking in a community that is dominated by English.

Interview excerpt 1: Tessa*

> R: I feel like especially white people/English-speaking white people, they just don't really get it. I know a lot of people who don't speak English [as a first language], they all speak English because it's the universal language. I feel like we're missing out. So I don't want to be another one of those.

For Tessa and many other learners within this learner group, language learning was a symbolic gesture through which she and other learners were attempting to broaden their cultural awareness. This means that these learners' investment in language learning is not necessarily connected directly with the goal of participating in a specific L2 community of practice. Rather, it is an act of differentiation from 'those' 'English-speaking white people' who lack understanding and empathy for other cultures. This particular type of investment in the process of learning aligns with a tendency to see language learning as something conceptual, rather than as something practical. This is aligned with data gathered by Schmidt (2014), whose research found that personal growth was a key factor for learners to choose to learn German at an Australian university.

Interview excerpt 2: Tessa*

> R: I think learning a language is just different because you can't just learn it for a test and then forget about it. You constantly have to build up on it and also I don't really speak about bacteria (laughs). I don't speak aloud ever on the science side of things.

Further reflecting this social investment, Tessa discusses the differences between learning German and her other university subjects, stating that a key point of difference was the social aspect of language, which requires frequent and active engagement. She describes this as something she has found difficult about language learning. She expressed difficulty in finding opportunities to engage with the language and to use the language in her life outside of class. She recognises that integrating German language use into her everyday communities of practice is beneficial to her language learning, yet she struggles to find and create opportunities to do so. In Interview excerpt 2, she comments that, with respect to her study of science, she 'doesn't really speak about bacteria' outside of class, thereby highlighting the contrast between her other subjects and German, which requires her to practise her out-of-class speaking. Learners experienced a disparity between what they expected to encounter as part of their university studies and the learning activities associated with language learning. Many academic subjects require learners to memorise facts, whereas language learning requires activities that are connected to learners' everyday communities of practice, beyond the academic realm. Sociocultural language learning theory emphasises that language learning involves the 'whole person' and forms part of one's life beyond the walls of the classroom (van Lier, 2004; Benson, 2019). However, interview data suggested that this strongly social view of learning was not always held by the learners themselves. Across the interviews, exemplified by David in Interview excerpt 3, many students described a desire to complete the formal elements of the course that were necessary to achieve a pass and to avoid any additional activities. While this is an approach adopted by many students across academia, for language learning it is particularly problematic. It is highly important that learners see the value of their informal, naturalistic out-of-class engagement with the language.

> *Interview excerpt 3: David*
>
> I: How do you learn German outside of the classroom?
>
> R: Revision. The *Vorbereitung* [homework activities]. But other than that, not really that much. I don't really consume that much German media outside of the/ Or like German texts outside of the classroom.
>
> I: Did you set any specific goals for yourself in the course?
>
> R: Aim for a pass? (laughs) […] Just keep rolling with it, just sort of get through the course.

Interviews further showed that learners are socially invested in communities of practice that form as part of their university studies, including those connected to their German tuition. Many students within this cohort knew each other, having begun learning German together the previous year. Various classroom and out-of-class communities of practice have been formed as a result of their German language courses. Such communities of practice have discourses—that is, habitual ways of using language—attached to them. Learners in these communities of practice share the mutual goal of learning German and have similar language abilities in German. Despite this, interview data indicated that learners often failed to see each other as potential learning resources or as potential German language speech partners.

> *Interview excerpt 4: Louise*
>
> I: Do you ever speak German together?
>
> R: I mean maybe like as a joke. But not like, 'Let's practise German together.'

I: Have you thought about doing that?

R: I don't know. We'd have to plan it! That'd be good! Why not use your friends who can speak German as a resource! But I don't know. We never do! (laughs)

In Interview excerpt 4, Louise describes speaking German outside of class with other learners in a joking way (line 2), and indicates that this is the only scenario in which she would speak in German with classmates outside of the classroom. Interestingly, she recognises the potential of learning with other students: 'Why not use your friends who can speak German as a resource!' (line 4). Despite her enthusiasm for learning German, she does not speak in German with other students outside of the classroom. In part, she appears not to realise the L2 learning resources that are available to her, and she does not use social strategies in order to create opportunities to access them. For example, she is particularly close with one classmate and it is likely, as was the case in Kurata's (2010) study, that Louise's social investment in the friendship outweighs her investment in improving her German.

Although many learners reported speaking German very little or not at all outside of the classroom, some learners had formed German-speaking communities of practice with German-speaking family members. In Interview excerpt 5, Sally describes using broken German with members of her family who have also learned German as an additional language.

Interview excerpt 5: Sally*

R: I'll say something [in German] and my dad will say something back like, *Was ist das?*

(laughs) Something really basic. And my brother and sister both did it in high school so we kind of have a pretty good knowledge of very basic German. (laughs)

I: You could have a conversation at the dinner table together! (laughs)

R: Hmmm about colours maybe! (laughs)

The family can act as a community of practice in which learners feel safe to play with language, though it appears that this form of language use is not necessarily strategically directed at improving one's language ability. Instead, the purpose of such encounters is more playful and for the enjoyment of a shared code, in a context where the correctness of language form is not of concern. Sally describes this activity as an enjoyable way to use her

ENABLING LEARNING

German, but she does not pursue these kinds of language exchanges to further her language learning. This is the case, despite her having been in the experimental group that received the strategy teaching.

4.2. Using social language learning strategies to participate in communities of practice

The initial questionnaire investigated the social strategies that learners were using to facilitate their naturalistic use of the L2 outside of class. A focus of this was on strategies for speaking, investigating which strategies learners used most frequently and which ones they were reluctant to use. Figure 7.1 shows a breakdown of learners' responses to individual questionnaire items. Learners reported frequently employing strategies that help them to maintain a conversation with a speech partner such as 'guessing from context' and 'keeping the conversation going'. Lesser used strategies included 'anticipating speech', 'changing the topic' and 'momentarily switching to English'.

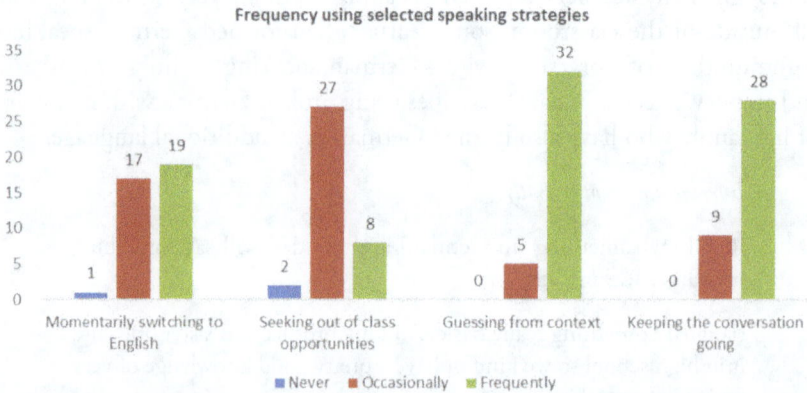

Figure 7.1 Learners' reported frequency using selected speaking strategies (n = 37)
Source: Compiled by author.

Most learners (73%, n = 27) only occasionally sought out opportunities to speak German outside of class. This outcome was also reflected in the interview data discussed earlier, where both a lack of realisation of the opportunities available and a lack of social investment in creating opportunities were described by learners. Figure 7.1 shows that learners regularly use a range of speaking strategies and are particularly willing to employ those which help them to continue their spoken interaction, once they have begun. However, learners appear to be less willing to initiate the creation of their own speaking opportunities, an activity which requires a higher degree of learner autonomy.

Learners described a range of social strategies that they had developed which allowed them to participate in L2 communities of practice while avoiding the necessity of face-to-face interaction. This is an important consideration for language learners, similar to those in Socket's (2014) study, who are geographically isolated from the larger L2-speaking population. In Interview excerpt 6, Adam describes his strategic use of video games as both a tool for learning German and way to foster naturalistic language use. Video games granted access to ways of speaking within a larger community of practice of 'nerds', as Adam identifies himself. Video games have allowed Adam to engage with the discourse of a community of practice which uses German and simultaneously reflects his own English-speaking community in Australia.

Interview excerpt 6: Adam

> R: Because I'm a nerd, I naturally gravitated towards video games. […] So, I would play through video games that I was familiar with in English, I'd just switch the language over to German. I chose games that have lots of dialogue, lots of speaking, lots of reading you have to do so you can understand, and story driven kind of things. So to progress you actually have to understand what's going on. […] It was overwhelming at first but I eased into it and so I had to pick up all these words from context.

Use of L2 media has given Adam the opportunity to engage in a meaningful and personally relevant way with German. He reflects on video games as having made significant contributions to his knowledge of and ability to use the L2. He discussed difficulties in finding and creating opportunities to speak the L2 outside of class face-to-face. However, this strategically sought out text-based activity has granted access to the L2 discourses that connected to the communities of practice with which he personally identifies. Employing such strategic behaviour in seeking out opportunities to use and engage with language in a meaningful and personally relevant way is motivating for learners and contributes to knowledge of the L2.

The interviews carried out with learners from both the experimental and control groups showed that learners do employ their own social strategies without explicit strategy teaching. However, others often do not recognise the potential language learning resources that already exist within their everyday communities of practice. This was true of both Louise, who did not receive strategy instruction, and Sally, who did. This indicates that even with the strategy teaching intervention, in relation to taking up opportunities to use the L2 outside of class, learners' social investment in relationships will often win out over their investment in building their German skills. Nevertheless, strategy teaching has the potential to make learners more aware of their language use choices, as discussed in the next section.

4.3. Teaching social language learning strategies

This section describes results taken from the post-strategy teaching questionnaire, which questioned both the group of learners who received strategy instruction (the experimental group) and those who did not (the control group). They were asked to reflect on their learning and strategy use throughout the semester. They also reported on the amounts of time spent on different types of out-of-class learning activities.

A key focus of the strategy teaching was on seeing other learners as potential language learning resources. Learners were encouraged to speak in German with each other outside of the classroom, including as part of ungraded homework tasks. Figure 7.2 shows learners' reported weekly time spent speaking German with other learners outside of class throughout the semester. Almost all (93%, $n = 14$) learners in the experimental group reported spending 30 minutes or more per week speaking German with other students. In contrast, under three-quarters (71%, $n = 10$) of learners in the control group reported doing this for more than half an hour weekly. Additionally, learners in the experimental group reported spending more time on receptive naturalistic learning activities such as reading books and watching television outside of class than learners in the control group.

This reflects in part the content of the homework assignments that were included in the strategy teaching sessions. However, the homework tasks given to learners as part of the strategy sessions only required them to engage in one activity type—reading, speaking, listening or writing—each week. The questionnaire results suggest that the homework activities initiated by strategy sessions helped learners to form ongoing habits for out-of-class learning.

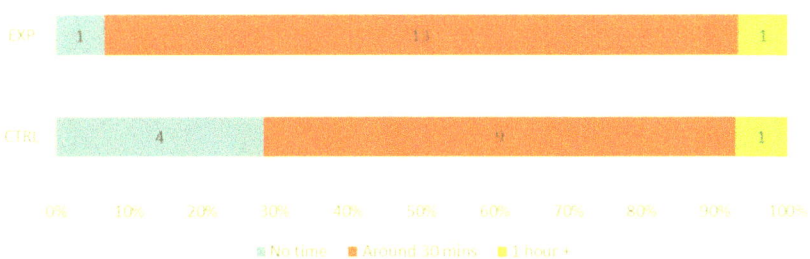

Figure 7.2 Weekly time spent speaking German with other students outside of class: A comparison of experimental (*n* = 15) and control (*n* = 14) groups
Source: Compiled by author.

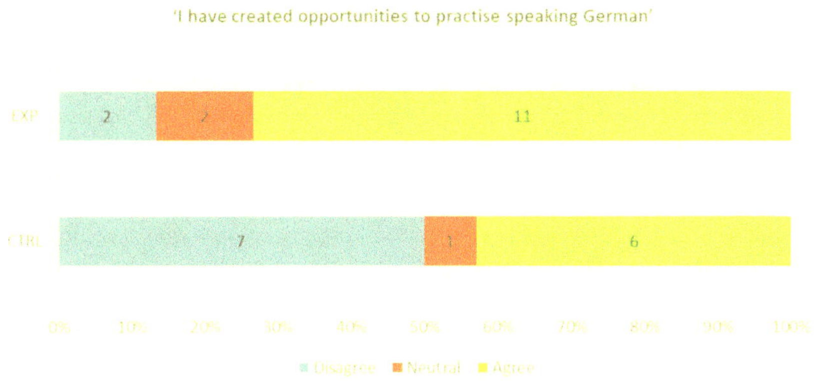

Figure 7.3 Learners' agreement with the statement 'I have created opportunities to practise speaking German': A comparison of experimental (*n* = 15) and control (*n* = 14) groups
Source: Compiled by author.

Figure 7.3 displays learners' agreement with the statement, 'I have created opportunities to practise speaking German'. Learners in the experimental group showed stronger agreement (73%, *n* = 11) with this item than the control group, of which less than half (43%, *n* = 6) expressed agreement. This suggests that the strategy teaching sessions prompted learners to create additional opportunities to practise using German outside of the classroom. Creating opportunities for language use was a strategy which learners used relatively less often, as already discussed with regard to Figure 7.1. The strategy sessions and associated homework tasks motivated learners to seek out opportunities for naturalistic language use where they otherwise would not have. In doing this, learners can build and participate in communities of practice whose habitual practices involve using German rather than solely English.

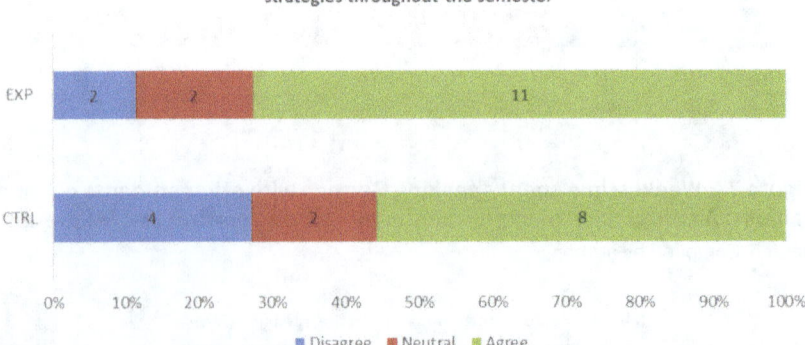

Figure 7.4 Learners' average agreement with statements about the development of social strategies throughout the semester: A comparison of experimental (*n* = 15) and control (*n* = 14) groups
Source: Compiled by author.

Learners' average agreement with statements about strategy development throughout the semester, shown in Figure 7.4, indicated that learners in the experimental group showed greater agreement with having developed social strategies throughout the semester. On average, across a range of items looking at different social strategies, almost three-quarters (73%, *n* = 11) of learners in the experimental group agreed that they had developed social strategies for out-of-class learning throughout the semester, whereas only 57 per cent (*n* = 8) of those in the control group expressed agreement on average with the same statements. That over half of the control group developed social strategies without explicit strategy instruction shows that learners will intuitively develop and use social strategies. However, the relatively short strategy sessions were able to prompt a larger proportion of learners within this learner group to actively develop social strategies to further their learning through naturalistic out-of-class language use.

The initial results of this small-scale action research project suggest that the teaching of social language learning strategies, even in very short sessions, unconnected to course assessment, has the potential to encourage students to increase their use of social strategies.

4.4. Research outcomes

The research results discussed have focused on learners' social strategy use outside of the classroom, their communities of practice and the potential of strategy teaching to prompt learners to use social strategies more frequently. The research outcomes are discussed below in relation to the guiding research questions.

Research question 1

> To what extent do learners use social strategies to facilitate using the L2 as part of their participation in communities of practice? How does this relate to their investment in learning the L2?

This investigation has indicated that learners do intuitively employ a range of social strategies outside of the classroom, particularly those that allow them to continue a conversation in the L2. However, they less frequently seek out opportunities to speak in the L2. Learners were highly invested in language learning as a symbolic action, showing a recognition of the need for empathy through cultural understanding. Many learners in this cohort are invested in language learning as an opportunity to gain knowledge, rather than practical ability or access to a particular community. Aligning with this investment, learners tended not to seek out L2-speaking communities of practice. Instead, the social strategies that learners employed facilitated largely receptive language use. Learners, such as Adam, sought out discourse in the L2 that allowed them to feel connected to the communities of practice with which they identified in the L1. Many learners discussed a lack of opportunities to speak. However, learners such as Louise were aware of other learners in their communities of practice who had the shared mutual interest in practising the L2. Nonetheless, most learners did not systematically attempt to shift the language of their communities of practice from English to L2. This can likely be attributed to learners' strong investment in social relationships being more powerful than their investment in making gains in their learning of the L2.

Research question 2

> What is the potential for the explicit instruction of social language learning strategies to influence learners' out-of-class activities and the use of the L2 in their communities of practice?

The results of a small-scale case study suggest that teaching social strategies has the potential to encourage students to see other L2 learners as learning resources. Questionnaire results show that the strategy sessions prompted learners to engage more frequently in naturalistic out-of-class language activities. This occurred in connection with informal homework tasks given to students, but these behaviours appeared to continue beyond those initial assignments. Additionally, learners who received strategy instruction agreed more strongly that they had developed social strategies throughout the semester. This indicates that at the very least the strategy teaching sessions have made learners more aware of these types of learning strategies and the ways in which they can contribute to their L2 learning. Strategy teaching can help learners to recognise language practices that they did not previously see as contributing to their language learning, and therefore to carry out these activities in a strategic and deliberate manner. Furthermore, it can help learners to recognise the language learning potentials in their pre-existing communities of practice. However, learners' social investment in a range of factors, as indicated by their desire to socialise versus their desire to learn, also plays a role in determining their use of the L2 within their communities of practice.

5. Conclusion and ways forward

This chapter has discussed the social strategies used to learn German by two classes of intermediate learners. It has considered the ways in which their social investment in factors such as a desire to gain conceptual knowledge, rather than specifically desiring to enter a particular German-speaking community of practice, influence the ways in which they engage with German outside of the classroom. Learners employ social strategies intuitively for social activities that they are invested in, which in the case of this learner group tends to be more focused on receptive use of the L2, such as through playing video games. They are reluctant to use strategies to go against the habitual behaviours of existing communities of practice in which they are socially invested, such as with other L2 learners, despite a shared desire to improve their L2 proficiencies. Teaching social strategies appears to have encouraged learners within this case study to engage more often in meaning-focused out-of-class learning. However, there were still potential learning situations that were not approached strategically, despite participation in strategy sessions. Future research is needed to investigate in greater detail the potential benefits of incorporating the teaching of social language learning strategies into the classroom. Additionally, future research could explore the effects of incorporating strategy-related learning into assessment to help to motivate learners to employ and reflect on their strategy use in a more directed way.

Acknowledgment

This chapter and the research behind it would not have been possible without the guidance and insight of my PhD thesis supervisor Professor John West-Sooby

References

Benson, P. (2019). Ways of seeing: The individual and the social in applied linguistics research methodologies. *Language Teaching, 52*(1), 60–70. doi.org/10.1017/S0261444817000234

Benson, P. & Reinders, H. (Eds). (2011). *Beyond the language classroom*. Palgrave Macmillan. doi.org/10.1057/9780230306790

Bernales, C. (2016). Towards a comprehensive concept of Willingness to Communicate: Learners' predicted and self-reported participation in the foreign language classroom. *System, 56*, 1–12. doi.org/10.1016/j.system.2015.11.002

Brosius, H., Haas, A. & Koschel, F. (2016). *Methoden der empirischen Kommunikationsforschung: Eine Einführung* (7th ed.). Springer. doi.org/10.1007/978-3-531-94214-8

Brown, H. D. (2007). *Teaching by principles: An interactive approach to language pedagogy* (3rd ed.). Addison Wesley.

Canagarajah, S. (2013). Negotiating translingual literacy: an enactment. *Research in the Teaching of English, 48*(1), 40–67.

Chamot, A. U. (2001). The role of learning strategies in second language acquisition. In M. P. Breen (Ed.), *Learner contributions to language learning: New directions in research* (pp. 25–43). Longman.

Chamot, A. U. (2007). Accelerating academic achievement of English language learners: A synthesis of five evaluations of the CALLA Model. In J. Cummins & C. Davidson (Eds), *The international handbook of English language learning* (Part I, pp. 317–31). Springer.

Chamot, A. U. (2009). *The CALLA handbook: Implementing the cognitive academic language learning approach* (2nd ed.). Pearson Education/Longman.

Chen, Y. (2007). Learning to learn: the impact of strategy training. *ELT Journal, 61*(1), 20–29. doi.org/10.1093/elt/ccl041

Cohen, A. D. (2014). *Strategies in learning and using a second language* (2nd ed.). Routledge. doi.org/10.4324/9781315833200

Cole, J. & Vanderplank, R. (2016). Comparing autonomous and class-based learners in Brazil: Evidence for the present-day advantages of informal, out-of-class learning. *System, 61*, 31–42.

Cotterall, S. & Reinders, H. (2004). *Learner strategies: A guide for teachers.* SEAMEO Regional Language Centre.

Council of Europe. (2019). *Common European Framework of Reference for Languages.* Council of Europe. Retrieved on 6 November 2019 from www.coe.int/en/web/common-european-framework-reference-languages

Creswell, J. (2003). *Research design: Qualitative, quantitative and a mixed method approach.* SAGE.

Deppermann, A. (2013). Editorial: Positioning in narrative interaction. *Narrative Inquiry, 23*(1), 1–15. doi.org/10.1075/NI.23.1.01DEP

Dörnyei, Z. (2003). *Questionnaires in second language research: Construction, administration and processing* (2nd ed.). Lawrence Erlbaum Associates.

Dörnyei, Z. (2007). *Research methods in applied linguistics: Quantitative, qualitative, and mixed methodologies.* Oxford University Press.

Eckert, P. & McConnell-Ginet, S. (1992). Think practically and look locally: Language and gender as community-based practice. *Annual Review of Anthropology, 21*(1), 461–88. doi.org/10.1146/annurev.an.21.100192.002333

De Fina, A. (2015). Afterword. In P. Deters, X. A. Gao, E. R. Miller & G. Vitanova (Eds), *Theorising and analysing agency in second language learning: Interdisciplinary approaches* (pp. 271–76). Multilingual Matters. doi.org/10.21832/9781783092901

Flick, U. (2011). *Triangulation: Eine Einführung.* VS-Verlag. doi.org/10.1007/978-3-531-92864-7

Gee, J. P. (1990). *Social linguistics and literacies: Ideology in discourses.* Falmer Press.

Georgakopoulou, A. (2007). Thinking big with small stories in narrative and identity analysis. In M. Bamberg (Ed.), *Narrative state of the art* (pp. 145–54). John Benjamins. doi.org/10.1075/bct.6.15geo

Guest, G., MacQueen, K. & Namey, E. (2012). *Applied thematic analysis*. SAGE. doi.org/10.4135/9781483384436

Gunning, P. & Oxford, R. L. (2014). Children's learning strategy use and the effects of strategy instruction on success in learning ESL in Canada. *System, 43*(1), 82–100. doi.org/10.1016/j.system.2013.12.012

Holliday, A. (1999). Small cultures. *Applied Linguistics, 20*(2), 237–64. doi.org/10.1093/applin/20.2.237

Huang, J. & Benson, P. (2013). Autonomy, agency and identity in foreign and second language education. *Chinese Journal of Applied Linguistics, 36*(1), 7–28. doi.org/10.1515/cjal-2013-0002

Joseph, J. E. (2016). Historical perspectives on language and identity. In S. Preece (Ed.), *The Routledge handbook of language and identity* (pp. 19–33). Routledge.

Kao, T. & Oxford, R. L. (2014). Learning language through music: A strategy for building inspiration and motivation. *System, 43*(1), 114–20. doi.org/10.1016/j.system.2014.01.003

Kayi-Aydar, H. (2014). Social positioning, participation, and second language learning: Talkative students in an academic ESL classroom. *TESOL Quarterly, 48*(4), 686–714. doi.org/10.1002/tesq.139

Kurata, N. (2010). Opportunities for foreign language learning and use within a learner's informal social networks. *Mind, Culture, and Activity, 17*(4), 382–96. doi.org/10.1080/10749030903402032

Lai, C. (2019). Technology and learner autonomy: An argument in favor of the nexus of formal and informal language learning. *Annual Review of Applied Linguistics, 39*(1), 52–58. doi.org/10.1017/S0267190519000035

Lai, C., Zhu, W. & Gong, G. (2015). Understanding the quality of out-of-class English learning. *TESOL Quarterly, 49*(2), 278–308. doi.org/10.1002/tesq.171

Lave, J. & Wenger, E. (1991). *Situated learning: Legitimate peripheral participation*. Cambridge University Press. doi.org/10.1017/CBO9780511815355

Lee, J. S. & Hsieh, J. C. (2019). Affective variables and willingness to communicate of EFL learners in in-class, out-of-class, and digital contexts. *System, 82*(1), 63–73. doi.org/10.1016/j.system.2019.03.002

Lee, K. R. & Oxford, R. L. (2008). Understanding EFL learners' strategy use and strategy awareness. *Asian EFL Journal, 10*(1), 7–32. www.asian-efl-journal.com/March_2008_EBook.pdf

van Lier, L. (2004). *The ecology and semiotics of language learning: A sociocultural perspective*. Kluwer Academic Publishers. doi.org/10.1007/1-4020-7912-5

van Lier, L. (2007). Action-based teaching, autonomy and identity. *Innovation in Language Learning and Teaching, 1*(1), 46–65. doi.org/10.2167/illt42.0

van Lier, L. (2011). Green grammar: Ways of languaging. *Taiwan Journal of TESOL, 8*(2), 1–21. www.tjtesol.org/attachments/article/374/1.pdf

Nakatani, Y. (2005). The effects of awareness-raising training on oral communication strategy use. *Modern Language Journal, 89*(1), 76–91. doi.org/10.1111/j.0026-7902.2005.00266.x

Norton, B. (2000). *Identity and language learning: Gender, ethnicity and educational change*. Pearson Education.

Norton, B. (2013). *Identity and language learning: Extending the conversation* (2nd ed.). Multilingual Matters. doi.org/10.21832/9781783090563

Norton Peirce, B. (1995). Social identity, investment, and language learning. *TESOL Quarterly, 29*(1), 9–31. doi.org/10.2307/3587803

O'Malley, J. M. & Chamot, A. U. (1990). *Learning strategies in second language acquisition*. Cambridge University Press. doi.org/10.1017/CBO9781139524490

Oxford, R. L. (1990). *Language learning strategies: What every teacher should know*. Heinle & Heinle.

Oxford, R. L. (2008). Hero with a thousand faces: Learner autonomy, learning strategies and learning tactics in independent language learning. In S. Hurd & T. Lewis (Eds), *Language learning strategies in independent settings* (pp. 41–63). Multilingual Matters. doi.org/10.21832/9781847690999-005

Oxford, R. L. (2017). *Teaching and researching language learning strategies: Self-regulation in context* (2nd ed.). Routledge. doi.org/10.4324/9781315719146

Preece, S. (2016). An identity transformation? Social class, language prejudice and the erasure of multilingual capital in higher education. In S. Preece (Ed.), *The Routledge handbook of language and identity* (pp. 366–81). Routledge. discovery.ucl.ac.uk/id/eprint/1476135/3/Preece_Chapter%2023_RHLI_final.pdf

Schmidt, G. (2014). Personal growth as a strong element in the motivation of Australian university students to learn German. *Australian Review of Applied Linguistics, 37*(2), 145–60. doi.org/10.1075/aral.37.2.04sch

Sockett, G. (2014). *The online informal learning of English*. Palgrave Macmillan. doi.org/10.1057/9781137414885

Wenger, E. (1998). *Communities of practice: Learning, meaning, and identity*. Cambridge University Press.

White, C. (2008). Language learning strategies in independent language learning: An overview. In S. Hurd & T. Lewis (Eds), *Language learning strategies in independent settings* (pp. 3–24). Multilingual Matters. doi.org/10.21832/9781847690999-003

Yoshida, R. (2013). Learners' self-concept and use of the target language in foreign language classrooms. *System, 41*(4), 935–51. doi.org/10.1016/j.system.2013.09.003

Part 3: Intercultural language teaching

8

Humanising translator and interpreter ethics for critical language users: A case of what the impartial model can learn from the 'empathetic' model

Maho Fukuno

Abstract

Translation and interpreting (T & I) is a social practice with various ethical implications. As the themes of translation, interpreting and intercultural communication become more prominent in Australian language and professional training, it becomes all the more important to address issues identified in T & I ethics training, including by taking a deontologist approach *un*critical of the rules and the apparent lack of relevance of ethics as part of a language program. This chapter asks how training on T & I ethics can be made more relevant and meaningful for all students, not only as T & I trainees but also more broadly as 'independent, proactive and critical users of languages' (Nakane & Hayes, 2021, p. 11). To start answering this question, I apply an ethical pluralism approach (Taylor, 2002) to the case of two distinctive role images of the interpreter: the impartial role image in Australia and the 'empathetic' role image in Japan. By elucidating some of the moral values and norms underpinning these contrasting role images, I demonstrate that recognising the cultural differences in interpreter ethics provides us with a space to (self-)reflect from an intercultural and pluralist perspective on normalised values and expectations, which leads to a more humanising translator and interpreter ethics and practice. I conclude that the T & I ethics class can create a low-risk environment for T & I students and critical language users to dialogically and self-reflectively engage in ethical heteroglossia and habituate the process of moral cultivation, which nurtures crucial competencies for global citizens.

Keywords: interpreters, translators, ethics, ethical pluralism, training, critical language users, empathy, Japan

1. Introduction

Translators and interpreters play a significant role in communications between people who belong to different linguistic and cultural communities and, therefore, in the exchange of knowledge and cultures. Yet translation and interpreting (T & I) is not practised in a social and cultural vacuum. The practice of T & I is always performed within certain sociocultural values and norms, and the norms of the T & I field are embedded in the values and norms that surround it. This means that some of the norms of T & I practice in one society may differ from those of T & I practice in another society, with each society possessing a somehow distinctive T & I culture.

Therefore, comparing T & I norms in differing cultures can provide us with new insights that allow us to reflect on our own familiar T & I norms and practices, no matter which culture(s) each of us is familiar with. This self-reflective practice can be useful not only in addressing practical issues present in the T & I field but also in cultivating our intercultural and ethical competencies in the university classroom as well as in professional training. Thus, training and dialogue on translator and interpreter ethics can be made more relevant and meaningful for a broad cohort of students, including those in the disciplines of languages and intercultural communication beyond T & I trainees. To explore this potentiality, I will apply an ethical pluralism approach to a comparative case study of interpreting culture in Australia and Japan, specifically in the fields of community interpreting in Australia and consultation interpreting in Japan. The case study focuses on interpreters' ethical roles; however, the approach to ethical reflection drawn from the case is intended to be applicable to both translation and interpreting.

I will first provide a background of T & I courses in Australian universities, raise issues of T & I ethics training and define the ethical pluralism approach applied in this study. I will then present a comparative case of ethical role images of the interpreter, specifically in the fields of community interpreting in Australia and consultation interpreting in Japan. After identifying the moral values and norms underpinning the different role images, I will apply an ethical pluralism approach to this comparative case study and argue that learning and examining new values and ideas from an intercultural perspective not only improves interpreter practice in a particular T & I field but also helps critical language users self-cultivate their own moral values and characters. Finally, I conclude by suggesting that the T & I ethics class should be harnessed as a safe environment for all of us to explore humanising translator and interpreter ethics and grow as global citizens.

2. Background

2.1. T & I course in Australian universities

T & I courses can be classified into two types that, in some cases, intertwine in students' study paths and program structures. The first type is those courses offered as part of a specialised T & I degree program for the purpose of professional training. In Australia, 12 universities[1] offer programs, such as master's degrees, graduate diplomas, diplomas and certificates in translation and interpreting, endorsed by the T & I certification body, the National Accreditation Authority for Translators and Interpreters (NAATI), as pre-requisites for NAATI certification testing for professional qualifications.

The second type comprises T & I courses offered as advanced or upper-advanced level language courses. For example, of the 43 universities in Australia, 22 offer Japanese language courses at advanced or upper-advanced

---

1   As of December 2021, the following universities offer NAATI-endorsed T & I programs: Macquarie University, Monash University, RMIT University, The Australian National University, the University of Melbourne, the University of New South Wales, the University of Queensland, the University of Sydney, the University of Adelaide, the University of Newcastle, the University of Western Australia and Western Sydney University. www.naati.com.au/services/endorsed-qualification/endorsed-qualification-institutions/.

levels.[2] Of these 22 universities, five of the Group of Eight universities[3] offer translation and/or interpreting courses, including the Japanese–English language pairing, as advanced or upper-advanced language courses (Table 8.1).

Table 8.1 List of T & I courses offered as an extension of language courses

University	Course title
The Australian National University	Japanese–English Translation
Monash University	Translating across Cultures
University of Melbourne	Japanese through Translation
University of Queensland	Japanese/English Interpreting and Translation
University of Sydney	Syntax and Translation

Source: Nakane & Hayes (2021, Appendix 2).

It can be anticipated that both types of T & I courses will become more relevant in Australian higher education and language learning for the following reasons. First, the intended learning outcomes of T & I courses support the aim of twenty-first-century higher education, in and beyond Australia—namely, educating global citizens (Oliver & de St Jorre, 2018). In view of the fact that T & I courses require the development of a high level of linguistic skills as well as critical perspectives and sensibilities in regard to diverse languages, people, cultures and societies, T & I courses are a suitable interdisciplinary field for nurturing the critical, analytic, reflective, communicative and intercultural competencies desired of global citizens. T & I courses, as well as language courses as the foundation of T & I, can contribute to this aim as a means for individuals as global citizens to communicate with one another, broaden and cultivate their perspectives and ethically engage with communities, cultures and nations. With the emphasis on global citizenship in language education, the traditional

---

2   Nakane and Hayes (2021, Appendix 1) list 19 Australian universities offering advanced or upper-advanced Japanese courses. Additionally, the university websites indicate that, as of 2021, the following three universities offer Japanese language courses at advanced level: Murdoch University (as in-country courses; www.murdoch.edu.au/study/courses/undergraduate/mj-jpna), University of Newcastle (www.newcastle.edu.au/degrees/bachelor-of-arts/handbook) and University of New England (www.une.edu.au/study/units/japanese-through-contemporary-culture-japn522).
3   The Group of Eight is a group of the following eight leading research-intensive universities in Australia: the University of Melbourne, The Australian National University, the University of Sydney, the University of Queensland, the University of Western Australia, the University of Adelaide, Monash University and the University of New South Wales (Group of Eight Australia, n.d.).

notion of 'language learners' juxtaposed with the 'native speaker' status is reconceptualised as 'independent, proactive and critical users' of language(s) (hereafter, critical language users) (Nakane & Hayes, 2021, p. 11).

Additionally, the attributes associated with global citizenship, such as engaging and collaborating with people from various cultural backgrounds, are desired by employers in Australia (Oliver & de St Jorre, 2018). This means that cultivating these attributes, especially through learning languages, intercultural communication, translation and interpreting, can lead to enhanced employability, which is the current target of the Australian government's higher education reforms (Department of Education, Skills and Employment, 2021). A further justification for offering T & I courses can be found in a strategy that advanced language courses apply to sustain the numbers of their enrolments—namely, by building a project-based course that accommodates multiple languages or students at a wider range of proficiency levels in the same course (Nakane & Hayes, 2021).

2.2. Ethics in T & I courses: Importance, issues and a question

The topic of ethics and code(s) of ethics is an integral part of the professionalisation of the T & I field and therefore an essential part of T & I training (Hale, 2007). Professional ethics and a code of ethics are particularly important for community-based translation and interpreting. Whether it is practised in a health, legal, education or public service domain, community translation and interpreting has direct implications for securing the human rights of the members of multicultural communities (Hale, 2007; Taibi & Ozolins, 2016), including communities in Australia and Japan, with different contents and implementations of multicultural policies. Therefore, it is critical that anyone who may work as a translator or interpreter in a multicultural society is aware of the ethical implications of their practice and has undertaken training in T & I ethics. In the Australian case, all NAATI-endorsed programs (the first type of T & I courses) are therefore required to include a class or course on T & I ethics and the code of ethics maintained by the T & I professional body, the Australian Institute of Interpreters and Translators (AUSIT, 2012). Furthermore, ethical sensitivity and thinking constitute an attribute that is not only desirable in professional translators and interpreters but also in critical language users who are able to engage ethically and constructively with global and local communities (Oliver &

de St Jorre, 2018). Therefore, T & I ethics training can form an important part of T & I professional training as well as of T & I courses offered as an extension of language studies (the second type of T & I courses).

However, previous studies identified several issues with T & I ethics training, which can be relevant in cases occurring in the Australian field of T & I ethics and university training. First, the approach to professional ethics is often reduced to a deontologist approach that views a code of ethics and its principles simply as rules to follow and overlooks the fact that applications of the code of ethics always require individual interpretation and judgement in specific intercultural situations (Drugan & Megone, 2011; Donovan, 2011; Martín Ruano, 2015; Lambert, 2018). As in critiques of Kant's categorical imperatives, it must be pointed out that ethical principles are inevitably the reflection of moral values and norms in specific cultures and societies (MacIntyre, 1981/2007; Martín Ruano, 2015).

In Australia, this issue is highly visible in the professional field of T & I training because of the mandatory inclusion of a professional ethics topic in NAATI-endorsed training. Some specialised T & I degree programs offer courses that adopt more analytic and critical approaches to T & I, such as the comparative analysis of various international codes of ethics (Monash University, 2021) or the evaluation of adherence to professional ethics in textual products of translation (University of Melbourne, 2021). However, the rules-focused discourse is exemplified by dilemma-triggering expressions, such as '[a]s an interpreter, I need to be impartial and accurate' and 'make sure you are familiar with the AUSIT Code of Ethics, which all NAATI interpreters are bound by' (Zhao, 2019). One of the primary objectives of Australian T & I training is to provide students with practical training suitable for passing NAATI certification test(s) (e.g. the Graduate Diploma in Translation offered by Western Sydney University). Therefore, the rules-focused approach and the lack of intercultural considerations in ethical thinking seem to stem from the epistemological norms set by the national certification system (NAATI), where ethical knowledge and understanding are categorised as an independent competency tested separately from intercultural competency (NAATI, 2019a; 2019b). Moreover, the AUSIT Code of Ethics (2012), knowledge of which is tested by NAATI or studied for as a pre-requisite for NAATI testing, is presented as a list of ethical principles. Therefore, those principles, although the term 'values' is used twice in the preamble (AUSIT, 2012, p. 4), seem to be commonly interpreted as rules to follow.

Second, when T & I ethics are viewed as a set of rules promulgated for the professional field (Drugan & Megone, 2011), it may seem less relevant to students who are taking T & I courses as part of their language program. This may be reflected in the fact that out of the courses listed in Table 8.1, only one T & I course offered by the University of Sydney mentions ethics in the course overviews (University of Sydney, 2021, Appendix A). A key element described in the overviews are the issues that arise from cultural and linguistic differences between English and Japanese. The Japanese through Translation course offered by the University of Melbourne lists intended learning outcomes that may include ethical thinking in T & I practice, such as '[c]ritically reflect on their own translation and interpretation practice between Japanese and English' and '[c]ritically reflect on and evaluate intercultural understanding in relation to translation and interpreting' (University of Melbourne, 2022, Appendix A). The course description of Japanese/English Interpreting and Translation offered by the University of Queensland refers to 'some professional aspects of the practice' which may also include ethical issues and considerations in T & I practice (University of Queensland, 2021, Appendix A). However, a specific focus on T & I ethics is absent from these courses that are structured as part of language programs. What, then, is the relevance of engaging with a professional code of ethics if I do not become a community translator or interpreter?

These issues lead to the following question that I aim to explore: How can training on ethics be made more relevant and meaningful for both T & I students and critical language users?

2.3. Ethical pluralism approach

I explore the possibility of a pluralist perspective on ethics that can provide a framework for thinking about diversity and heteroglossia in ethical thinking. The ethical pluralism approach proposed by Charles C. Taylor (2002) considers that the differences between two parties, societies or cultures enrich each other and help the parties' self-reflection, understanding and criticism, which leads to a fuller realisation of the self and of society. Taylor (2002, p. 191) proposed his approach of ethical pluralism based on the conviction that 'people can also bond not in spite of but because of difference'. Taylor's approach (2002) is heavily influenced by philosophers such as Herder, Durkheim, von Humboldt and Gadamar, who argued that humanity flourishes not in individual persons but in the communion of all human beings. In this view of humanity, the attempt to understand the other in an authentic way brings about an interest for each member of society as it leads them to a 'fusion of horizon' (Taylor, 2002, p. 192, drawing on Gadamer's term). At the fusion of horizon, we can then realise that *our* way of living and *their* way of living are, equally, two of many possible ways of living in the world, which leads to a self-understanding and constructive criticism of one's own way of living. In this way, 'the difference defines a complementarity' for humanity to flourish (Taylor, 2002, p. 191). It is because of differences that we can learn from each other's knowledge, capacity and practice and unite to realise a fuller potential of humanity.

Mutual enrichment can be achieved not from simply obtaining knowledge of differences but from the 'exchange and communion' between the parties together with self-reflection and examination (Taylor, 2002, p. 191). In this light, T & I students and critical language users are situated in an optimal position of interculturality. It is generally desired that advanced language users, including translators and interpreters, possess the intercultural knowledge and competency necessary to communicate freely at semantic and pragmatic levels as appropriate for various communicative situations. Therefore, they possess not only opportunities for ongoing learning, reflection and practice in and outside the classroom but also linguistic and cultural knowledge, experience and resources in multiple cultures with which to dialogise and reflect on moral values from a pluralist perspective. It is also through this intermediary position that translators can carry out the core of their professional purpose—namely, fostering cooperation between cultures (Pym, 2012). Thus, T & I courses dealing with the topic of ethics can provide a suitable space for students and teachers to reflect together on diverse moral and cultural value systems from a pluralist standpoint, learn from differences, and enrich their ethical judgement and sensibility from a space of cultural in-between.

The following section compares ethical role images of the interpreter in Australian community interpreting and Japanese consultation interpreting, and examines their cultural underpinnings. It then explores how an ethical pluralism approach to this type of cultural diversity in interpreter ethics can create a space for critical language users to cultivate dialogic perspectives on cultural and moral values in intercultural contexts and foster an ethically heteroglossic society.

3. Ethical discourses on the interpreter's role: A comparative case study

3.1. The impartial role image

In Australia, there seems to be a unified role image of the interpreter throughout the profession: that of the impartial interpreter who can accurately and fluently interpret a message from one language into another. Venuti (1995, p. 1) used the term 'invisibility' to highlight the dominant expectation placed on translators in Anglo cultures to produce a fluent translation that reads as if it was the original, and critiqued it as 'conceal[ing] the number of conditions under which the translation is made, starting with the translator's crucial intervention'. The interpreter in Australia is not free from this expectation. The discourse of invisibility sometimes even seems to suggest the ideal goal for the interpreter is to render the message between parties who do not share the same language so smoothly that they can communicate as if they shared the same language. This discourse is characterised by metaphors used to depict the role of the interpreter such as 'tube', 'conduit', 'channel', 'machine', 'telephone', 'window', 'bridge' and even 'bilingual ghost' (Hale 2007). Professional detachment from any parties involved in the interpreting context is thus considered an ideal moral quality of the interpreter (AUSIT, 2012, p. 9).

This role image focusing on impartiality and invisibility seems to be prevalent across different domains of interpreting, including conference, legal and community, and to be inscribed in a range of professional codes of ethics for interpreters around the world, including Australia (Hale, 2007; Angelelli, 2004; Lambert, 2018). The image is maintained and reproduced in the professional discourse as professional associations, training programs and certification organisations reference the impartiality principle inscribed in the codes of ethics with the purpose of prescribing what the interpreter's role should be. In the Australian case, it is enforced by the central code of ethics maintained by AUSIT.[4] The AUSIT Code of Ethics (2012, pp. 5–6) crystallises the impartial and invisible role image of interpreters and translators under the principles of impartiality and clarity of role boundaries:

---

[4] However, it must be noted that recent years have seen the development of health interpreter guidelines in Australia, which envisage a somewhat expanded role for the interpreter compared with the impartiality tradition. As examples, see Hlavac (2017), Australian Psychological Society (2013) and Migrant and Refugee Women's Health Partnership (2019).

> 4. IMPARTIALITY Interpreters and translators observe impartiality in all professional contacts. Interpreters remain unbiased throughout the communication exchanged between the participants in any interpreted encounter. Translators do not show bias towards either the author of the source text or the intended readers of their translation.
>
> 6. CLARITY OF ROLE BOUNDARIES Interpreters and translators maintain clear boundaries between their task as facilitators of communication through message transfer and any tasks that may be undertaken by other parties involved in the assignment.

This role image prevails despite numerous studies showing interpreters playing a co-participatory, active and visible role with the agency in the interpreted interaction (e.g. Iida, 2012; Wadensjö, 1995) and critiquing an overly simplistic view of impartiality and neutrality in the interpreter's practice (Lambert, 2018; McDonough-Dolmaya, 2011; Donovan, 2011; Maltby, 2010; Martín Ruano, 2015). The impartial role image can also put interpreters in ethically challenging situations where they are torn between their ethical, impartial role image and the expectations of their clients, who may expect, or who the interpreters think may benefit from, more emotional and empathetic support from them (Hale, 2007; Zhao, 2019).

3.2. The 'empathetic' role image

While the neutral and invisible interpreter image is widely shared in various parts of the world, including Australia, to the extent that Angelelli (2004, p. 13) refers to it as a 'professional ideology', a new model of interpreting called 'consultation interpreting' has emerged in Japan. The tasks and roles expected of a consultation interpreter are distinctively different from those associated with the interpreter role image prevalent in Australia. The differences between the roles expected of interpreters in Australia and those of consultation interpreters in Japan, outlined in this section, are analogous to the differences in the European Union (EU) between the roles of interpreters and those of intercultural mediators. Compared with the roles of interpreters as a registered profession in the EU, the roles of intercultural mediators are less clearly defined; however, the latter are differentiated from the former as entailing a 'more enriched means of communicating messages', beyond the accurate and complete meaning transfer between parties, to bridge between cultures in a form of facilitating communication, assisting in the resolution of conflicts or mediating to transform society for new intercultural relations (Theodosiou & Aspioti, 2015, p. 16). For ease of understanding, this section on consultation interpreting will draw on some comparisons with the EU's intercultural mediation.

While it can be said in the European context that interpreters and intercultural mediators are two distinctive roles for interpersonal communication between migrants and public service providers, (Theodosiou & Aspioti, 2015), consultation interpreting in Japan was developed as a subdomain of community interpreting developed by Tokyo University of Foreign Studies beginning in 2006. Commissioned by the Ministry of Education, Culture, Sports, Science and Technology (MEXT), the project identified issues and needs related to rapidly progressing multilingualism and multiculturalism in Japan,[5] and established the framework of professionals needed in Japanese society and the training mechanism for those professionals through research, education and social collaboration. One of the key professionals identified by the project was the 'consultation interpreter', who interprets for cases where linguistic and cultural minorities seek consultation with experts (Sugisawa et al., 2015, p. 187).

As the number of residents in Japan who do not have sufficient command of Japanese, the mainstream language, has increased, the administrative need to respond to diverse concerns and issues faced by residents has also increased. To address those concerns and issues, governments have organised professional expert consultation sessions. One type of session where consultation interpreters work is the 'relay expert consultation session'. A relay consultation session has professional experts in a range of domains ready to meet and help consultation clients. These experts include lawyers, solicitors, clinical psychologists, counsellors, social insurance consultants, tax accountants and labour counsellors. A client can see multiple experts as needed during one session. The relay expert consultation session was established on the basis of the understanding that the issues faced by non-Japanese residents can be so complex and multifaceted that one expert in one domain cannot fully assist them.

The common process by which a relay expert consultation session operates is as follows. When a client arrives at the venue, a consultation interpreter first conducts a short hearing session with the consultation client to identify

---

5   The number of non-Japanese citizenship holders in Japan increased by 44 per cent from 2,033,656 to 2,933,137 between December 2012 and December 2019, with a decrease to 2,887,116 in December 2020 (Immigration Services Agency of Japan, 2021).

their core issues. Based on the hearing sheet summarised by the interpreter, a matching coordinator identifies a list of appropriate experts, and the client and the interpreter meet with each of these experts. The fundamental purpose of a consultation interpreter is to resolve the client's issues in cooperation with other experts, as epitomised in the following aspects of the code of ethics for consultation interpreters (Sugisawa et al., 2015).

From the outset, the statement in the preamble and article 1 foregrounds that the aim of a consultation interpreter is to resolve the issues faced by the linguistic-cultural minority client and actively help improve their life.

> Preamble
>
> We, community interpreters, aim, at all sites of expert consultation sessions and foreign language consultation service desks, to read into and understand fundamental issues faced by linguistic-cultural minorities and to resolve those challenges in collaboration with other experts beyond the interpreting act between languages.
>
> Definition of consultation interpreting
>
> Consultation interpreting is a profession that plays a 'bridging role' that supports linguistic-cultural minorities through the means of interpreting and translating and links the minorities to the host society in the legal, administration, education and health domains specialised by community interpreting. (Sugisawa et al., 2015, p. 184 [chapter author translation from Japanese])

The aim of resolving the client's issues shows a similarity to one of the three types[6] of intercultural mediation—namely, assisting in the resolution of conflicts between migrants and public service providers (Theodosiou & Aspioti, 2015, drawing on Cohen-Emerique's theory of intercultural mediator for immigrants). However, a significant difference to be noted is that consultation interpreters' interventions are not framed as a conflict resolution between the migrant and the public service provider. Consultation interpreters serve, rather, as part of a supporting team with other professionals and service providers, to assist in resolving the migrant client's issues.

---

6   The other two types of intercultural mediation presented by Theodosiou & Aspioti (2015) are the mediation through facilitating communication and understanding between people of different cultures, as ensuring the prevention of conflicts, and the mediation through transforming social rules, based on the new intercultural relations that emerged in society.

Second, under the principle of technical skills, the consultation interpreter is expected to be an empathetic listener to the consultation client.

> 2-2 Technical skills
>
> The consultation interpreter conducts a hearing appropriately with the cardinal 'hearing' skills which consist of a skill of 'taking in' the information accurately, a skill of empathetic 'listening', and a skill of 'enquiring' to understand the problem by asking questions. (Sugisawa et al., 2015, p. 184 [chapter author translation from Japanese])

These skills are considered particularly important when the interpreter conducts the initial hearing session with the consultation client, because their role is to listen accurately and empathetically and to inquire, understand, unpack and analyse the full extent of the issues that the client faces (Sugisawa et al., 2015). Although the framing of conflicts differs between the two contexts, as discussed above, the importance of the hearing session is also identified in the EU's intercultural mediation, particularly for the purpose of building a shared understanding of the problem through the 'stories' of the migrant client and the public service provider (Theodosiou & Aspioti, 2015). However, in the case of consultation interpreting, because of the client-centred relationships between the consultation interpreter and other professional(s), the focus of the hearing session is on hearing the client's story and account. As also clarified in the preamble, these normalised tasks in consultation interpreting go beyond meaning transfer between languages.

Third, consultation interpreters are visible in the interpreted interaction. They are required, in respect of the principle of technical skills, to advise the expert when they judge that the expert's utterance cannot be sufficiently understood by the consultation client or that the client's utterance may possibly be misunderstood by the expert due to linguistic-cultural differences. Additionally, the principle of attitudes and manners requires the interpreter to play an active role in realising equal communication between the expert and consultation client by considering their different social statuses and positions. These interventions by the interpreter make the interpreter's presence clearly visible, in contrast with the professional ideology of an invisible interpreter.

2-2 Technical skills

...

- When the consultation interpreter judges from their standpoint that the utterance of the expert cannot be sufficiently understood by the consultation client, the interpreter explains the situation to the expert.

- When the consultation interpreter judges that the utterance of the consultation client can be misunderstood because of linguistic and cultural differences, the interpreter appropriately informs the expert of that and facilitates the communication.

2-3 Attitude/manner

... (The consultation interpreter) ensures equal communication is achieved by taking into account the differences of [social] positions between the parties involved. (Sugisawa et al., 2015, p. 184 [chapter author translation from Japanese])

A similar level of mediators' visibility can also be found in the EU's intercultural mediation, especially for the purpose of conflict resolution. The intercultural mediator, as the third party, is to create a new narrative shared between 'us', constituted by the migrant client and public service provider, to help both parties come up with solutions together (Theodosiou & Aspioti, 2015). In this process, the intercultural mediator is visible and expected to balance out the two parties' interests and objectives by means of empowerment, for which they need to deliberately balance out the relation between these parties. These works of active mediation differentiate intercultural mediators' roles, similarly to consultation interpreters', from those of invisible interpreters.

As reflected in these aspects of the code of ethics and similarities, and differences, with the EU's intercultural mediators, the resultant role image of a consultation interpreter is empathetic, advocative, proactive and visible. The role image and purpose of a consultation interpreter are thus in striking contrast with the ethical role image of the interpreter prevalent in Australia, which focuses on meaning transfer from an impartial standpoint, maintaining clear boundaries between the role of the interpreter and the roles of any of the other parties involved in the interpreting context. The Australian code further states that interpreters must maintain the emotions of the speakers in their interpreting without softening or enhancing the force of the message or language (AUSIT, 2012). However, interpreters are not expected to exercise their own emotions and empathy. Rather, the impartial role image prohibits the interpreter's bias, whether positive or negative, from affecting the interpreting practice. Therefore, in the Australian field, the interpreter's emotion and empathy can be considered unnecessary or even disturbing for ethical interpreting practice. Does this contrast then mean that one of these role images is morally wrong or unethical because it is not consistent with the counterpart's code of ethics? What factors underlie this contrast?

3.3. Cultural values and norms behind the impartial and 'empathetic' models

As mentioned in the introduction, interpreter practice and ethics do not exist in a sociocultural vacuum but are embedded in a broader social, cultural and political system. Therefore, an interpreter's ethics and role image can be viewed as a window into a system of social, cultural and political values and norms where the interpreter is situated. As the main aim of this chapter is to explore how a T & I ethics class can be made more relevant and meaningful for all critical language users, including T & I students, I focus on an example of moral values and an example of norms of social interaction as cultural factors[7] that underpin some of the differences between the 'empathetic' model in Japan and the impartial model in the predominantly Anglo field of Australian interpreting.

3.3.1. Moral value of *omoiyari* and empathy

'Culture' itself is a concept that has been developed and used in Western historical contexts for various purposes from the construction of national and social identities to the justifications for racism and colonialism (Riley, 2007). The definitions of the term in and beyond the Western tradition are, therefore, far from being unified and universal and its uses are pervasive not only in academia but also in social contexts involving groups sharing specific characteristics. One use of the term 'culture' is exemplified in the official English title of the Ministry of Education, Culture, Sports, Science and Technology (MEXT) of the Japanese government. The definition of culture by MEXT seems to centre on the idea of being inherited through

---

7   Among other underlying factors, for a cross-cultural comparison of approaches to moral standards, rules and regulations between the Chinese and Western (Australian and US) traditions, see Feng (2014); for a comparison between Australia and Japan of configurations and institutional contexts of T & I codes of ethics, see Fukuno (2020).

generations in Japan, embodied as heritage, such as arts and properties, and as practice, including language (Agency for Cultural Affairs, Government of Japan, n.d.). Simultaneously, culture can also be seen as a 'defining epistemological structure' of social anthropology and an essential concept to understanding the questions arising in humanities and social sciences (Riley, 2007, p. 21), including the fields of translation studies, linguistics and psychology. Situated in this epistemological tradition of 'culture', this study aims to elucidate cultural factors that may underlie the above-mentioned role images of interpreters. Thus, I find particularly relevant the definition of culture that Lawley et al. (2019) gave in their study on cross-cultural comparisons of emotional responses to support provision. Lawley et al. (2019, p. 2) defined culture as 'the system of meaning, folk beliefs, values, practices and customs' shared by a group of people; therefore, people in a culture form their own sets of values and value-based practices. With this in view, I argue that the emergence of the 'empathetic' model of interpreting in Japan reflects the distinct characteristics of a moral value of *omoiyari* in Japanese society, often glossed as 'empathy' in English.

Omoiyari can be defined as 'a kind of "intuitive" understanding of the unexpressed feelings, desires and thoughts of others, and doing something for them on the basis of this understanding' (Travis, 1998, p. 55). Travis (1992, cited in Travis, 1998), in a study of what constitutes 'a good person' in Japanese and Anglo-Australian societies, demonstrated that *omoiyari* is a core moral value in Japanese society. In Travis's study, *omoiyari* was the third most commonly ascribed term while 'empathetic' was not mentioned at all by Anglo-Australian respondents. Lebra (1976, p. 38) also maintained: 'For the Japanese, empathy (*omoiyari*) ranks high among the virtues considered indispensable for one to be really human, morally mature, and deserving of respect. I am even tempted to call Japanese an "*omoiyari* culture"'. These studies illustrate the significant importance of *omoiyari* as a value in Japanese society, in contrast with the importance placed on empathy in Anglo-Australian culture. As a core cultural value, *omoiyari* is often researched in relation to child and youth psychological development and training. For example, Koshiba et al. (2018) conducted a survey in 2017 which asked high school and university students in Japan how important they consider a range of virtues to be and to what level they think they have attained those virtues. The survey responses showed that *omoiyari* was ranked top in terms of both its importance and the participants' current level of attainment.

As mentioned above, *omoiyari* is commonly translated as 'empathy' in English, but there are distinct differences between their semantic components. For Travis (1998), the semantics of *omoiyari* are characterised by two main components: 1) One interprets and understands the unverbalised feelings, wants and thoughts of others through one's own intuition and 2) one actually does things for others based on this intuitive understanding. On the other hand, 'empathy' in English is represented by Travis (1998) as 1) one's ability to understand the way another person feels as a result of their bad experience and 2) putting oneself in that person's shoes and imagining how one would feel in the same situation.

The semantic descriptions highlight two main differences between the two values. First, *omoiyari* expects one to understand the other's unverbalised feelings and thoughts, while empathy does not have that specification. Second, with *omoiyari*, one is expected to act for the other based on intuitive understanding, while the focus of empathy is on understanding and imagining the other's feelings rather than acting in response to those feelings. These differences between *omoiyari* and empathy are argued in terms of communicative and interactional norms (Travis, 1998). In Japanese culture, indirect and intuitive communication is more normative, as opposed to the Anglo norm which values the explicit expression of one's own feelings and needs. Therefore, in Japan, understanding others' unsaid feelings, wants and needs through one's own intuition and acting for them without being asked are normative and considered an ideal form of interaction. In contrast, in Anglo society, the best way to understand another's feelings and needs is considered to be through the person's direct expressions; allowing the person their autonomy and their right to make decisions is more highly valued than acting for others.

I argue that this moral value of *omoiyari* makes the empathetic, advocative and proactive role image of a consultation interpreter rather desirable for ethical practice. The practice of a consultation interpreter, for example, reading between the lines of the consultation client's explanations, unpacking their problems and aiming to resolve their issues with the other experts, accords well with the core value of *omoiyari*. So does the interpreter's practice of advising the interlocutors of possible communication risk factors based on their own judgement, while the advice and explanations may be in turn crucial for the interpreter's *omoiyari*-based practice to be understood and accepted by the interlocutors. With the value of *omoiyari*, understanding each other's unsaid feelings, desires and needs and acting for others and having others act for oneself are perceived as a 'demonstration of mutual understanding of each other's feelings and desires, and thus [heighten] both one's sense of belonging to, and the closeness of, the group' (Travis, 1998, p. 69). Therefore, in light of the value of *omoiyari*, the 'empathetic' role image of a consultation interpreter is ethical. It is in turn a reasonable assumption that in Anglo society, where individual differences and autonomy are highly valued (Travis, 1998), what the consultation interpreter offers may be considered exceptional interventions, stepping outside of the interpreter's ethical role.

Hence, reflecting on the 'empathetic' role image of a consultation interpreter and their practice in contrast with the impartial and invisible role image of the interpreter (and the translator) in Australia provides critical language users with the space to think about differences in moral values between societies, which may cause them miscommunication challenges or ethical dilemmas. This is a valuable pedagogical opportunity for any intercultural communication beyond T & I contexts. These differences illustrated in the cases of *omoiyari* in Japan and 'empathy' in Anglo society subsequently led to the considerations of collectivistic and individualistic cultural schemata (Uchida & Kitayama, 2001). Considering that a key function of consultation interpreting is for the interpreter and other professionals to support the client, I now turn to differences in the perceptions of providing and receiving social support in collectivistic and individualistic cultures.

3.3.2. Collectivistic and individualistic perceptions of providing and receiving social support

Social support is defined as 'the perception or experience that one is loved and cared for, esteemed and valued, and part of a social network of mutual assistance and obligations' (Mojaverian & Kim, 2013, p. 88). The interpreter, client and expert(s) involved in an interpreting context are usually not in personally close relationships. However, the clients in many community interpreting contexts tend to have some kind of problem(s) they wish to resolve through the interpreted interactions and, therefore, are exposed to stressors. They are also often unable to, or prefer not to, seek support from close others in their social network, which is why they come to the interpreted session. Additionally, being unable to fully understand necessary information given in the mainstream language can detrimentally increase the level of stress and sense of helplessness and isolation they feel. Under these circumstances, what the interpreted session can provide is the feeling that one is cared for, is valued, and belongs to society—that is, social support.

Previous studies on cultural psychology show how emotional responses to the receipt and provision of different types of social support vary between individualistic, independent cultures (focusing on Europe), and collectivistic, interdependent cultures (focusing on East Asia) (e.g. Mojaverian & Kim, 2013; Lawley et al., 2019; Taylor et al., 2007; Kim et al., 2006). They also add to their analyses types of social support as variables (solicited vs. unsolicited, implicit vs. explicit, problem- or emotion-focused). Among various taxonomies of social support, the most relevant type of support for community interpreting contexts is unsolicited or solicited, problem-focused support, which aims to remove the cause of stress for the support recipient by providing advice or instrumental assistance whether requested or not (Lawley et al., 2019).

With regard to support receivers' perceptions, Mojaverian and Kim (2013) investigated variations in the effectiveness of solicited and unsolicited social support between European Americans and Asian Americans. They reported that Asian Americans were less likely to solicit support than European Americans and they experienced more negative effects from directly solicited support than European Americans (also see Taylor et al., 2007; Kim et al., 2006; Taylor et al., 2004). Further, the effects of receiving unsolicited support were more positive for Asian Americans than were those of receiving solicited support. This tendency to prefer and more effectively benefit from unsolicited support in collectivistic cultures can be linked to recipients' concerns about potential relational ramifications disturbing the harmony of the group (Kim et al., 2006; Taylor et al., 2004; Taylor al., 2007).

These studies do not focus specifically on Japanese culture. However, the receivers' preference for receiving unsolicited support without disclosing details of their problems seems consistent with the pro-social, collectivistic and harmony-driven nature of Japanese culture, where interdependence between group members is highly valued in both cultural practice and individual behaviours (Uchida & Kitayama, 2001). This tendency also seems to reflect the value of *omoiyari*, which expects one to understand the other's needs and act based on that understanding.

Holistically viewed, these considerations of moral values and the perceptions of receiving social support in the collectivistic and individualistic cultural schemata foreground how these cultural factors result in diverse practices and purposes of interpreting. In turn, these field-specific norms provide role image resources for interpreters. An exemplary phenomenon is the empathetic, advocative and proactive role image of a consultation interpreter, which is consistent with the moral values and interactional expectations considered important in Japan.

The discussion so far has provided some evidence that exploring the differences in interpreter ethics between cultures and societies in T & I ethics classes can provide critical language users with a conceptual window through which to recognise and self-reflect on moral values and interactional expectations normalised in the society where they are located and examine them from the position of the cultural in-between. The final section considers how the dialogue on cultural differences in translator and interpreter ethics and practices can transcend the recognition of ethical diversity and heteroglossia to the mutual enrichment and fuller realisation of humanity—namely, by humanising interpreter ethics.

4. Ethical pluralism approach for humanising translator and interpreter ethics

This section explores how we can apply an ethical pluralism approach to the diversity and heteroglossia in translator and interpreter ethics in order to humanise both interpreter practice and our ethical thinking. Focusing on the case of learning in the Australian context from the viewpoint of the 'empathetic' model in Japan, I argue for humanising translator and interpreter ethics in two ways: 1) making translation and interpreting practice more human-centred; and 2) cultivating our humanity through reflections on translator and interpreter ethics.

The humanising process in the first sense includes learning from the 'empathetic' model to contribute to ongoing discussions about the dilemmas that challenge both translators/interpreters and clients in Australia. For example, community interpreters report, in many professional development seminars, their emotional dilemmas of being torn between the clients' needs and expectations on the one hand and the professional role image of an impartial interpreter on the other. In some cases, the interpreter senses the client is left feeling lost with unresolved problems after the interpreted interaction with an expert, but at the same the interpreter feels obliged not to raise this concern (see the example in Zhao, 2019). These dilemmas, which are deeply connected with the interpreter's and the client's humanity, may be navigated better if the interpreter takes a more human-centred approach that embraces and utilises emotional understanding in the interpreting context. This approach may help the interpreter respond to such situations in a more emotionally sensitive, responsive and humanised way. The humanised approach taken by the interpreter may then bring practical solutions more efficiently and effectively to the complex and multilayered issues faced by the client.

As in the second sense of humanising, I argue that studying and examining heteroglossia in T & I ethics leads critical language users with advanced or upper-advanced language skills, including translators and interpreters, to cultivate their moral character and ultimately their humanity as professionals and as people. This effect is not limited to specific languages and cultures but is generalisable to any dialogic interactions between cultural and moral systems. As Vallor (2016) argued about techno-moral virtues, the self-cultivation of moral character is possible through cultivating the habits of understanding our relations to others, engaging in reflective self-examination, practising self-directed moral development, recognising morally salient facts in specific situations, executing prudent moral judgement and extending our moral concern and caring to other people in the appropriate situation and manner. When this process is projected onto the comparative case of interpreter ethics discussed in this study, it is revealed that examining new values and ideas and integrating aspects of them into one's T & I field and ethical schema provide a very similar process of moral self-cultivation to that proposed by Vallor (2016). For example, practising the above-mentioned humanised approach in the Australian context would require one to re-examine one's interpersonal relations to the other parties involved in the interpreting context; to make a moral judgement responsive and appropriate to the client and to other professionals' needs and the purpose of the interpreted session; to self-reflect on one's own beliefs, feelings and ideal moral self; and to decide to take a certain interpreting approach to action. Therefore, the ethical pluralism approach to cross-cultural diversity in translator and interpreter ethics provides continuous opportunities for translators and interpreters, trainees and, more broadly, critical language users to self-reflect on and cultivate their moral values and character, not only as professionals but also as individual humans—in other words, to humanise through ethical thinking.

However, the pluralist dialogue between diverse T & I ethics must include discussions of potential issues that may arise with the incorporation of new perspectives and values into the existing moral schema. As an example, it must be noted that the 'empathetic' model in Japan may be built on the assumption that a society is still largely homogeneous. Therefore, the members' feelings, desires and needs may also be considered largely homogeneous. However, the backgrounds, experiences, issues and needs present in society are, in reality, diverse, and the diversity becomes greater as the society becomes more multicultural. If sensitivity to the local diversity and ethical heteroglossia is absent, the 'empathetic' model risks becoming paternalistic, condescending, alienating, stereotyping or gatekeeping, depending on the interpreter's self-sufficient moral judgements (Iida, 2012). Can, then, the 'empathetic' or humanised model function effectively in multicultural Australia? What are the possible risks associated with the empathetic, advocative and proactive interpreter? How can one differentiate between ethical interventions and unethical ones? Discussions of the challenges, as well as the opportunities, of learning through the pluralist dialogue are also a critical part of enriching one's own ethical thinking and sensibility.

Above, I argued that learning and critically examining both familiar and new, or less familiar, values in translator and interpreter ethics by applying a pluralist approach can bring solutions to the practical challenges faced in translation and interpreting practice and professional training. Simultaneously, this ethical learning and examination from a pluralist perspective provides considerable opportunities for any critical language users, including students engaging in translation and interpreting at the advanced and upper-advanced levels of language courses and their teachers, through the dialogic process of intercultural ethical thinking. This self-cultivation and habituation of its process are themselves critical competencies of employable global citizens—in whom they can be further developed—citizens whom Australian higher education aims to nurture. To practise this process in the classroom, the class on T & I ethics as a part of language or T & I specific courses should be recognised and utilised as a low-risk, safe environment for T & I students and critical language users to freely engage in ethical heteroglossia, challenge one's existing values, learn from new values and ideas, and habituate the self-cultivation process of morality.

5. Conclusion

In the exploration of the different role images for interpreters that can exist in diverse cultures, it has become clear that cultural factors are inseparable from the ethical implications of T & I practice. The specific case studied, that of the impartial model in Australia contrasted with the 'empathetic' model in Japan, demonstrates how differently two cultures can construct and view the interpreter's role. It follows from this cultural difference that T & I ethics classes should be utilised as a safe space for students and teachers to recognise, (self)-examine and learn from intercultural moral possibilities, not only as part of their practical professional training but also as part of their moral cultivation. In turn, integrating the pluralist approach into T & I ethics classes makes translator and interpreter ethics more meaningful and humanising for all critical language users, not limited to T & I students, to grow as global citizens, who can effectively and sensitively operate in diverse linguistic and cultural communities.

I have limited the scope of this chapter to conceptually exploring the possibility of effective learning of T & I ethics for critical language users beyond the narrow context of professional training. Hence, I must leave to future studies further descriptions of inter-relations between social, cultural, institutional and political factors underpinning the differences in interpreter practice and ethics presented here. Future studies will also need to investigate how these observations are being, or can be, discussed in the classroom, as well as examine opportunities and challenges in curriculum design, interdisciplinary collaborations, and pedagogical grounds and devices.

Acknowledgments

I thank the editors and the anonymous reviewers for their insightful and constructive feedback. Any remaining deficiencies are my sole responsibility. This research is supported by an Australian government Research Training Program Scholarship.

References

Agency for Cultural Affairs, Government of Japan (n.d.). *What we do*. www.bunka.go.jp/english/index.html

Angelelli, C. V. (2004). *Revisiting the interpreter's role: A study of conference, court, and medical interpreters in Canada, Mexico, and the United States*. John Benjamins. doi.org/10.1075/btl.55

AUSIT (Australian Institute of Interpreters and Translators). (2012). *AUSIT Code of Ethics*. ausit.org/code-of-ethics/

Australian Psychological Society. (2013). *Working with interpreters: A practice guide for psychologists*. www.ausit.org/wp-content/uploads/2020/02/APS-Working-with-Interpreters-Practice-Guide-for-Psychologists_2013.pdf

Department of Education, Skills and Employment. (2021). *Job-ready Graduates Package*. Australian Government. www.education.gov.au/job-ready

Donovan, C. (2011). Ethics in the teaching of conference interpreting. *The Interpreter and Translator Trainer*, 5(1), 109–28. doi.org/10.1080/13556509.2011.10798814

Drugan, J. & Megone, C. (2011). Bringing ethics into translator training: An integrated, inter-disciplinary approach. *The Interpreter and Translator Trainer*, 5(1), 183–211. doi.org/10.1080/13556509.2011.10798817

Feng, M. (2014). Cross-cultural comparison on codes of ethics for interpreters. *US–China Foreign Language*, 12(1), 82–92. doi.org/10.17265/1539-8080/2014.01.009

Fukuno, M. (2020). Codes of ethics and professionalisation of translation and interpreting: Japanese and Australian cases. In *The Proceedings of the 30th International Japanese–English Translation, Cairns, 2019* (pp. 58–73). Japan Association of Translators.

Group of Eight Australia. (n.d.). *About the Go8*. go8.edu.au/about/the-go8

Hale, S. B. (2007). *Community interpreting*. Palgrave Macmillan. doi.org/10.1057/9780230593442

Hlavac, J. (2017). *Mental health interpreting guidelines for interpreters*. Monash University. research.monash.edu/en/publications/mental-health-interpreting-guidelines-for-interpreters

Iida, N. (2012). Taijin shien bamen no community tsuuyaku niokeru 'itsudatsu koui' no bunseki: Jirei houkoku bunseki o tooshite [Analysis of deviant behaviors in community interpreting at human support scenes through case study conversations and reports]. *Core Eshikkusu [Core Ethics]* 8, 27–39.

Immigration Services Agency of Japan. (2021). Statistics of residents with foreign citizenship. *E-Stat: Portal Site of Official Statistics of Japan*. www.moj.go.jp/isa/policies/statistics/toukei_ichiran_touroku.html

Kim, H. S., Sherman, D. K., Ko, D. & Taylor, S. E. (2006). Pursuit of comfort and pursuit of harmony: Culture, relationships, and social support seeking. *Personality and Social Psychology Bulletin*, 32(12), 1595–607. doi.org/10.1177/0146167206291991

Koshiba, T., Murase, M., Takeda, A. & Tsuchida, Y. (2018). Koukousei-daigakusei no doutoku eno ishikichousa [Attitudes of high school and university students towards morality]. *Kandagaigodaigakukiyou [the Journal of Kanda University of International Studies], 30*, 493–512.

Lambert, J. (2018). How ethical are codes of ethics? Using illusions of neutrality to sell translations. *The Journal of Specialised Translation, 30*(July), 269–90. jostrans.soap2.ch/issue30/art_lambert.php

Lawley, K. A., Willett, Z. Z., Scollon, C. N. & Lehman, B. J. (2019). Did you really need to ask? Cultural variation in emotional responses to providing solicited social support. *PLOS One, 14*(7), e0219478. doi.org/10.1371/journal.pone.0219478

Lebra, T. S. (1976). *Japanese patterns of behavior*. University Press of Hawaii.

MacIntyre, A. C. (2007). *After virtue: A study in moral theory* (3rd ed.). University of Notre Dame Press. (Original work published 1981)

Maltby, M. (2010). Institutional identities of interpreters in the asylum application context: A critical discourse analysis of interpreting policies in the voluntary sector. In M. Baker, M. Olohan & M. Pérez Calzada (Eds), *Text and context: Essays on translation and interpreting in honour of Ian Mason* (pp. 209–36). Routledge.

Martín Ruano, M. R. (2015). (Trans)formative theorising in legal translation and/or interpreting: A critical approach to deontological principles. *The Interpreter and Translator Trainer, 9*(2), 141–55. doi.org/10.1080/1750399X.2015.1051767

McDonough-Dolmaya, J. (2011). Moral ambiguity: Some shortcomings of professional codes of ethics for translators. *The Journal of Specialised Translation, 15*(January), 28–49. www.jostrans.soap2.ch/issue15/art_mcdonough.php

Migrant and Refugee Women's Health Partnership. (2019). *Guide for clinicians working with interpreters in healthcare settings*. culturaldiversityhealth.org.au/wp-content/uploads/2019/10/Guide-for-clinicians-working-with-interpreters-in-healthcare-settings-Jan2019.pdf

Mojaverian, T. & Kim, H. S. (2013). Interpreting a helping hand: Cultural variation in the effectiveness of solicited and unsolicited social support. *Personality and Social Psychology Bulletin, 39*(1), 88–99. doi.org/10.1177/0146167212465319

Monash University. (2022). *Handbook: APG5677—Professional ethics*. handbook.monash.edu/2022/units/APG5677?year=2022

NAATI (National Accreditation Authority for Translators and Interpreters). (2019a). *Certification scheme design summary: Interpreter certification pathway.* www.naati.com.au/wp-content/uploads/2020/09/INTERPETER-Certification-Scheme-Design-Summary.pdf

NAATI (National Accreditation Authority for Translators and Interpreters). (2019b). *Certification scheme design summary: Translator certification pathway.* www.naati.com.au/wp-content/uploads/2020/09/TRANSLATOR-Certification-Scheme-Design-Summary.pdf

Nakane, I. & Hayes, C. (2021). *Australian Network for Teaching Advanced Japanese Project Report.* Japanese Studies Association of Australia. asaa.asn.au/wp-content/uploads/2021/05/01_2021AdvJpnNetworkProject_Report_6May.pdf

Oliver, B. & de St Jorre, T. J. (2018). Graduate attributes for 2020 and beyond: Recommendations for Australian higher education providers. *Higher Education Research and Development, 37*(4), 821–36. doi.org/10.1080/07294360.2018.1446415

Pym, A. (2012). *On translator ethics: Principles for mediation between cultures.* John Benjamins. doi.org/10.1075/btl.104

Riley, P. (2007). *Language, culture and identity: An ethnolinguistic perspective.* Continuum.

Sugisawa, M., Naito, M., Iwata, K., Miki, K., Kamei, R., Miyagi, K. & Nakura, T. (2015). 'Soudan Tsuuyaku—Rinri Kouryou' Sakutei Ni Kansuru Kyoudou Jissen Kennkyuu [Toward the professionalisation of 'consultation interpreting'—Backgrounds of formulating a code of ethics]. *Tagengo-Tabunka: Jissen to Kenkyuu [Journal of Multilingual Multicultural Studies and Practices], 7*, 182–215.

Taibi, M. & Ozolins, U. (2016). *Community translation.* Bloomsbury Academic.

Taylor, C. C. (2002). Democracy, inclusive and exclusive. In R. Madsen, W. M. Sullivan, A. Swidler & S. M. Tipton (Eds), *Meaning and modernity: Religion, polity, and self* (pp. 181–94). University of California Press.

Taylor, S. E., Welch, W. T., Kim, H. S & Sherman, D. K. (2007). Cultural differences in the impact of social support on psychological and biological stress responses. *Psychological Science, 18*(9), 831–37. doi.org/10.1111/j.1467-9280.2007.01987.x

Theodosiou, A. & Aspioti, M. (Eds). (2015). *Research report on intercultural mediation for immigrants in Europe.* The European Union Erasmus+ & Train Intercultural Mediators for a Multicultural Europe. www.ec.europa.eu/migrant-integration/library-document/research-report-intercultural-mediation-immigrants-europe_en

Travis, C. (1998). *Omoiyari* as a core Japanese value: Japanese-style empathy? In A. Angeliki & T. Eizbieta (Eds), *Speaking of emotions: Conceptualization and expression* (pp. 55–81). Mouton de Gruyter. doi.org/10.1515/9783110806007.55

Uchida, Y. & Kitayama, S. (2001). Omoiyari syakudo no sakusei to datousei no kentou [Development and validation of a sympathy scale]. *Shinrigaku Kenkyuu [Japanese Journal of Psychology]*, 72(4), 275–82.

University of Melbourne. (2022). *Graduate coursebook: Translation and interpreting as product.* handbook.unimelb.edu.au/2022/subjects/tran90001

Vallor, S. (2016). *Technology and the virtues: A philosophical guide to a future worth wanting.* Oxford University Press. doi.org/10.1093/acprof:oso/9780190498511.001.0001

Venuti, L. (1995). *The translator's invisibility: A history of translation.* Routledge.

Wadensjö, C. (1995). Dialogue interpreting and the distribution of responsibility. *Hermes, Journal of Linguistics, 14*, 111–29.

Western Sydney University. (2020). *Academic handbook: Graduate Diploma in Translation.* hbook.westernsydney.edu.au/programs/graduate-diploma-translation/

Zhao, Y. (2019, November). Ethical dilemma. *NAATI News.* www.naati.com.au/news/ethical-dilemma/

Appendix A: T & I course overview (courses listed in Table 8.1)

Monash University. 2022. *Translating across Cultures.* handbook.monash.edu/2022/units/ATS3083?year=2022

The Australian National University. 2022. *Japanese–English Translation.* programsandcourses.anu.edu.au/2022/course/JPNS3013

University of Melbourne. 2022. *Japanese through Translation.* handbook.unimelb.edu.au/2022/subjects/japn30003

University of Queensland. 2021. *Japanese/English Interpreting and Translation.* programs-courses.uq.edu.au/course.html?course_code=JAPN3299

University of Sydney. 2021. *Syntax and Translation.* www.sydney.edu.au/units/JPNS3633

9

Teacher–student and student–student interaction in live online classes

Xiaoping Gao and Leimin Shi

Abstract

This chapter reports on a classroom-based study that investigated teacher–student (TS) and student–student (SS) interaction patterns in live online classes for teaching and learning Chinese as a foreign language (CFL). The participants were 59 students enrolled in three levels of CFL courses at an Australian university and their instructors. Data were collected from video recordings of the lectures and tutorials of three CFL subjects delivered via Zoom over a 13-week session. Results show that both the teachers and the students assisted with L2 knowledge construction through a variety of scaffolding strategies and interactional moves. The teachers executed more elicitations, recasts, explicit corrections and metalinguistic explanations in TS interactions, although they also served as facilitators and commenters as peers did in SS interactions. Findings lend support to the sociocultural theory by demonstrating how TS and SS interactions benefit L2 knowledge construction in formal CFL classes delivered in the synchronous computer-mediated communication (SCMC) mode. Results also provide evidence for translanguaging pedagogy by showing that the moderate use of L1 facilitates scaffolding, interaction and, therefore, L2 development. The study offers insights into pedagogical strategies for enhancing classroom interaction and learner engagement in live online classes.

Keywords: synchronous computer-mediated communication (SCMC), teacher–student interaction, student–student interaction, Chinese as a foreign language (CFL), use of L1, live online classes

1. Introduction

The COVID-19 pandemic has placed unprecedented challenges on the means of communication and education. Since April 2020, 186 countries have implemented nationwide closures, affecting about 73.8 per cent of the total enrolled students (UNESCO, 2020) and more than 220 million tertiary-level students worldwide (UNESCO, 2021). UNESCO's (2021) global survey shows that one of the major impacts of the COVID-19 pandemic on teaching and learning is the increase in online education. Due to COVID-19, nearly all face-to-face (F2F) classes worldwide have been transitioned to remote delivery to comply with social distancing requirements. Such an urgent transition to emergency remote teaching (i.e. a temporary shift of instructional delivery to an alternate delivery mode due to crisis circumstances) has placed enormous challenges on formal classroom learning, especially second language (L2) teaching and learning in which developing L2 learners' speaking skills through oral interaction is one of the central goals. For instance, previous studies found online courses might discourage teacher–student (TS) interaction, which is considered an important element in language learning (Ng et al., 2006). More recent studies under COVID-19 reported that students' performances in emergency online classes were affected by technological constraints (Muthuprasad et al., 2021), physical barriers (e.g. internet issues and learning space) and demands for self-discipline and time management abilities, which, in turn, affected students' mental health and motivation for learning (Gao, 2020). Although flexibility and convenience made online classes an attractive option during COVID-19, teachers' and students' satisfaction with online classes is dependent on quality and timely TS interaction, structured online class modules, technical support availability and modifications to accommodate the holding of practical classes (Nambiar, 2020). Because TS and student–student (SS) interactions serve as critical strategies and contexts for the facilitation of L2 acquisition (Philp, 2016), how to engage students through interaction in online classes has become an urgent topic for teaching practitioners and language educators who want to enhance learning outcomes. Although previous studies have examined interaction patterns and scaffolding strategies in F2F or synchronous computer-mediated communication (SCMC) modes within a blended learning environment, TS and SS interactions in the SCMC mode as a formal classroom setting remain under-researched, and this gap in the research partly motivated the current study to investigate the scaffolding strategies used by the instructors and their students in live online classes to facilitate L2 acquisition.

2. Literature review

2.1. Theoretical frameworks for classroom interaction

Classroom interaction has been one of the central concerns in L2 teaching and learning due to the demands of collaborative interaction in L2 classrooms (Lantolf & Poehner, 2014; Long, 1985; 1989; 1996; Loewen & Sato, 2018). Though grounded in two different theoretical frameworks—a cognitive approach based on Interaction Hypothesis (Long, 1985; 1989; 2018; Loewen & Sato, 2018; Long & Porter, 1985; Pica et al., 1996) and a sociocultural approach informed by Vygotskian sociocultural theory (Lantolf, 2000; Lantolf & Poehner, 2014; Storch, 2017; Vygotsky, 1978; 1981; 1986)—existing studies have achieved consistent results in finding that both TS and SS interactions are beneficial to L2 development (e.g. Lyster & Ranta, 1997; Philp et al., 2013; Loewen & Wolff, 2016; Ziegler & Mackey, 2017).

Research into SS interaction has also evidenced that SS interaction in the SCMC mode is as effective as in the F2F mode. Nevertheless, existing studies mainly focused on peer interaction in a laboratory setting for learning L2 English (e.g. McDonough, 2004), Spanish (e.g. Loewen & Wolff, 2016) or French (e.g. Lyster, 2002; 2019). Studies examining TS and SS interactions in SCMC formal classrooms remain scarce. To the best of our knowledge, no study has examined TS and SS interaction patterns in live online classes for learning Chinese as a foreign language (CFL). To fill this gap, this chapter reports on a qualitative case study that investigated TS and SS interaction patterns in CFL classes delivered via Zoom during COVID-19. The findings will contribute to a better understanding of how TS and SS interactions facilitate L2 knowledge construction in the SCMC formal classroom setting and provide insights into pedagogical strategies for enhancing student engagement and learning outcomes.

2.2. Sociocultural theory and scaffolding

The current study adopts a Vygotskian sociocultural theory (SCT) (Vygotsky, 1978, 1981, 1986) approach to address the research gap. SCT is a psychological theory that explains how mental capacities develop as an inherently social process mediated by a more capable human or artefacts. An SCT perspective views language learners as active agents who participate in the processes of developing higher-order capabilities with the assistance of more capable others (e.g. a teacher or peer) via scaffolding or mediation of physical (e.g. books, computers and the internet) or semiotic tools (e.g. language and gestures) that enable interactions to take place (e.g. Aljaafreh & Lantolf, 1994; Lantolf, 2000; Lantolf et al., 2018; Ohta, 1995; 2000). Central to SCT are the constructs of the zone of proximal development (ZPD), scaffolding, mediation and tools. The ZPD (Vygotsky, 1978) refers to the cognitive gap between what a novice can accomplish with and without assistance (Lantolf & Poehner, 2014). Scaffolding is a metaphor that refers to an expert's finely attuned and contingent assistance that is responsive to a novice's needs and helps the novice gain a higher order of understanding or capability in order to complete a challenging task that is unachievable independently (e.g. Maybin et al., 1992). Scaffolding has two characteristics: 1) dynamic assessment through diagnostic activities before and in between interventions, which helps the expert to find out the current state of the novice and to provide tailored support; 2) procedural facilitation that emphasises the appropriate and contingent support that the expert provides. The assistance should be temporary and cease once the less capable person has achieved a higher level of understanding in order to restore learner autonomy, since too much or too little assistance may be inappropriate or constrain development (Hermkes et al., 2018; Maybin et al., 1992; Mercer, 2002; Storch, 2017).

The current study adopted SCT as the theoretical framework for the following reasons. First, in SCT, scaffolding is closely related to constructivist theories, in which scaffolding is targeted not merely at outcomes but at the process of active knowledge construction. The current study is a classroom-based descriptive study that intends to reveal how the teacher and the peer student facilitate L2 knowledge construction in TS and SS interactions by focusing on demonstrating the dynamic scaffolding process and the nature of language-related episodes (LREs). Second, SCT views learning as a unity of affective and intellectual processes (Vygotsky, 1986) and acknowledges the use of both L1 and L2 as mediational resources in assisting knowledge construction and scaffolding. Like translanguaging pedagogy, it suggests that language learning is based on the learner's entire linguistic repertoire, including the use of L1, and acknowledges the positive impact of L1 use on L2 development (W. Li, 2018; Smith & Robertson, 2020; Wu, 2018). Third, LREs generated in the scaffolding process exemplify interactional moves and scaffolding features, and showcase how dialogic interventions enable a novice to gain new knowledge or the capabilities needed to accomplish a challenging task.

2.3. Interaction patterns in L2 classes

Interaction is an indispensable component in the L2 classroom. Research shows that interaction benefits L2 development, although its efficacy can be affected by many factors, such as modality (oral vs. written), mode (F2F vs. SCMC), task conditions and individual differences (e.g. L1, L2 proficiency, and motivation) (Loewen & Sato, 2018). Studies based on a sociocultural perspective revealed that negotiation for meaning and form that accounts for corrective feedback (CF) is an effective way to fulfil the pedagogical potential of communicative L2 classrooms (Lyster, 2002; 2019; Hall & Walsh, 2002; Jin, 2005; Nassaji & Swain, 2000). Consequently, the research focus of interaction studies has shifted to examining how and under what circumstances interaction is effective (Loewen & Sato, 2018), as interactional contexts may influence how individuals communicate. However, TS and SS interaction patterns may differ, since interlocutors have different linguistic capabilities and social relationships, which may, in turn, affect the provision, perception and acceptance of feedback in collaborative communication.

2.3.1. TS interaction patterns

With regard to TS interaction patterns, existing studies reported different interactional moves and structures in L2 classes. For instance, Long (2018) described an exchange structure that commonly emerged in TS interaction—IRF: 'I' stands for teachers' initiation, usually by closed, known information or questions; 'R' stands for students' response; and 'F' for teachers' feedback, usually in the form of praise or error correction. As Long (2018, p. 1) puts it, such a 'thinly disguised, rather boring, repetition drill' fails to effectively enhance students' communicative competence, as it is disparate from natural conversations in everyday life. However, some 'cost-free' adjustments to the first move of the IRF pattern can improve the quality of TS interaction, such as altering the proportions of displaying known information and referential questions (i.e. genuine questions to which teachers do not know the answer)

(Brock, 1986). Referential questions can elicit more turns, longer and more complex student utterances, and more communicative language use, so they are more likely to engage students in genuine communication and elaborate the input automatically. The current study adopted the adjusted IRF exchange structure as an analytical framework to analyse international moves in LREs generated in TS interaction. Previous studies that examined scaffolding features from an SCT perspective found that the teacher employed scaffolding features such as elicitation, recast, recap, rejection, elaboration, confirmation and repetition to provide the assistance needed in F2F classrooms (Gibbons, 2003; Hammond, 2001; Hammond & Gibbons, 2005; Lyster, 2002; Lyster & Ranta, 1997; Mercer, 2002). The current study adopted the above scaffolding features as a baseline to analyse TS interactions in the SCMC classroom setting.

2.3.2. SS interaction patterns

Group work and pair work that involve interactions and discussions are everyday activities in foreign language classrooms, since group and pair activities offer more opportunities and create a less stressful environment for students to practise the L2 (Long & Porter, 1985; Storch & Aldosari, 2013). Studies conducted within the SCT framework have analysed the nature of feedback that peers provided to each other, distribution of learner participation, nature of LREs, interaction patterns and learners' collaborations that lead to the co-construction of new language knowledge and solve language-related problems (e.g. Edstrom, 2015; Garcia Mayo & Zeitler, 2017; Swain, 2000; Swain & Lapkin, 2013; Swain & Watanabe, 2013). These studies have found that learners provided effective assistance using various scaffolding strategies, such as advising, requesting clarifications and providing mini grammar lessons when needed. Swain and Watanabe (2013) argue that peer–peer collaborative dialogue mediating L2 learning can be used as both communicative and cognitive tools in collaborative group interaction. Their findings suggest that interactive SCMC conditions place differential demands on L2 learners, which, in turn, impact the way in which L2 learners address LREs during task-based interactions. Golonka et al. (2017) investigated SS interaction patterns in L2 Russian SCMC classes. They found that students engaged in three types of interaction moves that might support language learning: 1) providing language-related assistance (e.g. self- or peer-correction, and negotiation for meaning), 2) using their partner as a resource (e.g. clarifying information, modelling language use or helping with unknown vocabulary), and 3) providing encouragement (e.g. responding positively to each other and eliciting information from a partner). The current study adopted Golonka et al.'s (2017) interaction patterns as the analytical framework for the analysis of SS interaction patterns in CFL online classes.

2.4. Interactional studies in the SCMC context

Interaction in the SCMC context has attracted growing attention in SLA since the last century (e.g. Chanier & Lamy, 2017; Chapelle, 1998; 2014; Chun, 1994; Kitade, 2000; Salaberry, 1996; 2000; Warschauer, 1997). Existing studies have uniformly demonstrated the benefits of computer-mediated communication for L2 development (e.g. Nassaji & Swain, 2000; Torres & Yanguas, 2021; Ziegler & Mackey, 2017), although they mainly focused on text-based (e.g. Blake, 2000; Chun, 1994; Storch, 2002), voice-based (Bueno-Alastuey, 2013) or video-based interactions (Yanguas, 2010). Some found that the interaction mode (SCMC vs. F2F) influenced the type of negotiations and learning outcomes in terms of modified output, successful uptake and communication strategies (Loewen & Wolff, 2016; Rouhshad & Storch, 2016), whereas others revealed no significant difference between SCMC and F2F in terms of the benefits of interaction for L2 development (Ziegler, 2016). Recent studies have confirmed that SCMC can effectively improve learner interaction when learners are physically isolated and thus has technological potential in future L2 learning environments (e.g. Lenkaiti, 2020; Junn, 2021).

In summary, previous studies have revealed that scaffolding strategies of TS and SS interactions in F2F or SCMC settings benefit L2 learning. However, classroom-based studies remain scarce, since existing studies are mainly experimental or quasi-experimental studies based on manipulated instruction in laboratory settings (e.g. Loewen & Wolff, 2016; Loewen & Sato, 2018). Researchers (e.g. Loewen & Sato, 2018; Mackey, 2012) call for more authentic classroom-based studies, as this line of research can provide high ecological validity and insights into the realities that teachers and students face in everyday practice. It is worth further investigating what scaffolding strategies are used in authentic SCMC classes and how they help L2 learners develop their linguistic competence. These have motivated the current study to investigate TS and SS interaction strategies in live online CFL classes during the emergency remote delivery period.

This study aimed to address the following research questions (RQ):

> RQ1. What are the TS interaction patterns in Zoom classes?
> RQ2. What are the SS interaction patterns in Zoom classes?

3. Method

3.1. Context

This study involved three levels of CFL courses offered at a mid-sized Australian university. The courses aimed to develop students' language skills (listening, speaking, reading and writing) and intercultural competencies. Weekly contact hours for first-, second- and third-year CFL courses were five, four and three hours, respectively. Due to the breakout of COVID-19, all courses were transitioned to remote delivery after three weeks of F2F teaching in the first semester of 2020. This study was based on the data collected from the second semester of 2020 over a 13-week teaching period. All CFL courses were delivered through a combination of live online classes via Zoom, video recordings, and interactive quizzes and learning resources on the course online learning platforms. All live Zoom classes were video-recorded, and recordings were made available on the course online learning platforms for students to review out of class after obtaining consent from the teachers and students as part of the course design. The textbooks of these courses were *Integrated Chinese*, volumes 1–3 (Liu et al., 2017a; 2017b; 2017c), depending on students' proficiency in Chinese, which ranged from elementary to upper-intermediate level.

3.2. Participants

Participants were students and their four teachers of the aforementioned CFL courses, including the authors of this chapter. The student participants were 57 undergraduates (32 females and 25 males) enrolled in one of the first-year (n = 28), second-year (n = 23) and third-year (n = 6) Mandarin courses. They were aged between 17 and over 60, with a mean age of 20. The students had varying L1 backgrounds: Australian English (n = 49), Vietnamese (n = 5) and Japanese (n = 3). Their proficiency in English was at native speaker or advanced level. At the time of investigation, they were studying towards a wide range of degrees and majors, including arts, international studies, law, international business and engineering. All the teacher participants were female and bilingual speakers of Mandarin and English with Mandarin as their L1 or dominant language. They had 5–25 years of experience teaching CFL in the English-speaking context.

3.3. Data collection

After obtaining human research ethics approval from the host institution, consent was obtained from both teacher and student participants to use their data from the Zoom recordings. The two authors, who were involved in teaching all three courses, watched all video recordings and selected episodes independently. A total of 60 hours of recordings (20 hours for each course) were selected. Auto-transcriptions of the selected Zoom classes were read through and edited by adding Chinese characters and pinyin tones while watching the selected recordings. Edited transcriptions were used for analysis. The transcription system is shown in the Appendix. The LREs were coded to identify the interaction patterns through a scrutiny of the transcribed data. For SS group activities in Zoom breakout rooms, only the groups that the teachers joined were recorded, and so only their data were analysed. This is one of the limitations of this study.

3.4. Data coding and analyses

The study adopted the following guidelines for coding scaffolding strategies. The contingent assistance must meet the following criteria: 1) a learner's successful completion of a task with assistance; 2) the learner's achievement of a greater level of independent competence as a result of the assistance (see Maybin et al., 1992; Hermkes et al., 2018). The two authors coded and identified interaction moves according to the IRF exchange structure (Long, 2018) and scaffolding features for TS interactions (Lyster, 2002) and SS interactions (Golonka et al., 2017), respectively. Where there was a disagreement on coding, the authors discussed and revised until an agreement was achieved. Coded data subject to unresolved disagreement were eliminated from the analysis. We adopted Lyster's (2002) CF strategies as a baseline because they were inclusive and clearly defined.

Most importantly, many previous studies have adopted this taxonomy, which enables us to compare our findings with existing findings generated in the F2F setting. However, scaffolding strategies that emerged in our study were far beyond the categories listed in Table 9.1, since classroom interactions are not confined to providing CF to learners' errors. We will refer back to this when reporting and discussing our qualitative results in Section 4. Coding schemes for scaffolding strategies, definitions and examples of TS interactions are shown in Table 9.1. Scaffolding strategies and examples for SS interactions are presented in Table 9.4, along with results (e.g. their numbers and percentages).

Table 9.1 Coding scheme for TS scaffolding strategies, definitions and examples

Scaffolding features	Definition	Example
Elicitation	To directly elicit correct forms from students by asking questions; or by pausing to allow students to complete the teacher's utterance; or by asking students to reformulate their utterance	T: xxx yòng Zhōngwén zěnme shuō ? [How to say xxx in Mandarin]? Nǐ de àihào shì …? [Your hobbies are …?] Qǐng zài shuō yí biàn? [Pardon?]
Recasts (conversational or didactic)	To repeat the student's utterance by highlighting the erroneous part with emphatic stress or using a rising intonation	S: Wǒ yi xiàkè jiù *qù* jiā [Once I finish class, I will go home.] T: Oh, Nǐ yí xiàkè jiù huí jiā [Once you finish class, I will go home.]
Metalinguistic explanations	To provide comments, information, or linguistic explanations on the well-formedness of the student's utterance without explicitly providing the correct form	S: Wǒ zuótiān *qù dàxué* [*I go to school yesterday.] T: Nǐ zuìhǎoshuō Wǒ zuótiān qù daxué le [You'd better say I went to school yesterday.] Because going to uni already happened, you should use le.
Explicit correction	To explicitly indicate an error and provide a correct form	S: Wǒ yi xià kè jiù *qù* jiā T: Oh, you'd better say Nǐ yi xiàkè jiù huí jiā because go home in Chinese is huí jiā (return home), not qù jiā
Repetition	To repeat the student's erroneous utterance, adjusting the intonation to highlight the error	S: Wǒ yǒu liǎng *kǒu* jiějie [I have two sisters.] T: Nǐ yǒu liǎng *kǒu* jiějie? [Do you have two sisters?]
Clarification requests	To indicate to the student that the message has not been understood or that the utterance is ill-formed in some way, and that a repetition or a reformulation is required	T: Nǐ de yìsi shì — ? [Did you mean — ?]
Confirmations	To confirm the correctness of learner's production	T: Duì, méicuò [Yeah, you are right.]
Confirmation checks	To confirm the learner's intended meaning	T: Qǐngwèn zhè xuéqī nǐ xué jǐ mén kè? [How many subjects are you studying this session?] S: Wǒ *xié shì*. incorrect pronunciation T: Duìbùqǐ, nǐ xué sì mén kè? [sorry, are you studying four subjects?] S: Yeah.

Scaffolding features	Definition	Example
Comprehension checks	To check if the student has comprehended	T: Nǐ dǒng le ma? [Do you understand?]
Paralinguistic signals	To use a gesture or facial expression to indicate that an error has been made or to assist in making corrections	S: Zhōngguó *cái* [Chinese food] T: Zhōngguó cài. Cài is the fourth tone, with the right hand moving sharply downwards to emphasise a falling tone.

Source: Compiled by author.

4. Results and discussion

4.1. RQ1 TS interaction patterns

RQ1 sought to reveal scaffolding strategies used in TS interactions in live Zoom classes. Table 9.2 presents the number (percentage) of instances of scaffolding strategies according to Lyster's (2002) taxonomy for CF strategies. It can be seen that recasts were the most used strategies to provide CF to learners' erroneous production. Didactive recasts were used more frequently than conversational recasts. This is because didactic instruction (asking students to read the text and answer questions) took place more frequently than conversation tasks involved in real-life tasks due to limited class time. Didactic recasts were frequently used to correct learners' non-target-like pronunciation (particularly tones), as reported in Gao (2021). This finding confirms that recasting is a time-efficient strategy that can avoid embarrassing learners. Unlike previous studies, explicit corrections and metalinguistic explanations accounted for a large proportion (26%). Explicit corrections were generally performed along with metalinguistic explanations to clarify the use of challenging grammar points or provide equivalent expressions in Chinese with their pragmatic functions or cultural backgrounds. The use of L1 allowed the teachers to efficiently stimulate more interactional moves.

Table 9.2 The numbers (percentages) of LREs in TS interactions by CF strategy

Category	N	%	Implicit	N	%	Explicit	N	%
Reformulations	895	75	Conversational recasts	224	19	Didactic recasts	368	31
						Explicit correction	102	9
						Explicit correction with metalinguistic explanation	201	17
Prompts	293	25	Repetition	43	4	Elicitation	136	11
			Clarification requests	81	7	Metalinguistic clue	18	2
						Paralinguistic signal	15	1
Subtotal	1188	100		348	29		840	71

Source: Compiled by author.

As Table 9.2 shows, CF strategies used in TS interactions follow the same pattern as reported in previous studies on adult EFL learners in Korea (Sheen, 2004) and ESL learners in New Zealand (Ellis et al., 2001)—that is, there were more explicit strategies than implicit strategies and more reformulations than prompts. However, the proportion of conversational and didactic recasts (50%) used in this study is much lower than those reported in the previous studies (i.e. 83% in Sheen, 2004; 68% in Ellis et al., 2001). This might be because the teachers provided more metalinguistic explanations in English to construct learners' new knowledge, which could not be gained from anywhere else. The proportion of elicitation (11%) is similar to those reported in the above studies (11% in Sheen, 2004; 13% in Ellis et al., 2001). However, as mentioned above, the current study focused on scaffolding strategies and interactional moves rather than merely providing CF to learners' erroneous production. Elicitation, as reported in Hammond and Gibbons (2005), included the teachers' initiation of dialogues using questioning techniques (e.g. referential questions) to elicit students' responses and production. This type of elicitation dominated TS interactions and occurred more frequently than elicitation functioned as a CF strategy (Table 9.2). Also, a single expression might reflect multiple scaffolding strategies, as shown in Table 9.3, which presents the LREs, interactional moves (IM) and scaffolding features during TS interactions in a third-year class.

9. TEACHER-STUDENT AND STUDENT-STUDENT INTERACTION IN LIVE ONLINE CLASSES

Table 9.3 TS interactional moves (IM), excerpts, and scaffolding features and functions

IM	LREs	Scaffolding feature (function)
I	T: Zuìjìn shéi yǒu shénme dǎoméi de shì ma? [Did anyone have any bad luck recently?]	**Elicitation** (information request)
R	S1: Lǎoshī [Ms/Teacher], I am not sure if I can say this in Chinese.	
F+TI	T: Hǎo [Okay], give it a try? Shì yi xià? [give it a try]	**Elicitation** (encouragement)
R	S1: Xià Xīngqīrì (.)// Wǒ kāichē (...) [next Sunday (.)// I drive (...)]	Self-questioning
F	T: Shàngge háishì xiàge? [last or next?]	**Clarification request & Elicitation** (eliciting self-correction) **& Recast** (adding a classifier 个)
R	S1: uh, xiàge? [uh, next]? last oh, no, shàngge [last]	(Self-correction)
F	T: Shàngge// shàngge xīngqītiān [Last, last Sunday]	**Confirmation & Recast**
R	S1: Shàngge xīngqītiān // Wǒ — uh, qù (-) gōng (-), uh gōngzuò [Last Sunday // I — uh, went to work] oh, no, what is work?	(Uptake) (Using teacher as a resource: helping with vocab)
F	T: Duì, gōngzuò, kāichē qù gōngzuò [Correct, work, drive to work]	**Confirmation** (providing language assistance)
	S1: Shàngge xīngqītiān [Last Sunday] I drove to work.	(Uptake)
I	S1: And, a kangaroo jumped out.	
R	T: Yìzhī dàishǔ tiào chūlái le [A kangaroo jumped out.]	Providing language assistance
I	S1: And hit on my car. And now, xiànzài [Now], hàide wǒ [made me] a week, yí gè xīngqī [one week], méiyǒu chē [have no car] hěn bù fāngbiàn [very inconvenient]	
I	S1: How to say kangaroo?	(Using teacher as a resource: helping with vocab)
R+I	T: Dàishǔ, yī zhī dàishǔ, the measure word for dàishǔ is zhī, yī zhī dàishǔ zhuàng shàng le nǐde chē, zhuàng huài le nǐde chē, duì bu duì? [kangaroo, a kangaroo, the measure word for kangaroo is zhī. A kangaroo hit your car and crashed your car, didn't it?]	Providing language assistance, **Metalinguistic explanations & confirmation checks** (providing language assistance)
R	S1: Duì, hàide wǒ xiànzài méiyǒu chē [Right. That made me end up with no car now.]	Confirmation (S1 uptake)

IM	LREs	Scaffolding feature (function)
I	S2: Lǎoshī, nǐ chī dàishǔ ma? [Ms, do you eat kangaroo?]	S2 uptake
R + I	T: Wǒ chī dàishǔròu ma? [Do I eat kangaroo meat?]	**Recast & Clarification check** (language assistance: negotiation for meaning)
R + I	S2: Duì, dàishǔròu nǐ xǐhuān ma? [Yep, do you like kangaroo meat?]	Confirmation (S2 uptake)

Source: Compiled by author.

After learning 'hàide' (to cause trouble or do harm, to cause or lead to an undesirable situation) in class, students were asked to talk about unfortunate incidents that they had encountered recently and their consequences (Table 9.3). TS interactions were in the form of a series of reacting moves in which the teacher reacted through commenting on what the student said or asking follow-up referential questions. The student used the teacher as a resource to provide language assistance. The teacher adopted a series of scaffolding strategies and helped the learner to complete a challenging task that could not be completed by herself alone. S1 not only expressed her own thoughts by using the target word (hàide) but also reviewed some words (shàngge xīngqītiān [last Sunday], gōngzuò [work]) and learned some new expressions (dàishǔròu [kangaroo meat]).

In Table 9.3, a single expression (e.g. Shàngge háishì xiàge? [last or next?]) contains several scaffolding strategies that fulfil multiple functions: clarification request, elicitation and recast. With the support of the teacher's confirmation, recast and provision of new words, S1 self-corrected her ill-formed expressions and told her real-life experiences in Chinese by using new words. Other students also gained new knowledge from their interactions. For instance, S2, as a listener, also picked up a new word (dàishǔròu [kangaroo meat]) and initiated a follow-up question to join the conversation. S2's referential question to the teacher (i.e. Lǎoshī, nǐ chī dàishǔ ma? [Teacher, do you eat kangaroo?]) indicated his uptake of the new word, 'dàishǔ' [kangaroo] after the teacher's provision to S1 and the whole class by repetitively speaking the sentences and typing them in characters and pinyin on the chat pad. S2's referential question initiated follow-up reacting moves on this interesting topic. The teacher corrected his expression with recast by replacing dàishǔ (kangaroo) with dàishǔròu (kangaroo meat) as the students had learned ròu (meat) in a previous lesson. S2 immediately picked up the word he was searching for in his follow-up utterances. The teacher's provision of new words and implicit correction of erroneous use scaffolded S1 and S2 to complete challenging tasks (i.e. telling real-life experiences and expressing their own thoughts using new words) beyond their existing knowledge and skills.

As indicated above, students in this study frequently asked the teachers to provide confirmation or metalinguistic explanations for their use of the L2. For example, after learning yǒuyìsi [interesting] in a first-year class, the teacher asked students to talk about their own learning experience in the main room. A student, S3, attempted this challenging task by telling her situation in Mandarin. Table 9.4 presents the LREs, IMs and scaffolding strategies used during the TS interaction. Although the teacher already provided implicit feedback using recast and praised her performance, S3 still insisted on asking the teacher to clarify whether her use of wàiguóyǔ [foreign language] was correct because she was struggling with it, and was not sure if her use of the word was 100 per cent correct. Her request triggered the teacher's explicit explanation, which helped S3 gain new knowledge after completing this task. From this scenario, we can see that the teacher's confirmation or response using repetition or 'hěnhǎo' [very good] is very vague. Even if a student had produced a target-like expression, s/he might not have fully acquired the form. The use of L1 helped both the teacher and students clear up their queries.

Table 9.4 LREs, interactional moves (IM) and scaffolding features in the TS interactions of a first-year class

IM	LREs	Scaffolding feature (interactional move)
I	T: Zhè ge xuéqī nǐ juéde zuìyǒuyìside shì nǎ mén kè? Wèishénme? [What is your favourite subject this session]? Why?	**Elicitation** (referential questions)
R	S3: Wǒ juéde zuìyǒuyìside shì Zhōngwén kè I think the most exciting subject is Mandarin.	S (response)
R+I	T: Wèishénme? [Why?]	**Elicitation**
R	S3: Yīnwèi... uh, yīnwèi... Because ...uh, because...	S encountered a challenge
I	T: You can use English if you have never learned the words in Chinese.	**Encouragement** (use of L1)
R	S3: Uh, kěshì, Wǒ shì yíxià, yīnwèi wǒ xǐhuān xuéxí xuexi uh, wàiguóyǔ [Uh, but let me try... Because I like studying, studying uh, foreign languages]	Output

IM	LREs	Scaffolding feature (interactional move)
F	T: Òu, yīnwèi nǐ xǐhuān wàiguóyǔ, hěnhǎo [Oh, because you like studying foreign languages. Very good.]	**Repetition** (providing feedback and praise)
I	S3: Is it the right word to say wàiguóyǔ [foreign language]?	Clarification request
R	T: Oh, you could say wàiguó yǔyán [foreign language] or wàiyǔ [foreign language] for short.	**Explicit explanation**
R	S3: Oh, wàiyǔ, xièxie nǐ [Oh, foreign language. Thank you.]	Uptake (understanding of new knowledge)

Source: Compiled by author.

The teachers in this study adopted various strategies in IRF interaction exchanges. Each interactional move might contain different strategies. Elicitation, recast, repetition, clarification and confirmation were used more frequently than rejection in the scaffolding strategies listed in the literature (Hammond, 2001; Hammond & Gibbons, 2005). According to some teachers, students were very shy to volunteer answers and take part in classroom interaction, particularly first-year students who had not built social networks with their classmates due to the outbreak of COVID-19 at the beginning of their studies. Therefore, the teachers encouraged students to speak in class to make them feel comfortable when interacting with others. They were inclined to employ more euphemistic ways to provide CF (i.e. 'What you said meant … It is better to say …') instead of using explicit negative comments (e.g. 'Zhèyàng shuō búduì', 'Nǐ shuō cuò le' [what you said was wrong or incorrect]). They were afraid that explicit rejection would demotivate students to participate in classroom interactions and continue their study of Mandarin. The students' reacting moves and responses shown in Tables 9.3 and 9.4 suggest that this strategy was well received.

In fact, in this study, students like S3 frequently asked the teacher to provide language assistance, which triggered the teachers' explicit explanations using L1. Students' requests for help and using the teacher as a resource have reduced the teachers' use of explicit corrections and avoided embarrassment on both sides. The teachers' bilingual competence enabled them to successfully answer students' questions and help students make progress in the online classroom setting.

4.2. SS interaction patterns

RQ2 examined the patterns of SS interactions in online classes. Table 9.5 displays the interaction strategies, examples and number (%) of LREs generated in SS interactions.

Table 9.5 SS interaction strategies, examples, and number (%) of LREs

SS interaction strategies	Examples	No of LREs	%
Providing language-related assistance		103	31
Peer-correction	S4: Nà, měicì dōu **de** dǎdiànhuà yuērén, máfán sǐ le [In that case, it is troublesome that we have to make a phone call for appointments every time.] S5: Cì, measure word, every time; děi have to. And yuē first tone.	32	10
Self-correction	S5: OK, děi, or just like hé and huò.	20	6
Negotiation for meaning	S5: Yeah. So I'd say 'bù hǎo yìsi, nà wǒ yě méi bànfa le. Nǐ bú yuànyì yùndòng, nà jiù pàng xiàqù ba!' [I am sorry. There is nothing I can do. If you don't want to exercise, you have to remain fat!] S4: What's 'bànfa le'? [What does 'bànfa' mean?]	51	15
Using their partner as a resource		178	54
Helping with vocab	S4: yǒu wait...duì, yígè kètīng, yígè chúfáng hé yígè wèishēngjiān [There are... Wait... Yeah, a living room, a kitchen and a bathroom.] Hold on. How to say 'it's very clean'? S5: Gānjìng [clean]	60	18
Providing language assistance (vocab, grammar)	S4: hěn gānjìng, érqiě dài jiājù [Very clean, including furniture] Uh...Uh...I forgot 'furniture' S5: 'furniture' is jiājù	72	22
Clarifying	Just what furniture could be...have what furniture?	46	14
Providing encouragement		50	15
Responding positively to each other	S5: Ok, all right. Perfect	37	11

SS interaction strategies	Examples	No of LREs	%
Elicitation	S4: 'furniture' is jiājù. Just what furniture could be…have what furniture? S5: 'kind', 'zhǒng', tāyǒushénme zhǒng jiājù? ['Kind', what kind of furniture does it have?]	13	4
Total		331	100

Source: Compiled by author.

SS interaction patterns that emerged in this study are similar to those identified by Golonka et al. (2017) in three broad categories. However, the most notable instances were 'using partners as resources' and 'providing language-related assistance' in the current study, but positive affect (e.g. encouragement), self-correction and partner correction in Golonka et al.'s (2017). This might be because Golonka et al.'s (2017) study was based on text chats of adult learners of Russian at an intermediate level. In contrast, our study was based on live chats of students across three different proficiency levels. The Zoom video platform is an effective channel for both oral and written communication (via video- and text-based chats on chat pad). It is easier to ask for help and provide assistance orally than typing. In addition, the difference might reflect the fact that the students in the same class of our study demonstrated slightly different linguistic competence, and more proficient learners were capable and willing to provide assistance to their peers. As shown in Table 9.5, S5 was more knowledgeable with regards to S4's questions and so performed as a 'teacher' or 'teaching assistant' to provide language assistance by using L1. SS interactions helped to clear up their confusions and assisted less capable students to complete a challenging task that they could not complete independently. There were some instances in which both or all students in one group were stuck or incapable of doing a task. They then asked the teacher for help when she entered their breakout rooms, leading to TS interactions. The findings of this study suggest that group work is a time-efficient pedagogical strategy, as SS interactions can engage students in meaningful learning and lead to better learning outcomes.

4.3. Use of L1

Scrutiny of LREs generated in this study reveals some common characteristics across TS and SS interactions. The first is the use of L1. As shown in Tables 9.2–9.5, L1 English was involved in both TS and SS IMs, although its use gradually declined from first-year to third-year classes. Both teachers and students used L1 to clarify, confirm, negotiate for meaning and provide metalinguistic explanations involving linguistic items beyond students' linguistic capacity. L1 was used to prevent the breakdown of conversation, ask for help and provide language assistance and metalinguistic explanations, which ensured the successful completion of communications in L2 Chinese.

Several reasons can be identified for the use of L1. First, the use of L1 was compatible with the goal of L2 education—that is, to cultivate bilingual or multilingual speakers rather than monolingual speakers of an L2 (W. Li 2018). As shown in LREs, the teachers' and students' use of L1 functioned as an advantage rather than a barrier to the promotion of TS and SS interactions in online classes. L1 served as a mediation tool to help the learners effectively develop their L2 competence through scaffolding in TS and SS interactions. Therefore, the findings provide empirical evidence for the SCT and translanguaging hypothesis.

Second, the use of L1 was determined by learner characteristics (e.g. cognitive competence and L2 proficiency). According to the teachers, they had tried their best to use L2 as much as possible following the convention in foreign language education. However, their actual use of L2 varied depending on students' proficiency, course content and the difficulty of tasks. Some teachers reported that a total ban of L1 would result in silence in class and hinder TS and SS interactions. It would be challenging to engage students with a relatively low level of proficiency in classroom interaction because they are adults with solid self-esteem and fear negative comments in front of the class, particularly in large groups.

Third, the participants' cognitive and bilingual competence made it possible to use L1. In many previous studies (e.g. Long, 2018; Hammond & Gibbons, 2005), scaffolding was mainly implemented in L2. However, the students in the current study were adult learners who had developed the cognitive ability to convey complex thoughts and ideas but had limited linguistic competence in L2 Chinese. As adult learners, they were keen to find out the rules and reasons behind language use (i.e. 'why say') to seek comprehensible input rather than just correct production (i.e. 'how to say') provided by recasts or explicit corrections. Therefore, the students constantly asked the teachers and peers to provide assistance in English. The teachers' bilingual competence enabled them to provide metalinguistic explanations and instructions in English, because the explanations in L2 Chinese would be far beyond the learners' linguistic repertoire. The common communicative language that the teachers and students share ensured that TS and SS interactions could scaffold learners to construct new knowledge successfully and efficiently based on their existing knowledge of L1. Therefore, this finding agrees with previous studies finding that L1 can be used as a useful mediation tool to facilitate L2 acquisition (Edstrom, 2015; J. Li, 2018; Storch, 2002).

4.4. Social relationships between interlocutors

A second common characteristic of TS and SS interactions was that both teachers and peers served as resources and providers of linguistic assistance when needed. This phenomenon might have reflected the social relationships between teachers and students in the Australian context, the less-competitive structure of the society or the learner-centred education system. Higher education is mostly a matter of interest, not social status. In the CFL language classes, the students treated their teacher as a resource to provide assistance as they did with their peers. They felt comfortable asking teachers to assist, just as if asking their peers for help. This situation might differ from the TS relationship in Asian contexts (e.g. Korea), where students tend to refrain from asking questions and fully respect the teachers' judgements and comments due to hierarchical cultural values. This might explain why recasts accounted for 84 per cent of the CF strategies used in Korean EFL classes (Sheen, 2004), while a relatively large proportion of explicit corrections and metalinguistic explanations were provided by the teachers in this study upon students' requests. Also, the students in this study tended to ask the teacher for help whenever the teacher entered their breakout rooms, because they believed that the teacher was more knowledgeable and helpful than their peers. They knew peers were unwilling or unable to provide explicit corrections to their erroneous expressions due to a lack of knowledge or confidence, or a desire to maintain harmonious social relationships with peers. Therefore, the students generally used the strategies of clarification, confirmation and providing new information to help peers.

4.5. Influences of online setting

Finally, the TS and SS interaction patterns also unveiled the influence of delivery mode on classroom interaction. For example, compared to those reported in previous studies (e.g. Lyster, 2002), the relatively low use of recasts (implicit CF strategies) and high use of explicit CF strategies in this study reflected the constraints of the online teaching setting on teachers' selection of scaffolding strategies. That is, interactive opportunities in Zoom classes are reduced compared to F2F classes due to technological (e.g. internet connection) and time constraints (e.g. extra time needed for breakout rooms) (e.g. Fraschini & Gonzales, this volume; Gao, 2020). Because using breakout room functions (i.e. opening, closing and entering each room) was overly time-consuming, teachers reduced the number of group work activities so as to make the most of the time with the whole class to provide metalinguistic explanations for key grammar points, explain common errors explicitly and address students' questions. Thus, because of time constraints, more explicit strategies were used than implicit strategies, and more reformulation strategies were performed than prompt strategies. Also, students' responses in the main room declined because some students were afraid to ask questions in front of the class in the main session. This is particularly true for first-year students who lacked community-building opportunities to work with their peers outside the classroom, because remote delivery commenced from the beginning of their studies. Thus, the teachers sometimes had to answer their own elicitation questions themselves with metalinguistic explanations.

However, there are some advantages to using Zoom in the online setting. For example, synchronous audio, video and written chats could be used simultaneously to develop students' reading and speaking skills, which helped their memorisation of new information through multiple input channels. The teachers could also type correct answers on the chat pad while providing detailed explanations verbally. Students could be asked to post their questions and type their responses on the chat pad. The written input and output not only ensured the flow of conversation but also helped students to learn characters and pinyin, including tone marks. As such, the chat pad and breakout room functions in Zoom effectively supplemented live online classroom teaching and facilitated TS and SS interactions in the online setting.

5. Conclusion

This study examined the patterns of TS and SS interactions in formal CFL classes delivered via Zoom. Drawing on SCT, the current study found that TS and SS interactions in live online courses demonstrated different patterns, although both TS and SS interactions scaffolded L2 knowledge construction and competence building. The teachers adopted more elicitations, recasts and explicit corrections with metalinguistic explanations to facilitate TS interactions, while both teachers and students served as resources, facilitators and commenters in online interaction. The findings lend support to SCT and translanguaging pedagogy by showing that the use of L1 facilitated the scaffolding process and that scaffolding, as a form of social mediation, effectively assisted learners in fulfilling challenging tasks which could not be completed independently. The results can be used as baseline data for comparison of TS and SS interactions in F2F and online settings in future studies. The study's findings contribute to the theoretical development of interaction studies based on the SCT by providing evidence from authentic CFL online classes.

Interaction is an essential topic in teacher education because of the growing evidence that it can play a critical role in enhancing teacher efficacy. The critical issue facing teachers is how to improve teaching quality and learning outcomes with pedagogy in changing circumstances (such as amid COVID-19) which may become permanent. It is now clear that simplistic pedagogical prescriptions cannot reflect the reality of teaching and learning. For this reason, the findings of this study enrich the guidelines of interaction in teacher education programs as a basis for teachers' reflection and exploration of interactional research.

This study has pedagogical implications for L2 teaching and learning in remote delivery. Though serving as an effective way to mediate L2 acquisition, interaction is a complex phenomenon. Its complexity is reflected in diverse patterns of interactional moves surrounding issues relating to the who, how, when and where of interaction. Our findings suggest that teachers should familiarise themselves with effective scaffolding strategies and actively implement them into their teaching practices to facilitate TS and SS interactions and improve learning outcomes. The teacher also plays a crucial role in ensuring the quality of the collaborative dialogue among learners. Teachers need to develop their questioning techniques to incorporate various scaffolding strategies and referential questions that stimulate learners' responses and provide effective feedback. Thus, teachers could assist students in internalising the target-like use of linguistic forms through real-life communicative dialogues and enhance their communicative competence in expressing their thoughts. Teachers should be aware of individual differences and consciously adopt various strategies and communicative tasks to stimulate SS interaction and mitigate student anxiety. The moderate use of L1 is a mediation tool to prevent the breakdown of conversations, reduce students' anxiety and embarrassment, and facilitate TS and SS interactions. Given the potential of online learning platforms in future education, teachers should equip themselves with technical skills and explore innovative teaching approaches to promote TS and SS interaction and maximise learning outcomes.

Finally, teaching is a form of social mediation. This study suggests that teachers' and students' motivation and affective factors might have influenced the quality of interactions in the online classroom setting. Not only interlocutors (teachers and peers) but also tools (e.g. Zoom) play a significant role in mediating the development of L2 competence. We call for future studies to examine the effects of affective and contextual factors and teachers' and learners' perceptions of interactions in the SCMC mode. We believe that participants' self-reports could provide further insights into why TS and SS interactions were executed, as we revealed in this study, and how to improve their execution in the future to facilitate L2 learning in both F2F and SCMC contexts.

References

Aljaafreh, A. & Lantolf, J. P. (1994). Negative feedback as regulation and second language learning in the zone of proximal development. *The Modern Language Journal, 78*(4), 465–83. doi.org/10.1111/j.1540-4781.1994.tb02064.x

Blake, R. (2000). Computer-mediated communication: A window on L2 Spanish interlanguage. *Language Learning and Technology, 4*(1), 111–25. doi.org/10125/25089

Brock, C. A. (1986). The effects of referential questions on ESL classroom discourse. *TESOL Quarterly, 20*(1), 47–59. doi.org/10.2307/3586388

Bueno-Alastuey, M. C. (2013). Interactional feedback in synchronous voice-based computer-mediated communication: Effect of dyad. *System, 41*(3), 543–59. doi.org/10.1016/j.system.2013.05.005

Chanier, T. & Lamy, M. N. (2017). Researching technology-mediated multimodal interaction. In C. A. Chapelle & S. Sauro (Eds), *The handbook of technology and second language teaching and learning* (pp. 428–43). Wiley Blackwell.

Chapelle, C. (1998). Multimedia CALL: Lessons to be learned from research on instructed SLA. *Language Learning and Technology, 2*(1), 21–39. doi.org/10125/25030

Chappell, P. (2014). Engaging learners: Conversation- or dialogic-driven pedagogy? *ELT Journal, 68*(1), 1–11. doi.org/10.1093/elt/cct040

Chun, D. M. (1994). Using computer networking to facilitate the acquisition of interactive competence. *System, 22*(1), 17–31. doi.org/10.1016/0346-251X(94)90037-X

Edstrom, A. (2015). Triads in the L2 classroom: Interaction patterns and engagement during a collaborative task. *System, 52*(August), 26–37. doi.org/10.1016/j.system.2015.04.014

Ellis, R., Basturkmen, H. & Loewen, S. (2001). Learner uptake in communicative ESL lessons. *Language Learning, 51*(2), 281–318. doi.org/10.1111/1467-9922.00156

Gao, X. (2020). Australian students' perceptions of the challenges and strategies for learning Chinese characters in emergency online teaching. *International Journal of Chinese Language Teaching, 1*(1), 83–98. doi.org/10.46451/ijclt.2020.06.04

Gao, X. (2021). Oral corrective feedback on Mandarin pronunciation in live online classes. In Y. Zhang & X. Gao (Eds), *Frontiers of L2 Chinese language education: A global perspective* (pp. 90–109). Routledge. doi.org/10.4324/9781003169895

García Mayo, D. P. & Zeitler, N. (2017). Lexical language-related episodes in pair and small group work. *International Journal of English Studies, 17*(1), 61–82. doi.org/10.6018/ijes/2017/1/255011

Gibbons, P. (2003). Mediating language learning: Teacher interactions with ESL students in a content-based classroom. *TESOL Quarterly, 37*(2), 247–73. doi.org/10.2307/3588504

Golonka, E. M., Tare, M. & Bonilla, C. (2017). Peer interaction in text chat: Qualitative analysis of chat transcripts. *Language Learning & Technology, 21*(2), 157–78. doi.org/10125/44616

Hall, J. K. & Walsh, M. (2002). Teacher–student interaction and language learning. *Annual Review of Applied Linguistics, 22*, 186–203. doi.org/10.1017/S0267190502000107

Hammond, J. (Ed.). (2001). *Scaffolding teaching and learning in language and literacy education*. Primary English Teaching Association.

Hammond, J. & Gibbons, P. (2005) Putting scaffolding to work: the contribution of scaffolding in articulating ESL education. *Prospect, 20*(1), 6–30.

Hermkes, R., Mach, H. & Minnameier, G. (2018). Interaction-based coding of scaffolding processes. *Learning and Instruction, 54*, 147–55. doi.org/10.1016/j.learninstruc.2017.09.003

Jin, S. H. (2005). Analysing student–student and student–instructor interaction through multiple communication tools in web-based learning. *International Journal of Instructional Media, 32*(1), 59–67.

Junn, H. (2021). L2 communicative competence analysis via synchronous computer-mediated communication (SCMC) as an alternative to formal classrooms. *Innovation in Language Learning and Teaching, 17*(1), 15–31. doi.org/10.1080/17501229.2021.1895802

Kitade, K. (2000). L2 learners' discourse and SLA theories in CMC: Collaborative interaction in internet chat. *Computer Assisted Language Learning, 13*(2), 143–66. doi.org/10.1076/0958-8221(200004)13:2;1-D;FT143

Lantolf, J. P. (Ed.). (2000). *Sociocultural theory and second language learning*. Oxford University Press.

Lantolf, J. P. & Poehner, M. E. (2014). *Sociocultural theory and the pedagogical imperative in L2 education: Vygotskian praxis and the research/practice divide*. Routledge.

Lantolf, J. P., Poehner, M. E. & Swain, M. (Eds). (2018). *The Routledge handbook of sociocultural theory and second language development*. Routledge. doi.org/10.1080/13670050.2019.1652559

Lenkaitis, C. A. (2020). Technology as a mediating tool: videoconferencing, L2 learning, and learner autonomy. *Computer Assisted Language Learning, 33*(5–6), 483–509. doi.org/10.1080/09588221.2019.1572018

Li, J. (2018). L1 in the IRF cycle: a case study of Chinese EFL classrooms. *Asian-Pacific Journal of Second and Foreign Language Education, 3*(1), 1–15. doi.org/10.1186/s40862-017-0042-y

Li, W. (2018). Translanguaging as a practical theory of language. *Applied Linguistics, 39*(1), 9–30. doi.org/10.1093/applin/amx044

Liu, Y. Yao, T-c, Bi, N-P, Ge, L. & Shi, Y. (2017a). *Integrated Chinese volume 1 textbook* (4th ed.). Cheng & Tsui Company, Inc.

Liu, Y. Yao, T-c, Bi, N-P, Ge, L. & Shi, Y. (2017b). *Integrated Chinese volume 2 textbook* (4th ed.). Cheng & Tsui Company, Inc.

Liu, Y. Yao, T-c, Bi, N-P, Ge, L. & Shi, Y. (2017c). *Integrated Chinese volume 3 textbook* (4th ed.). Cheng & Tsui Company, Inc.

Loewen, S. & Sato, M. (2018). Interaction and instructed second language acquisition. *Language teaching, 51*(3), 285–329. doi.org/10.1017/S0261444818000125

Loewen, S. & Wolff, D. (2016). Peer interaction in F2F and CMC contexts. In M. Sato & S. Ballinger (Eds), *Peer interaction and second language learning: Pedagogical potential and research agenda* (pp. 163–184). John Benjamins. doi.org/10.1075/lllt.45.07loe

Long, M. & Porter, R. (1985). Group work, interlanguage talk and second language acquisition. *TESOL Quarterly, 19*(2), 207–28. doi.org/10.2307/3586827

Long, M. (1989). Task, group and task-group interactions. *University of Hawaii Working Papers in ESL, 8*, 1–26.

Long, M. H. (2018). Interaction in L2 classrooms. In J. I. Liontas (Ed.), *The TESOL encyclopedia of English language teaching* (vol. 8, 1–7). John Wiley & Sons.

Lyster, R. (2002). Negotiation in immersion teacher–student interaction. *International Journal of Educational Research, 37*(3–4), 237–53. doi.org/10.1016/S0883-0355(03)00003-X

Lyster, R. (2019). Effective scaffolding and questioning techniques. In D. J., Tedick & R. Lyster (Eds), *Scaffolding language development in immersion and dual language classrooms* (pp. 129–49). Routledge. doi.org/10.4324/9780429428319-9

Lyster, R. & Ranta, L. (1997). Corrective feedback and learner uptake: Negotiation of form in communicative classrooms. *Studies in Second Language Acquisition, 19*(1), 37–66. doi.org/10.1017/S0272263197001034

Mackey, A. (2012). *Input, interaction and corrective feedback in L2 learning*. Oxford University Press.

Maybin, J., Mercer, N. & Stierer, B. (1992). 'Scaffolding' learning in the classroom. In K. Norman (Ed.), *Thinking voices: The work of the National Oracy Project* (pp. 186–95). Hodder and Stoughton.

McDonough, K. (2004). Learner–learner interaction during pair and small group activities in a Thai EFL context. *System, 32*(2), 207–24. doi.org/10.1016/j.system.2004.01.003

Mercer, N. (2002). Developing dialogues. In G. Wells & G. Claxton (Eds), *Learning for life in the 21st century: Sociocultural perspectives on the future of education* (pp. 141–53). Blackwell. doi.org/10.1002/9780470753545.ch11

Muthuprasad, T., Aiswarya, S., Aditya, K. S. & Jha, G. K. (2021). Students' perception and preference for online education in India during COVID-19 pandemic. *Social Sciences & Humanities Open, 3*(1), 100101. doi.org/10.1016/j.ssaho.2020.100101

Nambiar, D. (2020). The impact of online learning during COVID-19: students' and teachers' perspective. *The International Journal of Indian Psychology, 8*(2), 783–93.

Nassaji, H. & Swain, M. (2000). A Vygotskian perspective on corrective feedback in L2: The effect of random versus negotiated help on the learning of English articles. *Language Awareness, 9*(1), 34–51. doi.org/10.1080/09658410008667135

Ng, C., Yeung, A. S. & Hon, R. Y. H. (2006). Does online language learning diminish interaction between student and teacher? *Educational Media International, 43*(3), 219–32. doi.org/10.1080/09523980600641429

Ohta, A. (1995). Applying sociocultural theory to an analysis of learner discourse: Learner–learner collaborative interaction in the zone of proximal development. *Issues in Applied Linguistics, 6*(2), 93–121. doi.org/10.5070/L462005219

Ohta, A. S. (2000). Rethinking interaction in SLA: Developmentally appropriate assistance in the zone of proximal development and the acquisition of L2 grammar. In J. P. Lantolf (Ed.), *Sociocultural theory and second language learning* (pp. 51–78). Oxford University Press.

Philp, J. (2016). New pathways in researching interaction. In M. Sato & S. Ballinger (Eds), *Peer interaction and second language learning: Pedagogical potential and research agenda* (pp. 377–95). John Benjamins. doi.org/10.1075/lllt.45.15phi

Philp, J., Adams, R. & Iwashita, N. (2013). *Peer interaction and second language learning.* Routledge. doi.org/10.4324/9780203551349

Pica, T., Lincoln-Porter, F., Paninos, D. & Linnell, J. (1996). Language learners' interaction: How does it address the input, output and feedback needs of L2 learners? *TESOL Quarterly, 30*(1), 59–83. doi.org/10.2307/3587607

Rouhshad, A. & Storch, N. (2016). A focus on mode. In M. Sato & S. Ballinger (Eds), *Peer interaction and second language learning: Pedagogical potential and research agenda* (pp. 267–89). John Benjamins. doi.org/10.1075/lllt.45.11rou

Salaberry, M. R. (1996). A theoretical foundation for the development of pedagogical tasks in computer mediated communication. *CALICO Journal, 14*(1), 5–36. doi.org/10.1558/cj.v14i1.5-34

Salaberry, M. R. (2000). L2 morphosyntactic development in text-based computer-mediated communication. *Computer Assisted Language Learning, 13*(1), 5–27. doi.org/10.1076/0958-8221(200002)13:1;1-K;FT005

Sheen, Y. (2004). Corrective feedback and learner uptake in communicative classrooms across instructional settings. *Language Teaching Research, 8*(3), 263–300. doi.org/10.1191/1362168804lr146oa

Smith, H. J. & Robertson, L. H. (2020). SCT and translanguaging-to-learn: Proposed conceptual integration. *Language and Sociocultural Theory, 6*(2), 213–33. doi.org/10.1558/lst.36955

Storch, N. (2002). Patterns of interaction in ESL pair work. *Language Learning, 52*(1), 119–58. doi.org/10.1111/1467-9922.00179

Storch, N. (2017). Sociocultural theory in the L2 classroom. In S. Loewen & M. Sato (Eds), *The Routledge handbook of instructed second language acquisition* (pp. 69–83). Routledge.

Storch, N. & Aldosari, A. (2013). Pairing learners in pair work activity. *Language Teaching Research, 17*(1), 31–48. doi.org/10.1177/1362168812457530

Swain, M. & Lapkin, S. (2000). Task-based second language learning: The uses of the first language. *Language Teaching Research, 4*(3), 251–74. doi.org/10.1177/136216880000400304

Swain, M. & Lapkin, S. (2013). A Vygotskian sociocultural perspective on immersion education: The L1/L2 debate. *Journal of Immersion and Content-Based Language Education, 1*(1), 101–29. doi.org/10.1075/jicb.1.1.05swa

Swain, M. & Watanabe, Y. (2013). Languaging: Collaborative dialogue as a source of second language learning. In C. A. Chapelle (Ed.), *The encyclopedia of applied linguistics* (pp. 3218–3225). Blackwell Publishing Ltd. doi.org/10.1002/9781405198431.wbeal0664

Torres, J. & Yanguas, Í. (2021). Levels of engagement in task-based synchronous computer-mediated interaction. *Canadian Journal of Applied Linguistics, 24*(2), 234–59. doi.org/10.37213/cjal.2021.31319

UNESCO. (2020). *COVID-19 educational disruption and response.* Retrieved on 10 November 2021 from en.unesco.org/themes/educationemergencies/coronavirus-school-closures

UNESCO. (2021). *COVID-19: Reopening and reimagining universities, survey on higher education through the UNESCO National Commissions*. UNESCO. unesdoc.unesco.org/ark:/48223/pf0000378174.locale=en

Vygotsky, L. (1981). The genesis of higher mental functions. In J. Wertsch (Ed.), *The concept of activity in Soviet psychology* (pp. 144–88). Sharpe.

Vygotsky, L. (1986). *Thought and language*. MIT Press.

Vygotsky, L. S. (1978). *Mind in society: The development of higher psychological processes*. Harvard University Press.

Warschauer, M. (1997). Computer-mediated collaborative learning: Theory and practice. *The Modern Language Journal, 81*(4), 470–81. doi.org/10.1111/j.1540-4781.1997.tb05514.x

Wu, W. (2018). A Vygotskyan sociocultural perspective on the role of L1 in target language learning. *Cambridge Open-Review Educational Research e-Journal, 5*(November), 87–103.

Yanguas, Í. (2010). Oral computer-mediated interaction between L2 learners: It's about time! *Language Learning & Technology, 14*(3), 72–93. doi.org/10125/44227

Ziegler, N. (2016). Synchronous computer-mediated communication and interaction: A meta-analysis. *Studies in Second Language Acquisition, 38*(3), 553–86. doi.org/10.1017/S027226311500025X

Ziegler, N. & Mackey, A. (2017). Interactional feedback in synchronous computer-mediated communication: A review of the state of the art. In H. Nassaji & E. Kartchava (Eds), *Corrective feedback in second language teaching and learning: Research, theory, applications, implications* (pp. 80–94). Routledge. doi.org/10.4324/9781315621432-7

Appendix: Transcription system

//	pause during the on-going interaction
[]	use of L1 / English translation
(…)	a pause of one second or less marked by three full stops
?	rising intonation, questions
Underscore	utterances for target scaffolding strategies

(Writing)	give an explanation of what is happening in the background
Italicised	non-target-like forms
Bold	scaffolding strategies
()	functions of interactional moves

10

Equipping Australian Defence Force (ADF) members with the ability to influence the outcome of interactions conducted in an intercultural environment

Anna Ivanova

Abstract

The Australian Defence Force School of Languages (DFSL) is the primary training centre for the delivery of Languages Other Than English (LOTE) training within the Australian Defence Force (ADF). It is important that the curriculum design, development, delivery and evaluation optimise the effectiveness and efficiency of ADF LOTE capability to enhance Australia's projection of 'soft power' in protecting its national interests. DFSL course packages are designed to support multiple LOTE, which enables standardised courses to be developed and delivered in various target languages, in response to evolving ADF priorities. These packages are later contextualised to reflect the target countries' cultural contexts. The purpose of the LOTE Strategic Engagement (SE) course is to prepare selected ADF members for overseas representational postings and to produce graduates with sufficient command of the target language and a sufficient level of cultural knowledge to act as communication facilitators in routine and non-routine military settings at the strategic level. SE duties require interaction with foreign government, defence and industry organisations and individuals. In this chapter, I will focus on a number of course design solutions aimed at supporting SE graduates' future contribution to the building of strategic relationships.

Keywords: interculturality, language course design, intercultural communication, rapport-building, strategic engagement

1. Introduction

Recognition has been growing of the importance of cultural knowledge for Languages Other Than English (LOTE) learners and the need to cultivate learners' communicative competence through cultural teaching (Liddicoat & Scarino, 2013; Wilson & Wilson, 2001; Xue, 2014). Because our cultural and linguistic knowledge affects the ways in which we think, behave and interact, imprecise interpretation of a target language cultural norm or linguistic expression can lead to miscommunication or communication breakdown, which could potentially have serious implications in the civilian world and be absolutely critical in the military context. Liddicoat (2008) argues that language issues arise in communication both within coalitions of allies and in interaction with local people in theatres of conflict. On the other hand, a deeper understanding of the target country's cultural nuances can help reduce the risk of military confrontation, assist with the task of interoperability with key partners and improve the coordination of responses to shared international challenges, including terrorism, humanitarian assistance and disaster relief. It is also key to boosting a nation's soft power, which can be a force as effective and motivating as traditional military hard power (Nye, 2002).

The Australian Defence Force's (ADF) focus on international engagement and language requirements has never been greater, as reflected in the *2016 Defence White Paper*. This chapter discusses international engagement as an important part of the Australian government's approach to building international partnerships and stresses the importance of 'strengthening Defence's international engagement and international defence relationships and arrangements' (Department of Defence, 2016, p. 21). By implication, the provision of LOTE training within ADF is part of Australia's projection of 'soft power'.

The Australian Defence Force School of Languages (DFSL) is a unique LOTE training institution that exists to serve ADF needs and therefore is purely vocational with a military focus. Apart from the method of selecting prospective students, which consists of a compulsory pre-course language aptitude testing process, the internal course design and development process, small classes and full-time intensity of DFSL courses are clearly the school's defining features (Deck, 1999; Surachestpong, 2016). To achieve the levels of LOTE proficiency and cultural knowledge required for ADF members' future workplace tasks, time needs to be spent on targeted tasks that are identified in the design process and implemented in class by highly experienced language teachers.

DFSL language programs aim to minimise chances of intercultural communication breakdown by equipping ADF personnel with knowledge of the target language and culture as well as communicative strategies, which increase their ability to influence the outcomes of interactions conducted in an intercultural environment. The 46-week-long LOTE Strategic Engagement (SE) course prepares selected ADF members for overseas representational postings, including embassy and foreign staff college positions, and aims to produce graduates with sufficient command of LOTE and a sufficient level of cultural knowledge to act as communication facilitators within routine and non-routine military settings at the strategic level. SE duties are performed in diverse contexts and require interaction with foreign government, defence and industry organisations and individuals.

Most SE students start the course with no target language proficiency and, after completing a range of concurrent modules for six hours per day over the 46-week period, reach what is described as an 'Intermediate' or 'Generally effective' level of proficiency by the end of the course. As limited LOTE and cultural awareness of SE job incumbents can have potentially very serious implications for the ADF, the course designers put considerable thought into creating multiple solutions to address this issue while most efficiently meeting ADF requirements.

This chapter will outline different SE course development and delivery solutions, which are based on DFSL course designers' understanding of language teaching and learning as an intercultural venture. The solutions include an intercultural awareness module, a focus on rapport-building language and language required to conduct business relating to SE plans and activities, the introduction of military terminology and workplace task-specific modules.

2. Intercultural awareness learning outcome

The DFSL SE course is designed for military learners with no prior knowledge of the target language or culture. It comprises multiple learning outcomes (LOs). LOTE skills are taught in conjunction with an intercultural awareness LO called 'Work collaboratively in an intercultural context to support SE tasks'.

As they progress through the language-specific LOs, SE learners will also be acquiring intercultural knowledge and developing intercultural communication skills, which are critical in equipping SE graduates with the ability to influence the outcome of interactions conducted in an intercultural environment. The intercultural awareness LO has a significant attitudinal component, as well as underpinning knowledge and skills required to work collaboratively in an intercultural context. Students are required to participate in intercultural events, multiple rapport-building and workplace-based role-plays, and visits involving the target language culture. The content of this module is intended to be interwoven with all of the other LOs on this course; however, teachers can choose to address certain aspects of the module in stand-alone lessons.

As part of this module, SE students learn about the importance of cultural awareness and the significance of intercultural communication, various factors shaping the national/regional identity of people in the target country (e.g. history, values, attitudes, norms, social structure and status, customs, social conventions), and strategies that can be used to facilitate intercultural communication. The requirement to apply these strategies is built into SE course assessment rubrics. In this way, information is collected on students' ability to show interest and respect, ask questions to seek clarification, withhold judgement, adapt responses and so on.

SE students are encouraged to reflect, discuss, engage in multiple tasks and draw on their own experiences when working on this module of the course. As part of their studies, they are also encouraged to critically examine their own culture as well as the target language culture. As Liddicoat and Scarino (2013) argue, LOTE learning is 'an act of learning about the other and about the self and of the relationships which exist between self and other' (p. 2). To successfully pass this LO, the students need to apply culturally appropriate target language and behaviour, as well as strategies to facilitate intercultural communication through a number of assessment events. They are also required to share target culture and intercultural knowledge and experiences with their classmates.

This module is designed to assist SE graduates with the task of moving between different linguistic and cultural systems and to enable them to embrace the new cultural identity that LOTE learning inevitably moves them to take on.

3. Rapport-building language

The development of rapport-building language is specifically built into the SE course design to support graduates' future contributions to relationship building. This LO introduces the target language knowledge and skills required to build rapport with native speakers, build general conversational fluency, and engage in basic conversations relating to daily life and the military. SE students are taught to apply appropriate social and cultural conventions when engaging in conversations to build rapport (e.g. eye contact, body language and gestures, formal and informal greetings and leave-taking expressions), appropriate use of honorifics (terms of address), social norms regarding physical contact (e.g. handshakes, public displays of affection), appropriate rapport-building topics and expressions, differences in male–male, male–female and female–female interactions, and so on. All these conventions obviously differ according to the language and cultural background of the speaker. SE students are taught vocabulary, language patterns and structures used when asking and answering questions related to personal information, titles and naming systems, and much more.

Even though the bulk of rapport-building language teaching occurs during the foundation phase of the SE course, provision is made for the continual practice of rapport-building skills throughout the course, particularly general conversation skills. The requirement to engage in casual conversations in multiple scenarios is built into the second-phase workplace task-based module of the SE course.

4. Military terminology module and workplace task-specific modules

Kramsch (2008) argues that the focus in language teaching cannot be just on teaching a linguistic code, but should also be on teaching meaning. When it comes to meaning in the military context, there are of course further complications and interconnected dimensions. When military personnel from different countries meet and engage in workplace interaction, not only do they represent different cultures, but they also represent different military organisations with their respective agendas and strategic priorities, as well as some of the sub-cultures within these organisations (i.e. army, navy or air force). To achieve their communication goals, ADF members must perform the extremely complex task of interpreting linguistic and cultural codes at these multiple levels.

Wilson and Wilson (2001, p. 77) argue that communication is a 'socially and jointly constructed (inter)action of which power is an indissoluble part' and that 'intercultural communication on a global level is steeped in relations of power and domination'. These points are particularly accurate and relevant in the military context. To assist ADF members with the complex task of intercultural communication, DFSL course designers introduced a range of military-specific modules in the SE curriculum. The 'Apply basic military terminology in rapport-building conversations' module teaches SE students how to apply relevant military terminology in a range of contexts. Students participate in multiple role-plays involving small talk relevant to military life, as well as deliver a presentation in the target language on certain aspects of the ADF.

The second phase of the SE course covers eight main military-related themes: 1. Military equipment, 2. Military personnel, 3. Politics and society, 4. International defence relations, 5. Security, 6. Military role, issues and operations, 7. Religion and economy, and 8. Ceremonies. Within each theme, there are a number of sub-topics. Through these themes, SE students learn about defence cooperation and joint military training between Australia and the target language country, contemporary political issues in Australia and the target language country, defence policy and strategic direction in both countries and much more.

The aim of these themes is to develop the students' language proficiency in SE-related topics to the highest possible level, to ensure they have the necessary language and cultural knowledge and skills to engage with their counterparts on these topics in the target language. The length of time to spend on each theme, and on each topic within each theme, is not prescriptive, as the importance of the various themes and topics varies from target country to target country. Therefore, it is up to each language department to determine the priorities and order of themes and topics most appropriate to their language, while ensuring that all themes are covered.

One of the skills identified in the SE training needs analysis is the ability to express both agreement and disagreement with others. As the students' ability to express agreement and disagreement improves, more complex expressions are introduced, enabling the students to 'soften' how they express disagreement to maximise the chances that their disagreement is received well and to avoid causing offence or tension: for example, 'I can see what you mean, but have you thought about …?'; 'I'm not sure you're quite right about that'; 'What about …?'; 'I appreciate where you are coming from, but from my perspective…'. All DFSL language departments are encouraged to use debate language-task format and role-plays of military meetings in which the parties are required to discuss opposing views while monitoring triggers for offence and misunderstanding. Lesson materials also contain guidelines for explaining the inability to provide an immediate spoken response to a question, which may be due, for instance, to difficulties in articulating a response in a target language or to not knowing the answer.

Bennett (1986) argues that participants in intercultural training programs expect not only specific knowledge about a foreign culture and the linguistic and behavioural habits of its members, but also, above all, guidance on how to proceed in intercultural situations. DFSL courses aim to provide ADF members with interaction-relevant knowledge that will enable them to perform effectively in their future SE jobs. The 'Communicate in target language in support of SE tasks' LO is built around real-life tasks and topics that DFSL graduates are likely to discuss in their future jobs. In this module, SE students are required to apply their linguistic and cultural knowledge when completing a range of activities replicating SE job tasks. They are required to discuss topics of mutual interest with their target country's military counterparts and conduct business relating to SE plans and activities. Conducting business related to SE plans and activities involves discussions of various aspects of ADF plans and policies, logistics arrangements, combined operations, security, and so on, as well as writing related texts. As part of this module, SE students are also taught how to acknowledge differences of opinion and attitudes, how to show interest, raise concerns in a tactful manner, minimise the possibility of misunderstanding and use turn-taking procedures appropriately. This part of the course is linked closely to the 'Apply language learning strategies in context' module.

Students' knowledge and attitudes are assessed through a range of tasks. For example, the students are required to make arrangements for and escort visitors in culturally appropriate ways—using appropriate opening and closing salutations, polite expressions and forms of address when writing messages related to visit arrangements (including when misunderstandings regarding visit arrangements occur), using appropriate gestures, facial expressions and eye contact, and so on. SE students are also presented with a problem and asked to negotiate a solution to this problem as part of a role-play. The ability to negotiate a solution is one of the assessment criteria used for this task and one of the examples of the training situation in which SE students are asked to demonstrate their skills in influencing the outcome of an interaction.

5. Language learning strategies module

Another module that is taught concurrently with the rest of the SE curriculum is the 'Apply selected study and language learning strategies in context' module. Even though the main focus of this module is on the specific strategies that support SE students' acquisition of vocabulary, grammar, speaking, listening, reading, writing, translating and interpreting skills, language-enabling strategies that can facilitate communication are also covered.

As most DFSL students reach Intermediate level target language proficiency by the end of the SE course, it is crucial to teach them simplifying skills that they can use when communicating concepts, ideas and meanings within their level of language capability. These include the use of circumlocution, breaking complex sentences into simpler ones, adapting language register as appropriate and so on.

Because people often misread signs and intentions when crossing cultural borders, it is important to ensure that DFSL students are able to employ strategies to check common understanding—paraphrasing, questioning, echoing, use of confirmatory statements and so on. For example, when asking for specific information, SE students are taught to include questions designed to enable the questioner to distinguish between fact and opinion, such as 'Is this your opinion?' and 'What is this information based on?', or to repeat back what has been said.

All these strategies are incorporated with language teaching as appropriate throughout the course, and students are required to demonstrate their abilities in a range of assessment tasks.

6. In-country training module

It is hard to question the transformative value of in-country training for LOTE learners. Angulo (2010), for example, in her investigation into the experiences of undergraduate students from the University of Texas at Austin (UT) who were engaged in study abroad programs, concluded that studying abroad was a 'unique and transformative experience' for participants (Angulo, 2010, p. 85).

In-country training is one of the final SE LOs, and is conducted over two weeks in a target language country. In-country training further assists DFSL students with the development of their rapport-building skills and intercultural knowledge. The purpose of in-country training activities is to provide SE students with language and cultural learning opportunities that can only be gained in-country, through interaction with members of target language speech communities. During in-country training, students do two very important things: 'they communicate with native speakers trying to be equal to them and at the same time absorb all cultural nuances they need' (Coalition of Distinguished Language Centers, 2015, p. 76).

While in the country, DFSL students have the opportunity to practise and improve their language skills by interacting with people with many different accents and paces of speech. The overriding motivation behind in-country training is to immerse the students in the target country language and culture so as to improve their ability to interact effectively and, ultimately, to prepare them for their future SE workplace tasks.

Preparation for in-country training is built in throughout the course. For example, when preparing for the task of discussions with members of the target language community, SE students choose a topic that interests them and is related to one of the eight themes covered in the 'Communicate in target language in support of SE tasks' LO. When choosing the topics, they are asked to consider what aspects of the target language culture they wish to explore, what specifically they want to learn and why, and what they already know about the topic. They are also expected to consider the backgrounds of the people they would like to talk to, a requirement being that they include both males and females of different socioeconomic backgrounds, different ages, different occupations and, if possible, different areas of the target country. Students discuss with their teachers any linguistic and cultural difficulties they might face in holding these discussions and strategies they might be able to employ to overcome these difficulties if/when they arise. They then research the approved topic while reflecting on their own ideas and feelings about it. The students receive a great deal of information on possible discussion stages (greetings, 'ice-breaking' comments or questions/rapport-building exchanges, explaining the purpose of the discussion, introduction of the topic and so on), but are asked to remember that they need to keep an open mind in case the discussions go in different directions from what they expect. After consulting with teachers individually, the students factor any suggestions for improvement into their plans. The last stage of their preparation is the presentation they give to the class about their plan for their discussions. Their final presentation should demonstrate their competence in establishing rapport with, and gaining the trust of, the other person; asking and answering questions about each other and the discussion topic, including personal views; and practising courtesies appropriate to the context—for example, thanking people for their assistance and taking leave appropriately. Students are also encouraged to use technology and engage with target language communities as part of this preparation.

SE students are required to complete a range of activities while in the country—for example, participate in local group activities, talk to people from different professions, conduct and record individual discussions with members of the target language community on a chosen topic, and plan, prepare and undertake a community–military engagement activity. The students are expected to apply their intercultural communication skills while completing these activities. DFSL teachers accompanying their students on in-country training observe and collect evidence of completion of each of the required activities, and ensure all the assessment checklists are completed.

The effectiveness of in-country training for students is, in large part, affected by the attitude and dedication of the students themselves. Therefore, DFSL students are advised that a positive, exploratory and proactive attitude towards learning will enable them to make the most of the opportunity to improve their language skills provided by in-country training. Davidson and Lekic (2010) argue that the immersion setting of in-country training programs represents an acquisition-rich environment in which intensive interaction with language and culture leads to significant proficiency gains. Ongoing positive feedback from DFSL in-country training program participants supports this view.

A wide range of development and delivery approaches is used to introduce the above solutions in DFSL courses. DFSL teachers apply a diverse range of lesson types, class activities and teaching models in their courses. Teachers' experiences show that an approach that combines various teaching models and ways of organising and presenting course content maximises outcomes for DFSL trainees undertaking intensive LOTE courses from diverse defence and personal backgrounds with a range of preferred learning styles. DFSL course design documents ensure consistency across multiple LOTE courses but offer enough flexibility to course developers and deliverers to accommodate different learning and teaching styles and needs.

At DFSL, technology is also considered an integral tool in intercultural language teaching that offers access to a wide range of authentic and contemporary resources for LOTE education and allows for synchronous and asynchronous online intercultural engagement practice. As Kern and Develotte (2018, p. 2) argue, the use of visual media is essential to:

> distinguish between cultural learning, which implies acquiring knowledge about another culture, and intercultural learning, which involves reflection on one's personal engagement with multiple cultures and developing an awareness of one's cultural assumptions and interpretative logic in relation to those of others.

7. Conclusion

LOTE learners are always engaged in intercultural communication and thus are always moving towards the intercultural identity which Liddicoat and Scarino (2013, p. 29) describe as the site where '[t]he borders between self and other are explored, problematized, and redrawn'. Integrating intercultural capabilities into SE course language teaching and learning at

DFSL is of fundamental importance. In their strategy-level military jobs, DFSL SE graduates will rely on their acquired intercultural knowledge, skills and attitudes to exert influence in the international arena through subtle means rather than through traditional military hard power (Hinchcliffe, 2009).

DFSL as an institution recognises the need for an intercultural focus in language learning and has developed a solid practice of intercultural teaching. DFSL's SE curriculum integrates a range of course development and delivery solutions designed to help DFSL graduates build relationships in their future jobs, including the intercultural awareness module, rapport-building language and language required to conduct business relating to SE plans and activities, military terminology and workplace task-specific modules. To consolidate their linguistic and intercultural skills, SE students participate in in-country training, which provides an authentic and diverse training environment with linguistic and cultural interaction experiences not possible in Australia. In-country training activities are designed to give SE students real insights into the target country's culture and opportunities to further develop their linguistic and cultural knowledge and skills.

While there is definitely a place in DFSL's SE curriculum for cultural facts that give key insights into the target language culture, the key focus is on the real-life workplace application of cultural knowledge and the ability of DFSL graduates to engage effectively with their military counterparts. This is why intercultural awareness is taught and assessed concurrently with the rest of the SE curriculum.

Just as languages and cultures are constantly evolving, so too is our understanding of the nature of language teaching. Australian Defence Force's strategic priorities are also constantly changing. Lovell (2017, p. 88) observes that in today's world 'soldiers are increasingly asked to do much more than fight in armed conflicts'. Today, soldiers act as peacekeepers and as emergency responders; they are required to negotiate and to develop trust. This is why it is crucial for DFSL course designers to be conscious of the need to be responsive and adaptable to constantly changing ADF requirements, and to systematically review the school's teaching and learning priorities and practices. The ultimate goal is to enhance ADF LOTE capability, which will, in turn, strengthen Australia's international strategic partnerships.

References

Angulo, S. (2010). *Trading cultures, transforming lives: Positive change during study abroad*. VDM Verlag Dr. Müller.

Bennett, J. M. (1986). Modes of cross-cultural training: Conceptualizing cross-cultural training as education. *International Journal of Intercultural Relations, 10*(2), 117–34. doi.org/10.1016/0147-1767(86)90002-7

Coalition of Distinguished Language Centers. (2015). *What works: Helping students reach native-like second-language competence*. Virginia Institute Press.

Davidson, D. & Lekic, M. (2010). The overseas immersion setting as contextual variable in adult SLA: Learner behaviors associated with language gain to level-3 proficiency in Russian. *Russian Language Journal, 60*(1), 55–78. scholarsarchive.byu.edu/cgi/viewcontent.cgi?article=1173&context=rlj

Deck, D. (1999). *Development of an intensive integrated curriculum of teaching Indonesian to foreign speakers: An Australian perspective* [Conference paper].

Department of Defence. (2016). *2016 Defence White Paper*. Australian Government. www.defence.gov.au/sites/default/files/2021-08/2016-Defence-White-Paper.pdf

Hinchcliffe, M. (2009). Soft power and the role of the ADF in shaping the Australian security environment. *Australian Defence Force Journal, 179*, 7–12.

Kern, R. & Develotte, C. (Eds). (2018). *Screens and scenes: Multimodal communication in online intercultural encounters*. Routledge. doi.org/10.4324/9781315447124

Kramsch, C. (2008). Ecological perspectives on foreign language education. *Language Teaching, 41*(3), 15–17. doi.org/10.1017/S0261444808005065

Liddicoat, A. J. (2008). Language planning and questions of national security: An overview of planning approaches. *Current Issues in Language Planning, 9*(2), 129–53. doi.org/10.1080/14664200802139356

Liddicoat, A. J. & Scarino, A. (2013). *Intercultural language teaching and learning*. Wiley Blackwell. doi.org/10.1002/9781118482070

Lovell, D. W. (2017). Creating strategic corporals? Preparing soldiers for future conflict. *Australian Defence Force Journal, 201*, 88–92. www.defence.gov.au/sites/default/files/research-publication/2017/201_2017_May_Jun.pdf

Nye, J. (2002). *The paradox of American power: Why the world's only superpower can't go it alone*. Oxford University Press. doi.org/10.1093/0195161106.001.0001

Surachestpong, I. (2016). *A needs assessment of intensive language teaching at the ADF School of Languages* [Unpublished PhD dissertation]. Victoria University, Australia.

Wilson, S.-X. & Wilson, J. (2001). Will and power: Towards radical intercultural communication research and pedagogy. *Language and Intercultural Communication, 1*(1), 76–93. doi.org/10.1080/14708470108668064

Xue, J. (2014). Cultivating intercultural communication competence through culture teaching. *Theory and Practice in Language Studies, 4*(7), 3–7. doi.org/10.4304/TPLS.4.7.1492-1498

Index

Entries in *italics* refer to figures; entries in **bold** refer to tables.

Aboriginal and Torres Strait Islander people 7, 94, 96
    community lives of 112–13
    funding to attend universities 109
    as language workers 97–9, 103,114–15, *see also* Indigenous language workers; studying their own languages
    teacher training for 101
    see also Australian Indigenous languages
Academy of Active Learning Arts and Sciences 128
accountability
    and flipped approach 127, 132–3, 142, **143**
    in Indigenous language education 103
active learning 127–8, 133, 144
ADF (Australian Defence Force) 264–5, 268, 274, *see also* DFSL
agency
    and flipped approach 127, 131–2
    teachers' 16, 33
agreement and disagreement, expressing 269
AILI (Australian Indigenous Languages Institute) 7, 94–5, 105–6, 112–14
    origins of 106–8
    programs 2019–2020 110–12
    statistics from events **111**
    travel scholarships 108–9

ALS (Australian Linguistics Society) 98, 106–7, 114–15
American Indian Language Development Institute 104
Anglo-Australian culture 220–2
ANU (The Australian National University) 17, 46–7, 208
    and Indigenous languages 108
    learner expectations survey 44, 46–7, 52–3, 60–2
    T & I courses at 207
anxiety 16, 18, 160, 255
Arrernte language 102
Asia literacy 81–3
Asian languages
    cross-institutional teaching 158
    education programs in 64, 68
    teaching and learning in Australia 3–4, 81–2
    in Western Australia 69
Associate Degree in Indigenous Languages and Linguistics 108
ATAR (Australian Tertiary Admission Rank) 84
attitudes and manners, in consultation interpreting 217–18
audiovisual materials 25–6, 46, *see also* video resources
AUSIT (Australian Institute of Interpreters and Translators) 209–10, 213, 218

Australia, interpreting culture in 206–7, 213–14, 218–19, 224–7
Australia in the Asian Century White Paper 82
Australia-Korea relations 68
Australian Federation of Modern Languages Teachers Association 56
Australian Indigenous languages 94–6
  future of 114–15
  teaching at universities 102–4, 107, 112–13
  training teachers of 100–2, *see also* Indigenous language workers
Australian Linguistics Institutes 98
Australian universities
  classroom environment in 17–18
  Indigenous languages in 94, 102–4, 106, 112–13
  L2 learning motivation in 14–17, 21, 32
  language studies in xv–xvi
  language teaching and learning in 1–5
  T& I courses in 207–11, **208**
authentic materials, and L2 motivation 27, 35, 78
autonomy, personal 221–2, *see also* learner autonomy

Bachelor of Indigenous Language and Linguistics 107–8
Batchelor Institute 107–8, 110
beginner learners 6
  biographical information **20**
  see also first-year students
best practices xvi, 5, 132, 164
bilingual competence 248, 251–2
bilingual education 98
Bininj Kunwok language 102
Bow, Cathy 7, 108
breakout rooms 163–6, 168, 241, 250, 252–3
Brown, Josh 6

Cameron, Tracey 110
Cantero, Manuel Delicado 6
Caruso, Marinella 7
CDU (Charles Darwin University) 107–8, 110
CEFR (Common European Framework of Reference for Languages) 48–9, 51–3, 56, 183
  student familiarity with *52*, **52**
CF (corrective feedback) 49, 53–4, *54*
  in online classes 237, 241, 243–4, 248, 252–3
CFL (Chinese as a Foreign Language), online teaching of 235, 239–54
Chinese language: learning in Australia 1–2, *see also* CFL
CILLDI (Canadian Indigenous Languages and Literacy Development Institute) 104–5
clarification requests 238, 246, 248, 252
classical languages xv
classroom interactions
  for L2 learning 237–9
  theoretical frameworks for 235
classroom social climate 17, 33
codes of ethics, for T & I 209–10, 213, 216, 218–19
CoEDL (Centre of Excellence for the Dynamics of Language) 109
cognitive competence 251
collaborative activities 97, 130, 163
collectivistic and individualistic cultures 222–4
Commonwealth funding gap 2, 71
communication breakdown 264–5
communicative competence 18, 33–4, 36, 237, 255, 264
communities of practice 178–9
  language learners' 7, 181–2, 186–92, 194–6
community interpreting 206–7, 215–16, 222–4
competence, need for 130

computer literacy, and flipped approach 133, 136, 138–9, 146–7
computer skills 98, 112
computer-assisted language learning 146, 158
computer-mediated communication 239, *see also* SCMC
confirmation requests 238, 247–8, 252
constructivist theories 236
consultation interpreting 206–7, 214–18, 221–2, 224
conversational activities, task-based 35–6
Council of Australian Government (COAG) 81
Course-specific Motivational Components 17, 22, 24–7, **25**, 31–2, 36
COVID-19 pandemic
   and Korean language study 67–8, 71, 83
   and L2 learning motivation 25, 37
   and online teaching 126, 159–60, 169–70, 234–5, 240
   and social interactions 248
   and study abroad 67
critical language users 207, 209, 211–12, 219, 222, 224–7
cross-cultural comparisons 219–20
cross-institutional collaborations 7, 171
cultural activities, and L2 motivation 27, 30
cultural awareness 187, 265–6
cultural differences, in interpreting ethics 206, 218, 224, 227
cultural knowledge 8, 76, 212, 264–5, 269, 274
cultural learning 273
culture, definitions of 219–20
curriculum matching 161–3
Curtin University 69, 71
CWLC (Center for World Languages and Cultures) 161, 164

demotivation 17, 19, 34
deontologist approach 210
DFSL (Defence Force School of Languages) 8, 265–6, 268–7, *see also* SE (Strategic Engagement) course
Digital Language Shell 103
digital literacy *see* computer literacy
digital tools 37, 50–1
dilemma-triggering expressions 210
Diploma of Indigenous Language Work 108
Directed Independent Language Study program 161–2
discourses, in communities of practice 178, 181, 188
D'Orazzi, Giuseppe 6
DU (University of Denver) 158, 161–3, 169, 171

effectiveness, of flipped approach 129, 139–42, **140–1**
EFL (English as a Foreign Language) 129–30, 244, 252
Elfving-Hwang, Jo 6
elicitation 238, 244, 246, 248, 250, 253–4
emotions
   in interpreting 218–19, 224–5
   in online environment 160
empathetic role image 205, 214–22, 224, 226–7
empathy
   cross-cultural 187, 195
   Japanese and Anglo-Australian understandings of 219–22, *see also omoiyari*
employability 72, 79, 96, 209
employment prospects, and learning Korean 75–6, 80
encouragement 87, 238, 250
English language, L2 communities of practice 182

279

enjoyment
  in flipped learning approach 133, 137–9, **138–9**
  and L2 learner motivation 16–17, 32–3, 36
enrichment, mutual 212, 224
e-textbooks 164, 169–70
ethical pluralism approach 206–7, 211–12, 224–5
ethical thinking 210–11, 224–6
ethics, professional 209–12, 225–7
  see also codes of ethics
e-tivities 134, 139–43, 145
EU (European Union) 214–15, 217–18
everyday language activities 77, 80
exchange programs 17, 28–9, 34–5
explicit corrections 243, 248, 252, 254
extra-curricular activities 14, 17, 29–30, 34, 36
eye contact 167, 267, 270

face-to-face classes, interaction patterns in 234–5, 237–41, 253–4
face-to-face interaction 36, 86
  and flipped approach 130, **138**, 143–5, 147
  avoiding 191
  in online teaching 160, 163
  patterns of 234–5, 237
  and SCMC 238–9
false beginners 85
feedback
  corrective *see* CF (corrective feedback)
  in flipped classroom 126, 129–30, 132, 134–5
  implicit 247
  on Indigenous language teaching 107, 111
  in online learning 166–7, 170–1
  word cloud for *54*
First Languages Australia 94–5, 100–1, 115

first-year students, expectations of 6, 44–9, *48*, 53, 56
flashcards 50, 55
FLCA (foreign language classroom anxiety) 16
FLE (foreign language enjoyment) 16–17, 33, 36
flexibility
  of flipped approach 126, 136, 138–9, **139**, 141
  and Indigenous language training 94, 99, 105, 114–15
Flinders University 19
flipped learning approach 7, 86, 126–7
  definition 128
  main learning phases of 133–5, *134*
  pedagogy of 145–7
  and performance 128–32
  student perceptions of 136–45, 151–6
form-focused activities 77–9
Framework for the Teaching of Aboriginal Languages and Torres Strait Islander Languages 100
Fraschini, Nicola 4, 7
French language
  L2 learning motivation for 14–15, 18–20, 23–4, 29–31, 34
  learning in Australia 2
Fukuno, Maho 7

Gamilaraay language 102, 108, 110
Gao, Xiaoping 8
gender, and Korean language learning 74, 80
German language
  L2 learning motivation for 14–15, 19–20, 23–4, 26–7, 29–30, 34
  learner communities of practice 186–90
  learning in Australia 2
  social language learning strategies 178, 183–4, 190–4, *193*, 196
Giacon, John 108, 110

global citizens 8, 207–9, 226–7
Go8 (Group of Eight) universities 15, 19, 46, 208
Gonzales, Adriana 7
grade point average (GPA) 72, 86
grammar teaching, and flipped approach 129, 131
Griffith University 19
group chats 36
group dynamics 15, 17
group work 238, 250, 253
Group-specific Motivational Components 15–16

Hajek, John 2–3
Hawai'i 103
health interpreters 213
heritage learners 1, 65, 67, 73, 86
heteroglossia, ethical 8, 211, 225–6
hidden curriculum 142
Higher Education Support Amendment (Job-Ready Graduates and Supporting Regional and Remote Students) Bill 2, 71
high-level language activities 77–8, 80
Hindi 1, 84
horizon, fusion of 212

Ideal L2 Self 14, 36
ideal moral self 225
identity construction 16
ILA (Indigenous Languages and Arts) funding 96, 98, 107–8, 110
immersion, and L2 learner motivation 35
impartial role image 213–14, 219, 224
Inceoglu, Solène 6
in-class activities 16, 128, 132
in-country training 271–4
independent learning, and flipped approach 127, 131–3, 147
Indigenous language workers 7, 94, 96
 career pathways for 106
 linguistic training for 97–9, 112–14
 travel scholarships for 108–9
Indigenous languages xvi, 7
 of North America 104–5
 teaching and learning 103
 see also Australian Indigenous languages
Indigenous people, of Australia *see* Aboriginal and Torres Strait Islander people
Indonesian language 1–3
inductive teaching 130–1, 133
informal learning, online 180
Institute for Collaborative Language Research 104
Interaction Hypothesis 235
interaction patterns 234–5, 237–9, 241
interactional moves (IM) 244–7, **245–8**
interactive activities 26–7, 135
interactive learning 86, 130
intercultural awareness 266, 274
intercultural communication 206, 209, 222
 in DFSL training 266–7
intercultural competence xvi–xvii, 6, 37, 159, 208, 210, 240
intercultural identity 273
intercultural knowledge 212, 266–7, 271, 274
intercultural learning 273
intercultural mediation 214–18
intercultural teaching 7, 269, 273–4
intercultural understanding 211
interculturality 212
interdisciplinarity xvii
international collaboration 161
interpreting: role images of 213–20, *see also* community interpreting; consultation interpreting; T & I
investment 14, 182, 186–90, 192, 195–6
invisibility, of interpreters 213
IRF (initiation, response, feedback) 237–8, 241, 248

Italian language
    flipped learning approach 7, 126–7, 130, 135–7, 146
    L2 learning motivation for 14–15, 19–20, 24, 26–7, 29–31, 34
    teaching and learning in Australia 2, 18–19
Ivanova, Anna 8

Japan, interpreting culture in 206–7, 214–15, 219–21, 223–4, 226–7
Japanese language
    in Australian universities 207–8
    L2 communities of practice 182
    learning in Australia 2
    T & I training for 211
JRGP (Job-Ready Graduates Package) 81, 83

KAFTA (Korea–Australia Free Trade Agreement) 68
Kant, Immanuel 210
Kaurna language 102
Kaurna Warra Pintyanthi 109
Kinder, John 4
Korea *see* North Korea; ROK
Korean language
    courses taught in Western Australia 6, 69–71, *70*, 84–7
    demographics of learners 73–5, **74**
    learning activities 77–80, **77**
    learning script of 167, 169
    motivations for learning 64, 69, 72–6, **75**, 78–80, **79**
    online teaching and learning 158, 160–2, 164–70
    promotion in Australian education 82–3
    speakers in Australia 65–7, **66**
    teaching and learning in Australia 1, 3
Korean popular culture 64, 67, 69, 75, 80, 82–3

Korean Research Centre of Western Australia 83
Korean studies 3, 68–72, 74, 76, 83, 86–7
K-pop 67, 69, 82, *see also* Korean popular culture
Kriol 110

L2 Learning Experience 14–15, 17, 20, 28, 33–4, 36
L2 learning motivation *see* learning motivation
L2 Motivational Self System 14
language activities, categories of **77**, 78
language crisis 2–3
language documentation 98, 105
language learning resources 44, 49–50, 56
    frequency of use **51**
    for Indigenous languages 101
    using partner as 238, 249–50
    using teacher as 246, 248
language learning techniques 45, 49–50, 56
language peers, successful 55
language policy xvii–xviii, 95
language revitalisation 7, 94–6, 98, 100–2, 104–5, 109
language structures 155, 181
language study xv–xvi
language teachers 4–5
    for Indigenous Languages 7, 95, 101
    in L2 learning environment 16
    in tertiary sector xv–xvii
    see also teacher education
language-related assistance 238, 246, 248, 250–1
languages and cultures xvi–xvii
LCNAU (Languages and Cultures Network for Australian Universities) xvii, 2, 4, 56, 107
learner autonomy
    in flipped approach 127, 130–1

and learning strategies 179, 181, 191
and scaffolding 236
and task-based learning 35
videos on 44, 49, 53
learner training 132
learning activities
    in flipped approach 127
    Korean language student preferences for **77**, 78
    and learning motivations **79**
learning environments 5–6
    and L2 motivation 15–19, 32–6
learning experience xv
    in flipped approach 136
    see also L2 Learning Experience
learning materials, real-life *see* authentic materials
learning motivation 14–15, 36–7;
    and Asian languages 72, 82
    contributions of motivators 21–36, **32**
    in flipped approach 130
    and formal learning environment 15–17
    and learning activities 78, **79**
    and online courses 234
    research design 19–21, **21**
    and social language learning strategies 185
    see also Korean language, motivations for learning
learning outcomes
    and beliefs 130
    in DFSL 266–7, 269, 272
    and interaction patterns 234–5, 239, 250, 254–5
    and learning strategies 179
    realistic expectations for 6
    in T & I courses 208, 211
learning strategies 26, 178–9, 270–1
    developing 49, 55
    frequency of use *190*

see also social language learning strategies
learning styles 24, 273
lesson materials, translation of 23
lesson pace 25–6
linguistic analysis 97–8, 112
linguistic and cultural minorities, in Japan 215–18
linguistic knowledge 104, 264
linguistic proficiency xvi–xvii
linguistic skills 98–9, 101, 208
linguistic training, for Australian Indigenous languages 95, 97–8, 105
live interaction 7
Living Languages 98, 109, 113–14
LMS (learning management systems) 47, 135–6, 164, 169
Lo Bianco, Joseph 3–4, 81
LOTE (Languages Other Than English)
    cultural knowledge for 264, 266–7
    funding for 69–70
    in-country training for 271, 273
    in primary schools 87
    in United States 161
    see also DFSL
Lowe, Kevin 105, 108
LREs (language-related episodes) 236–8, 241, **244**, 247–51, **248–50**
Lund University 161

McEwen, Tanya 110
Macquarie University 207
meaning-focused activities 180
mediational resources 236, 251–2, 255
metacognitive awareness 129, 133
metacognitive language learning strategies 181
metalinguistic explanations 243–4, 247, 251–4
method of studying 44–5
MEXT (Ministry of Education, Culture, Sports, Science and Technology) 215, 219

micro-credentials 114
military terminology 265, 268–70, 274
Monash University 15, 208
    T & I courses at 207
moral character 225
moral values and norms 207, 210, 212, 219–25
movies
    and L2 learner motivation 27, 35
    and student expectations 50
multicultural and multilingual identities 18, 36
multiculturalism, and T & I ethics 209, 226
multilingualism 1, 215

NAATI (National Accreditation Authority for Translators and Interpreters) 207, 209–10, 231
NALSAS (National Asian Languages and Studies in Australian Schools) 3, 81–2
NALSSP (National Asian Languages and Studies in Schools Program) 3
narrative inquiry 165
National Aboriginal and Torres Strait Islander Languages Teaching and Employment Forum 94
National Indigenous Languages Convention 94
National Indigenous Languages Survey 95
National Languages Campaign (2022-2023) 4
native speakers, interviews with 35
naturalistic language use 180, 191, 193–4
NCP (New Colombo Plan) 3, 83
Netflix 50, 82
neutrality 214
New South Wales
    Indigenous languages in 95
    Korean speakers in 65–7, **66**
    language learning in 1

New Zealand 103, 244
Nicola Fraschini 6
NILR (National Indigenous Languages Report) 95–6
non-Latin scripts 167, 169
North America, Indigenous languages of 95, 104–5, 112–14
North Korea 65, 82
Northern Territory 97
Northwest Indian Language Institute 104

office hours, online 171
omoiyari 219–23
online activities
    in flipped approach *see* e-tivities
    grading 160
online classes
    design and planning 160
    interaction patterns in 234–5, 240, 248, 253–5
online content delivery 47, 105, 126, 137–9, 254
online courses 112, 159, 234
online interaction 8, 159, 254
online teaching
    post-pandemic considerations 169–70
    retaining student attention in 166–7
    and scaffolding strategies 253
    synchronous 158–61, 163–6, 170
    time management in 167–8, 234
oral language activities 77–8
Ought-to L2 Self 14
out-of-class language use 178, 180–2, 186–8, 192–4, *193*, 196

pair work 168, 238
partner correction 250
Patji-Dawes Language Teaching Award 4
Peer Assisted Study Scheme 31
peer feedback 53–5, 131, 168

peer scaffolding 168
peer-educators 164
peer-tutoring, online 171
Pitjantjatjara language 102
placement tests 73
Polycom system 165
post-class activities 127, 133, 139
PowerPoint 165
pre-class activities 128–9, 131, 134–5, 142, 145, 147
professional ideology 214, 217
professionalisation 7, 100, 106, 209
pronunciation teaching 48–9
PULiiMA Indigenous Language and Technology Conference 110, 114

Queensland University of Technology 19
Quigley, Mary Grace 7

rapport-building language 265–8, 271–2, 274
recasts 238, 243–4, 246–8, 252–4
Reconciliation Action Plans 96
referential questions 237–8, 244, 246
reflective journals 165–8, 170
regular practice, learning benefits of 126, 142, 146
rejection, as scaffolding feature 238, 248
relatedness 130
relay expert consultation session 215
remote language centres 109
repetition, as scaffolding feature 238, 247–8
RMIT University 207
ROK (Republic of Korea) 64, 68, 70, 82–3
role images 207, 212–14, 218–24, 226
Romeo, Nicoletta 110
Rudd Report 81
Run Lola Run 27
Russian language 161, 238, 250

satisfaction
    and computer literacy 146
    and flipped approach 130, 132–3, 137–9, 143–4
scaffolding 236–7
    in F2F and SCMC 239
    in flipped approach 128–9, 133
    and interaction patterns 238
    in online teaching 166, 168
scaffolding strategies 8, 234–5
    in online setting 239, 241, 253–4
    and student–student interactions 238
    and teacher–student interactions **242–3**, 244–7, **245–8**
school context 15, 17
School of Australian Linguistics 97
Schools Curriculum Standard Authority 87
SCMC (synchronous computer-mediated communication) 235, 237–9, 255
SCT (socio-cultural theory) 188, 236–8, 251, 254
SE (Strategic Engagement) course 8, 265–74
secondary education, language teaching and learning in 1, 3
self-confidence 18
self-correction 250
self-cultivation 225–6
self-determination theory 130
self-discipline 234
self-narratives 165
self-reflection 16, 158, 165, 211–12, 225
self-regulation 131–3, 147
Shi, Leimin 8
social engagement 180–1
social interaction, norms of 219
social language learning strategies 7, 178–83, 189, 195–7
    and communities of practice 190–2
    developing *194*

teaching **184**, 192–6
social learning 178
social media 37, 42, 46–7, 50, 108–9, 180
social mediation 254–5
social networks 36–7, 222, 248
social support 222–3
sociocultural language learning theory *see* SCT
sociolinguistic competence 34
Sogang University Korean Language Education Centre 164
South Korea *see* ROK
Spanish language
    and flipped learning approach 130–1
    L2 learning motivation for 14–15, 19–20, 24, 26–7, 34–5
    learning in Australia 2
speech recognition, automatic 55
Strasek, Priscilla 110
strategy instruction 178–9, 183–5, **184**, 190–6
student engagement 139, 235
student interaction
    in online learning 159, 166–7
    see also student-student (SS) interactions; teacher-student (TS) interactions
student-centred approach 6, 49, 127, 130
student-student (SS) interactions
    in breakout rooms 241
    and LREs **249–50**
    in online setting 8, 159, 234–5, 253–5
    patterns of 237–9
    and scaffolding 241
    and SCT 236
    and social relationships 252
    use of L1 in 251
study abroad 271
    COVID-19 preventing 67
    and L2 learner motivation 35

in UWA/DU Korean course 162, 164
study at home, and L2 learner motivation 35
symbolic action, language learning as 187, 195
synchronous communication 160
computer-mediated *see* SCMC

T & I (translating and interpreting) 206–7
    courses in Australia 207–9, **208**, 231
    ethics training 209–11, 219, 224
    humanising ethics 224–7
    and interculturality 212
    invisibility of 213
    see also interpreting
T & I ethics 224
TA *see* teaching assistants
Tamil language 1, 84
Taylor, Charles C. 211
teacher education
    for Indigenous languages 94–5, 98, 100–2, 105, 112
    interaction in 254
Teacher-specific Motivational Components 15, 17, 22–4, **22**, 31–3, 36
teacher–student (TS) interactions 34
    LREs in **244**
    in online setting 8, 159, 234–5, 253–5
    patterns of 237–9, 243–8
    and scaffolding 241–3, **242–3**, **245–8**
    and SCT 236
    and social relationships 252
    SS interactions leading to 250
    use of L1 in 251–2
teaching assistants 163–4, 250
teaching experience 45, 54, 158–9
technical skills, of consultation interpreting 217–18

technology-enhanced language learning 158
testing, in online learning 169
Three-level Framework of L2 Motivation 15, 16
time management 167–8, 234
transcription conventions 185–6, **186**, 261–2
translanguaging 8, 236, 251, 254
translation and interpretation ethics 8
translation drills 23
Triebel Lecture 2
Troy, Jakelin 103

University Context 17, 22, 28–32, **28**, 34, 36
University of Adelaide 109, 183, 207–8
University of Melbourne 3, 19, 208
    Breadth Subject mode 17, 34
    T & I courses at 207, 211
University of New South Wales 207–8
University of Newcastle 3, 107, 207
University of Queensland 19, 207–8, 211
University of Sydney 101, 207–8, 211
UWA (University of Western Australia) 2, 208
    Broadening Unit model 17, 34, 135
    flipped approach at 126
    hybrid Korean language course 158, 161–3, 169
    Italian language at 18, 135, **136**
    T & I courses at 207
    traditional Korean language courses at 65, 69–74, *70*, **74**, 86

van den Bos, Jackie 110
Verdina, Federica 7
VET (vocational education and training) 98–9, 113
Victoria, language learning in 1
video conferencing 159, 165

video games, and language learning 191, 196
video resources
    in flipped approach 129, 134, 137–41, 143–5
    and student expectations 44–50, 52–6
virtual classroom 160, 166, 168
Vygotsky, Lev 235–6

Western Australia
    Indigenous languages in 101
    Korean language teaching and learning in 6, 64, 69–71, *70*, 84–7, 158
    Korean-speaking community in 65–7, **66**
    language curriculum in 1, 84–5
    and ROK 68–9
    see also UWA
Western Sydney University 107, 207, 210
wikis 159
Williams, Greg 108
Wiradjuri language 102

Xiaoping, Gao 8

Yolŋu languages 102–3, 108, 110
YouTube 46, 50, 55
Yu, Tao 6

Zoom classes 164–6, 255
    interaction patterns in 235, 239–41, 243, 250, 253
ZPD (zone of proximal development) 236

www.ingramcontent.com/pod-product-compliance
Lightning Source LLC
Chambersburg PA
CBHW052046220426
43663CB00012B/2459